# Two Penn orth

# of

# Poison

# PENNY DEVERILL

This book is published by Penny Deverill who reserves the right to be acknowledged as the author.

Although this book is a work of fiction it is based on real facts and events surrounding the death, by poison, of Thomas Worlock of Bitton, Gloucestershire and the subsequent execution of his wife Rebecca at Gloucester Gaol in 1820.

Most of the characters portrayed are real people, however any resemblance to persons, living or dead, who are unconnected to the event is entirely coincidental.

Printed by MPS Printing (Bristol) Ltd – Tel/Fax: 0117 967 2517

Bound by Rhogar

Typeset by Simon Barrington Design.

Front cover designed by Nico Hattton & Niki Hatton-Williams

ISNB978-095624290-7

*This book is dedicated to three people;*

*Thomas and Rebecca, without whom there would be
no story, in the hope they eventually found the
happiness denied them in life and my father,
who always said I could do it.*

While I breathe I have hope.
*(Translated from a Latin Quotation).*

# CHAPTER ONE

"*Dearly beloved we are gathered here to bring about the joining of this man to this woman.*" So said Reverend Ashton, Curate of St. Mary the Virgin, to the small congregation gathered before him on May 5<sup>th</sup> 1776. The groom was John Worlock, Butcher, Bachelor of the Parish of Bitton, his bride Martha Prigg, Spinster from the nearby hamlet of Swineford.

The Priggs ran a small holding and were well known local hauliers, whereas the Worlocks remained something of a mystery. Some thought they simply arrived from Marshfield looking for work in the village; others suggested they were from Wotton under Edge where there was a cluster of yeomen Worlocks. All agreed they were friends of the village baker William Hulburd and his brother John the butcher, who both hailed from Marshfield, as the latter had taken on their young son as his apprentice and had given him a home. However by the time John Worlock reached his late teens he was running the business on his own, travelling throughout the neighbouring villages slaughtering animals on farms and smallholdings, an accepted member of the community.

In between hiring out their horse and carts the Priggs kept most of the larger houses supplied with their provisions and although far from affluent they remained a large contented brood. Thanks to Mary Prigg her four girls were all skilled in dairy work whilst her three boys knew they were expected to help father as best they could and, come milking time, to be ready to carry pails of fresh creamy milk on wooden yokes across their broad ever growing shoulders down to the dairy where their sisters were waiting. Martha knew little else until she reached her late teens and began showing great expertise as a seamstress so that by now she was as much in demand for her skills with a needle as for her butter and cheese. Eighteen months ago her elder sister Hannah married Charles Willis and, like all young girls, she dreamt of the time when it would be her turn.

John was keen on female company but, working long hard hours often away from home left little or no time for courting. Things improved when he began using the old outhouse across the yard for a slaughterhouse but even then few girls were interested in someone who spent his days killing animals.

With the lengthening spring days and an increasing number of animals going for slaughter visits by the young butcher played a prominent part in Martha's dreams. Should she spy a lone cow or the occasional pig wandering aimlessly on its own segregated from the others, she instinctively knew the poor creature was destined for John Worlock and although she felt nothing but pity for the wretched animal it made her heart skip a beat to think she would be seeing him again. Unfortunately, John only saw the young daughter of one of his customers, his immediate plans did not include marriage especially to a girl he considered a child.

Unbeknown to the pair their friendship had not gone un-noticed and whilst they failed to realise they were meant for each other Mary Prigg saw the spark and eagerly anticipated talk of marriage before very much longer. Of course the Priggs did everything to encourage things along; when they knew John would be paying them a visit or delivering their butchered meat the whole family gathered in the kitchen whilst Martha innocently brought in a cake along with a liberal serving of her home made cream and a jug of her special cider. All eyes then watched for his reaction as she took her seat in the far corner of the room where, thinking no one could see her, she would gaze longingly at him.

With the approach of her twenty-first birthday life was changing, visits to Bitton other than to attend Church became less frequent as she spent her time helping at home in the dairy or, as often as not, sitting in a quiet corner working on the delicate stitches of some important dress. Should John arrive to carry out his gruesome task he would courteously ask after her until towards the end on November when, as usual, he asked after her he was politely informed,
*"She be too busy workin on a portant gown which gotta be done afore Christmus."*

The two rarely met during the next few weeks which was just as well because deep in her heart Martha felt such a one way love too painful to bear. Absence, however, can sometimes make the heart grow fonder and John began to miss her company until, on the rare occasions they did meet, he finally realised she was no longer a child but a very handsome young woman. Now, instead of accepting excuses for not seeing her, whenever he called to discuss business he always managed to bring her name into the conversation.

Early December found the pair so busy satisfying the needs of the big houses they rarely met and it was not until Christmas Day, at Church and then later sat around the Priggs large kitchen table that they met socially for the first time in almost two months. Determined for romance to blossom Mary Prigg invited John to spend the day with them rather than be on his own in his lonely hovel and from the way they hardly left each others side even the Prigg men folk noticed and asked, *"What on earth be stoppin the young fool frum askin t'marry er?"* every time one of them found themselves alone with Mary and out of earshot from the rest on the family.

January came as everyone waited patiently for John to propose. Heavy snow made travelling difficult and visits were rare, especially when the weather turned so severe people actually perished as they walked the treacherous frost covered lanes. John was given more time until Mary Prigg, supported by her other daughters, decided they could wait no longer and took a hand in things by casually hinting how Martha might be moving in with relatives at nearby Twerton on the pretext of improving her dressmaking skills.

The plan worked, just as they had hoped, the thought of losing her prompted John to ask if he could call and before the month had passed, for permission to marry her. In early March the couple saw Reverend Elwes and whilst he was happy to call the Banns he suggested his Curate perform the Service.

Although far from poor, with daughters still at home and the prospect of more weddings, the Priggs could not afford a grand affair and Martha, acutely aware of the cost of a special dress and new bonnet, remembered her friends had married in their best Sunday clothes and decided she had the skills at her fingertips to make her own. Her dress was therefore simple yet suitable for Church, future family weddings and, when the time came, the Christenings of all their children. John, along with his friends and supporters, strolled up the short lane to the Church to find most of the village waiting for them. Amongst the crowd were those who had known the couple since their early teens and thought they made a perfect match.

Meanwhile, as John lead his little party down the path and through the West door underneath the one hundred foot 14th Century tower of St. Mary the Virgin the few guests waiting inside could only guess what the bride's family felt at the prospect of their daughter marrying such a hard working prosperous young man.

The Priggs arrived, singing and laughing, aboard two wagons festooned with flowers as befitted the occasion. Martha followed in a specially borrowed chaise looking radiant in her plain cream cotton dress, her hair hanging loosely over her shoulders and around her plump little face, new straw bonnet tied under her chin with yellow ribbon, small bow pox in her hands a blaze of colour with spring flowers freshly picked from the garden that morning.

Slowly walking down the aisle Martha glimpsed her future husband waiting for her at the large altar step beneath the Rood Screen and instinctively tightened her grip on her posy. It was early spring and quite warm for the time of year even so she felt herself shiver a little as she started her journey towards married life. She had been told very little about what was expected of her as a wife and prayed she would not disappoint her new husband but, knowing how much she loved him, she silently promised to make him a worthy wife. Reaching John she smiled and immediately felt her face grow hot as she blushed at the sight of this handsome man who was about to vow to love her till death did them part. Feeling calm and composed at last she reached out for John's outstretched hand and together they turned to face Reverend Ashton.

Standing in the Vestry next to her husband Martha could barely remember saying 'I do' such was her excitement. Reverend Ashton had the Marriage Register open in front of him and had already completed his part before handing John a fine quill pen with which to sign his name in his clear small sloping hand. It was now her turn and although she had never been taught her letters she took great care when making her mark. John's friend, Thomas Gingell, followed by Churchwarden John Wright then added their names as witnesses before Mr and Mrs John Worlock made their way up the aisle to be greeted by more friends sitting in the back of the Church before emerging into the spring sunshine where they strolled amongst their guests, accepting good wishes and congratulations. The wedding party then clambered back aboard their decorated wagons, John and Martha alone in their chaise, to return to Swineford for the wedding breakfast. As the horses trundled onwards so more villagers came out of their houses to greet them until, with much waving, shouting and laughter, the happy couple led their guests out of Bitton towards her old home where people were already arriving ladened down with food and drink.

It was getting dark before, after much eating, drinking and dancing, the couple made to leave for their home in Bitton. When their betrothal was announced the Priggs suggested they move in with them after their wedding but John always vowed to take his bride back to the only home he knew, the cottage where he had lived since his arrival in Bitton. Back then it was a hovel and as the wedding drew nearer it was clear little had changed…it was still a hovel. Throughout the past months family and friends had worked hard to make the place habitable, the scullery walls were lime washed, Martha made curtains from colourful leftover material whilst John repaired all the old bits of furniture they had been given. Living on his own he had no use for either a bedroom or front parlour, finding it much more convenient to live in the scullery in front of the range but, with May 5th looming ever nearer, he reluctantly accepted time and money would only allow them to furnish one of the bedrooms, the other would have to wait since Martha was insisting the front parlour be furnished, *"Soze we got zumwhere t'ask people in t'sit,"* she would say when asked why.

Standing alone in the cottage a week before the wedding, with Martha's bright curtains at the windows and her rag rugs on the floor, John recalled there had been no such luxuries when his family first moved here, times were hard but at least there was a roof, albeit a leaky one, over their heads and no one starved.

*4*

Nor were they separated like those in the Poor House, they stayed together never complaining, working hard and suffering bad winters, aware there were other homeless families ready to take their place. Now, thanks to the Hulburds, he was fully accepted by his fellow businessmen, earned a decent living and was soon to marry a popular local girl who would hopefully give him sons to carry on the business. With only days to go before the wedding John reluctantly accepted he had let the place deteriorate and maybe, despite all their hard work, Martha might prefer to live with her family after all. However, his future wife determined to have John all to herself and decided it had been too late to change anything.

The bridal carriage, resplendent with its coachman suitably dressed for the occasion, arrived and Mr and Mrs John Worlock were unceremoniously thrown aboard to ribald jokes, cheers and shouts. Giving Martha one last hug the Prigg men shook John's hand, warning him,
*"You take proper care of our Martha mind."*
*" I ope thee knows I better than t'doubt that,"* was the swift reply.

Then, standing back, the Priggs and their guests sent the pair off in the customary raucous way!

A few days before John and Martha celebrated their first wedding anniversary a carriage made its way up the short curved drive leading to Lower Farm, Saltford, home of the Flower family. Inside sat Mary Francis, her widowed father Richard, her older sister Susannah and her mother's widowed sister Aunt Ann Tippett, whilst alongside on horseback, as if guarding Queen Charlotte herself, rode her two brothers Richard and William. Behind them came a smaller carriage loaded with cow skin trunks, bonnet boxes, band boxes, bags and luggage amongst which was a very precious item indeed …her wedding gown.

The front of the large three storey house came into view allowing Mary to lean out of the window as she saw her aunt and cousins waiting for them, all the while anxious to seek out one very special person she knew was also there waiting for her, Lamorock Flower, her future husband. Richard Francis was the first to alight to be welcomed warmly by his widowed sister in law Ann Flower and her sons George, whose home Lower Farm now was and his elder brother Lamorock, who had inherited Boyd Mill over in Bitton from their late father and where he now lived. Richard, William, Susannah and Aunt Tippett were already making their way inside leaving Lamorock to help his fiancée from the carriage. Once he released Mary from his arms his mother moved forward to welcome her niece and future daughter in law in an equally loving embrace.

The wedding was set for two days hence and there was still much to be done; however, for the moment the family disappeared inside the house leaving Mary and her fiancé standing alone by the carriage. Lamorock was the elder by five years and had known his fiancée from childhood, the couple had grown up together more like brother and sister than first cousins. He barely remembered his father because he was only four, his brother George only three, when he had tragically died. Mary on the other hand had been seven when she lost her mother and still had her memories, however the years in between had been full of wonderful family gatherings, both at Kelston where Aunt Ann lived or Bitton where Mary lived with her father, brothers and sister. But it was here at Saltford where all her special memories lay and it was because of those special memories that they had chosen to marry at the little Church of St. Mary next door to Lower Farm.

Lower Farm had been the Flowers home ever since an earlier Lamorock first leased part of it in the 15th century before buying a third of it along with about 110 acres of enclosed land for £102.12s. Two generations later another Lamorock and his bride, Susanna, chose to settle on the other side of the River Avon in Bitton where they raised their six children. When the couple later bought Boyd Mill, a large dwelling house, water gristmill and other plots of land, they became owners of one of the oldest mills in Golden Valley, dating back to Doomsday. In later years another, the aptly named New Mill, was built further up the valley but, like its neighbour, it relied on the fast flowing River Boyd to power its waterwheel. Their paternal grandmother, Rebecca Smallcombe, came from an old Kelston family and it was to the tiny village, nestling under the vast rolling hills of Lansdown, that she and grandpapa George Flower returned following their marriage and where their five children, including the bride's mother Mary and the groom's father George, were born and baptized.

Naturally as the eldest son it was George on whom the family centred their attention and following his marriage to another Kelston girl, Ann Croom, he returned home fully expecting to remain at his father's side, never suspecting how, within a year, that father would be dead.

Forty nine year old Grandpapa George was carried to the small Norman Church of St Nicholas to be laid to rest in the family grave under the old yew tree on the very day his son and daughter in law should have been celebrating their first wedding anniversary. Sadly their grief did not end there because five months later tragedy struck again with the death of twenty five year old Susannah and once more the Flowers made their sad way to that familiar old churchyard to lay her to rest near her father.

Grandmamma Rebecca passed her remaining years surrounded by family and friends like the Harringtons and Huddlestons. She saw her surviving children make good matches, Ann married Stephen Tippett, Mary married Richard Francis a gentleman of independent means from Northstoke, George was happily settled with Ann leaving her youngest son John a bachelor and likely to remain so just like the uncle after whom he was named. Six years later death called on the Flowers again with the death, at thirty six, of young George and the family again gathered around the extended family plot alongside Kelston Church and watched as he was laid with his father and sister leaving Ann a young widow with two sons under five.

The family, especially Mary Francis, supported her and as Mary's family increased so all the cousins were encouraged to visit each other....under the benevolent gaze of Grandmamma Rebecca whilst Ann rarely missed an opportunity to instil in them the importance of their birthright. However, any dreams the widowed Ann may have had for a long family bond were cruelly shattered when first her mother in law then, three years later, her closest confidante and friend Mary Francis died. Richard Francis and the children remained in Bitton enabling him to divide his time between his positions as Surveyor of the Highways, Overseer of the Poor and occasionally sitting as a member the Court Leat Jury. Ann Flower contented herself at Kelston, visiting and organising her bachelor sons' households from time to time, however neither showed any desire to find themselves a wife despite her constant hints or suggestions that she find one from amongst her circle of friends.

On a wider scene, the ill tempered skirmishes between England and America lead to a tax increase on tea imported from the Colonies, boiling over into the Boston Tea Party, putting the price of decent tea out of reach of poor folk and then often only available from smugglers provided you were prepared to pay anything from 9/- to 10/6 a pound. However, the poor folk of Bitton paid little heed to tea parties they much preferred the fermented juice of the apple and, thanks to its two large orchards, Boyd Mill was now supplying cider apples at a rate of 145 bushels a year whilst cider production was returning 'grate gane'. Meanwhile, further up Golden Valley, changes had taken place at the New Mill, it was no longer a Boring Mill but a Leather Mill and, whilst they freely admitted to having no fear of competition, Lamorock and his brother could foresee problems because there would surely come a time when the River Boyd, fast flowing as it was, simply would not power two waterwheels.

Mary was still legally a minor, needing her father's consent to marry but once this was given it was further decided to dispense with calling the Banns and apply for a marriage licence.

With the Flowers immersed in their wedding plans over at Saltford so folk across the river in Bitton prepared to welcome home the young Master and new Mistress of Boyd Mill, a strange state of affairs since nearly everyone had known them both since they were children and had watched them grow up.

Bitton was not the most attractive of places, true it had the pretty little River Boyd trickling through but that was only because further up the valley all its power had already been spent turning two water wheels. A potholed track, which turned to mud at the merest hint of rain and proved almost impassable during the winter months, divided the village. Near the Church lay the Rectory, the Vicarage and a Tithe Barn, further on past Micklemead, Sideham, Edenfield and Holmemead was the fast flowing River Avon. It was here some labourers' hovels, all in desperate need of repair, could be found along with one or two larger cottages complete with outhouses and small paddocks. To the North lay Golden Valley with Boyd Mill, New Mill and the steep track leading to Upton Cheyney, Beech, Wick, Lansdown and ultimately Bath.

Although there was much to be done before the wedding all that would have to wait because this evening there was to be a small family celebration, then tomorrow morning Lamorock and Mary were to see Reverend Slater to finalise the wedding service before hosting an afternoon tea party for their tenants, employees and business colleagues whom it was impossible to invite to the wedding because the Church was far too small. Later that evening Richard and Ann would entertain Flowers gathered from all over Somerset to a family supper.

Mary awoke on her wedding day with the memory of the previous night still fresh in her mind. Various cousins, aunts and uncles had joined those already gathered at Lower Farm where, naturally, Flowers ale played a big part in their celebrations. For those not staying overnight, either as guest of Ann at Lower Farm, at a neighbouring Inn or would be leaving before it became too dark to travel safely and chose not to risk the potency of the family brew, a special wedding mead of honey ginger and elder flower, fused with a sprinkling of fresh yeast, had been prepared well in advance.

Despite reaching her bed very late last night she was the first to rise, wrapping herself in her mother's old thick shawl and undressed hair tumbling about her shoulders, she crept from her room to wander barefoot around the old house still silent in the early dawn. In the Solar Hall, scene of last nights celebrations and where later today she would return with her family as Mrs Lamorock Flower, daylight was beginning to streak through the two light windows in the North and East walls. Continuing her walk she came to the 13th century wall painting of the Virgin and Child where, pausing for a moment, she decided to offer up a silent prayer. The sound of a door slamming downstairs brought her back from her thoughts and she decided to return to her room, it wouldn't be proper for anyone, especially her beloved Lamorock, to see her before the ceremony.

Safely back in her room there was no point in returning to her bed, instead she crept over to the large fireplace where, with trembling fingers, she reached up and traced the carved initials LF and AF 1637 left by those ancestors who, when they took the risk in buying this old house, laid the foundations for her future. Curled up in a chair, staring at the cold burnt out embers of last night's fire, she patiently waited for her sister and aunts to arrive.

Mary's wedding dress was made of rich ivory silk brocade dotted with flowers in pale purple and pink silks, the bodice was low cut and adorned with an eschelle stomacher decorated with matching bows of decreasing size from which the skirt, supported by a wide hoop, reached delicately down to her dainty feet. Her poke bonnet was trimmed with the same material as her dress and was complemented by an exquisite lace veil, in her tiny hands she held a small posy of hand picked flowers and, as if to say she would have approved, Papa had given her the necklace Mamma wore on her wedding day. Susannah and Aunt Ann had suggested a slightly more elegant gown but Mary felt her choice was perfect and taking one last look at herself in the cheval mirror in the corner of the room, from her mass of curly hair piled high on her head with one or two small wisps framing her small neck, around which she now wore her mothers necklace, down to the matching heeled silk slippers on her feet, the finished effect was exactly how she always planned to look on her special day.

In another part of the rambling old house the groom and his party were also preparing for the big day. Their tailor had used the best expensive soft velvet from which to make their new jackets, George, William and Richard chose black whilst Lamorock decided on dark blue lined with cream silk underneath which he wore a cream sleeveless waistcoat embroidered with coloured silk flowers and pure linen shirt, however all four refused to entertain any suggestion that their outfits be complemented by fashionable knee breeches, silk stockings and high heeled buckled shoes. The luckless tailor was firmly reminded how they were country gentlemen not effeminate fops, the kind of which were seen parading around Bath these days!

By the time Mary and her father finally made their way downstairs everyone had left for Church, walking through the silent rooms and out through the door leading to the garden she glanced up at another fireplace and more carved initials, A.A.F, L.F. and E, left by the same ancestors. Strolling arm in arm into the afternoon sunshine down the well worn path towards the walled gate through which generations of Flowers walked to Church from this, their family home, she could see St Mary's and glancing back at the house one last time she looked up at the roof with the rams head on one gable end and the lion at rest on the other. Family legend said they were religious symbols, the lamb for sacrifice, and the lion for victory.

Father and daughter entered through the West Door and began their slow short walk past Flowers from all over Somerset till they reached Lamorock and his supporters waiting for them on the altar steps. Lamorock bowed slightly to his future father in law then taking hold of Mary's hand he placed it gently on his arm as they stepped forward to face Reverend Slater. Meanwhile from the front pew Ann Flower and Ann Tippett, noticing Mary's necklace and knowing how much her mother and Lamorock's father would have approved of the union, could do nothing to stem tears of joy from streaming down their cheeks.

The newlyweds, William, George and Reverend Slater signed the Register in the peace and quiet of the Vestry, thus joining a long line of family names already written in this and earlier volumes, before Mr and Mrs Lamorock Flower prepared to lead their guests back to Lower Farm for their wedding breakfast. Passing the front pew Mary dropped a small curtsey whilst Lamorock reached out to brush a gentle kiss on the back of his mothers delicately gloved hand before doing exactly the same to Aunt Tippett. Everyone then joyfully made their way towards the West door, past elaborate wall memorials to their ancestors to begin the short walk home. Rather than return through the family entrance the couple allowed their guests to lead them towards the main gates, half way up the Church path they stopped briefly to gaze over the gently sloping valley towards Kelston where, in the distance on the other side of the River Avon, they could just pick out the tower of St Nicholas beneath which in its quiet little churchyard most of their family including Mary's mother, Lamorock's father and both grandparents lay. Lamorock, sensing what must be going through her mind, squeezed her tiny hand before guiding her gently towards their old family home.

Celebrations carried on well into the evening with Flowers ale and more wedding mead flowing freely until Lamorock announced,
*"Mary and I must prepare to leave or we will not arrive at Bitton, from where we are to begin our honeymoon tomorrow,"* before dark adding, *"they are expecting us there for supper at 9 of the clock."*

Although the sun was still hazy it was not what you could call a warm evening, it was early spring and there was a chill in the air. Back in her room, wrapped in Mamma's warm woollen old cloak, brought specially from Bitton, her wedding bonnet replaced by a calash tied firmly under her chin, Mary nervously waited for her husband to join her.

Lamorock closed the door quietly behind him and turned to look at the young girl who was now his wife, a girl he had known since the day she was born and with whom he had spent most of his growing years. Life changed so much when his father died but Mary was always there, showing concern for him whenever they met and she more than most understood the family business. Once their betrothal was announced there had been little time to spend alone, now they had the rest of their lives. Smiling he held out his arms towards her, as they turned to walk past that same fireplace with its familiar carvings he was sure their ancestors had already given them their blessing before, opening the door, together they walked downstairs to where a loaded phaeton was waiting to take them away to their future.

John Worlock emerged, exhausted and splattered in blood, from the ramshackle old shed he used as his slaughterhouse glad to have despatched the last half dozen lively bullocks sent down from Cully Hall Farm, to find Martha waving excitedly towards him from the kitchen door. When they first married she often joined him around mid-day to sit on the wall to eat a bit of food together but these days she chose to stay indoors. He knew the sufferings of the animals distressed her and feared bad news because there was little else to tempt her this close to dead animals, until he saw the wide grin on her face and the unopened letter she was frantically waving in the air,
*"Look what Mister Flower frum th'Mill ave sent us John....an,"* pointing to the ragged little urchin, scuffing his worn hand me down boots against the wall, *"is boy as bin told t'wait fur a answer!"*

As he broke the seal John could think of no reason why one of his best customers would want to write to him the day after returning from his honeymoon but, as Martha could not read, it was left to him to announce,
*"Well, t'is a invertation t'take tea wiv sum other gentlemun n their wives t'morra afternun"* and, with a glint in his eye, he continued, *"well, Martha Worlock, do e wanna go then?"* earning him the swift reply,
*"Do I wanna go, Oh John Worlock theese be a mischivus man an no mistake, course I d'wanna go!"*

*"In thik case we'd better tell thik young-un,"* pointing to the youngster now pacing impatiently up and down outside their gate, *"ow Mr n Mrs Worlock ould be onoured,"* chuckled her *"mischivus man of a husband."*

As Martha scurried away to give the boy give their answer John tried to wash off what animal blood he could at the pump before walking across the yard and together they discussed whether to tell their neighbours about their invitation to take tea with Mr and Mrs Lamorock Flower.

Everything was all hustle and bustle as they turned to walk down the sloping drive towards the house. The choking thick dust from the grinding corn that met them was over powering whilst the thundering noise from the water wheel was deafening and, as it was a very dry afternoon, the debris churned up by the wheels of the delivery wagons only made matters worse. The L shaped Mill House, with its massive wheel at the end, meant the newly weds were living amongst all this dust and noise. On either side of the drive were various outbuildings for animals, a dairy and stabling for Lamorocks' horses and somewhere for Mary to keep his wedding gift, a new gig to replace the old one she had inherited from her mother.

As invited guests they went in through the front door. John had never been in this part of the house before, he always made his deliveries to the kitchen from where you could see the two large orchards, the garden and, further on, the millpond fed by the River Boyd which in turn powered the waterwheel. Climbing the curved wooden staircase in the middle of the house they made their way towards the parlour on the first floor, as they walked so John contemplated how things might have been, had he not worked hard at building up his business he might well have been one of Lamorock's labourers working in all that dust instead of his invited guest this afternoon. Employment in and around Bitton was limited to agriculture, one or other of the mills dotted along the River Boyd and mining the Millgrit, Rag, Buff and Parrot deep seams of coal discovered in the Valley. Although mining had started in a very small way back in the 13th Century serious commercial working had begun in 1726 so that by now these pits formed part of the Kingswood Coalfield.

Martha viewed everything with amazement as they walked along the passage to where their hosts and fellow guests were waiting. Like John she had been here many times with the family deliveries before her marriage but had never been inside the Millhouse and she was in awe of what she saw. Flowers gazed down from portraits hanging on oak panelled walls, there were carved stone fireplaces and some of the floors were even covered in carpet! Martha could do nothing but enviously wish there were portraits and carpets in their cottage instead of bare boards in the one habitable bedroom and cold flagstones downstairs. The nearest thing they had to carpets were her rag rugs but, be that as it may, she could not understand why anyone chose to live in such a noisy house when there were more peaceful places their money could have bought them. The two young couples were not exactly close friends, although all four had known each other since childhood and Lamorock particularly admired the way John had built up his business from such humble beginnings.

The newlyweds welcomed them warmly and Mary introduced them to the other guests, *"I am sure you will already be acquainted with Mr and Mrs Bush, my sister Susannah and my brothers William and Richard Francis,"* she cooed as she guided Martha about the room, *"and over there"*, glancing towards an elderly eccentric looking lady, *"is, of course, my aunt, Mrs Anne Tippett."*

Martha knew most of them, however there were those, like the Newtons from Barrs Court and the Pearsalls from Willsbridge House whom she only knew by name, little believing that one day she would be taking tea with them.

Never had she been in such a room; the delicate wall coverings of dove grey and pale yellow were enhanced by the polished steel grate and marble chimneypiece which positively gleamed as the afternoon sun streamed through the windows. Fortunately they faced up the drive towards the lane, had the room overlooked the Mill there would have been little chance of any light, however powerful, finding its way through all the grime and dust. Though there were chairs and sofas on which to sit Martha noticed the ladies preferred to stand or walk about the room chatting to one another. Watching and listening to the confident way in which John spoke to people, gently guiding her by the arm as he did so, filled her with pride for this adored 'mischivus man' she had married.

Once everyone was gathered the young kitchen maid brought in a kettle of hot water, Mary reached for a small key from a reticule hanging from her waist and unlocked an exquisite mahogany inlaid tortishell caddy, one of their many wedding gifts, took out some of its precious contents and mixed some tea in a delicate silver urn for her guests. Martha recognised the young girl, (in fact if it were not for her and John the child's widowed mother and numerous siblings would starve because they often sent them meat scraps), and walked over to speak to her, *"How's thy muther, tell her there be zum scrag ends if she d'want t'send thy brother up."*

The room suddenly went deathly quiet and everyone stared at her but it was only when she saw John look at her and slightly shake his head that she realised they were in the company of those who would never dream of passing the time of day with their kitchen maid nor care if her large fatherless family starved, especially when being entertained by their Master and Mistress in their own drawing room!

Mary served her guests with their tea before inviting them to help themselves to some small cakes piled high on large delicate china plates on the fully extended satinwood and rosewood cross band tea table in the corner of the room. Once again Martha could only imagine life in this house, she had a few special china cups and plates t'is true but they were nothing like the ones from which she was now eating and drinking. She also soon discovered she had nothing in common with any of the other wives either; however, if only for John's sake, she did her best to show an interest in their conversations hoping they would eventually include her. Sadly hardly any of them as much as acknowledged her presence. Mary, dressed in her favourite pale blue, her hair tied up with a matching bow and her mother's necklace around her neck, was the most charming of young hostesses mingling with her guests despite being constantly in demand from those wives who felt it their right to receive her personal attention.

Mercifully it was soon time to leave, although some of the guests had driven there in their own gigs no one offered to take John and Martha home, in fact they all seemed in an inordinate hurry to avoid them but what did it matter the pair preferred to walk anyway. Arm and arm they took the shorter route across the fields talking all the while about the afternoon so that by the time they reached their cottage they thought they knew why Martha, in particular, had been snubbed especially since John recalled being pressed several times,
*"Your wife is one of those Priggs from Swineford, a local dressmaker, is she not?"* was one question.
*"Yes, that be correct."*
*"Why in God's name, if you want to succeed in business, could you not find one with a useful inheritance and enough of an education to know it bain't done to treat a servant as your equal, especially in front of her mistress,"* was another.
*"A more suitable choice would have ensured she could be relied on to make a half decent attempt at knowing what to do in company,"* came yet another, more of a statement than a question.

Lying in each others arms later that night they both blamed the other women for deeming the wife of a lowly butcher and the daughter of a common carter unsuitable for their exalted company. Gently stroking her hair John forlornly tried to explain,
*"I cud ave sid ow busy thy family be these days an ow they be thinkin bout buyin another cart n yung hos but we might need them sort a people fer the bizness, so I didn't make zum scuse fur us t'leave or say summut I ould regret later."*

Martha snuggled up against John and whispered,
*"Oh dussent take on so, how wuz we t'know we ould be spendin th'afternun wiv a bunch of ambitious selfish wumen, dust thee know thik gown Missus Bush*

*were wearing were three yers old, well"*….. pausing only to take breath before John even had chance to say it was not the sort of thing he was expected to notice… *"I do and I shud know cuz I made it fur er afore thee n me wuz wed an it bain't been altered ner mended since…I might not know me letters nor ow t'read ner write proper but I got thee John Worlock an as fur all they people an their gimcracks up there t'day theese didn't marry me fur me money nor fur what we Priggs brung to thy business."* Finally, following another swift intake of breath, she declared, *"So what if I weren't dressed s'elegant as what they wuz, least I were tidy an me dress weren't in no need of a needle n thread!"*

After her first disastrous visit to Boyd Mill Martha vowed never to go there again, should she need to speak to Mary there would be ample opportunity at Church on Sunday but as there was no reason for them having anything to talk about, neither of them had children nor did they share the same circle of friends, the only thing Mary might possibly want to discuss was dressmaking and, as she was at pains to tell everyone, she had an excellent dressmaker in Bath to make all her gowns, even that was highly unlikely.

# CHAPTER TWO

**M**ay became June then July until, after Church one morning Mary took Martha to one side,
*"I have some wonderful news; I am to have a child in February."*

Martha put on a very brave face struggling to find the right words,
*"Me n John be thrilled at thy news,"* before making some lame excuse to leave.

All through summer and early autumn Martha desperately tried to avoid Mary, the sight of her blossoming figure depressed her more than anyone imagined.

Winter found John working very long hours as well as attending Parish meetings, sometimes with Lamorock Flower and Richard Francis who was once again Surveyor of Highways, leaving Martha on her own. She often walked the mile into Swineford to be with her family but if the weather was really bad it was not always safe to walk even that short distance, in desperation and with some reluctance she took up her dressmaking again, something she had vowed not to do when she became the wife of a successful butcher. However, in agreeing to take up her sewing needle she was adamant it would only be for clients of her choosing and still leave time to visit Swineford.

When Martha left home the Priggs took in a girl from the village and, willing though the child was, it was clear it would be some time before she reached Martha's standard, therefore any help with the milking and churning was always welcome. On one such visit a concerned Mary Prigg, noticing how pale her normally robust daughter was looking, asked if she was sickening for something or was business so bad John was forcing her to take on too much work. Martha assured her mother that John was as caring and thoughtful as ever, adding how she enjoyed her sewing because it took her mind off other things. Looking to change the subject the young dairymaid walked past carrying a pail of warm milk straight from the cow giving Martha the chance to swiftly suggest,
*"Cum on Muther, we bain't got time t'talk bout sewing, there be churnin t'do."*

As the sweet smell of the fresh creamy liquid drifted past her nose Martha was filled with an uncontrollable urge to be sick and, turning on her heels, rushed outside for some fresh air. On her return she sheepishly pre-empted their knowing looks,

*"Well, don't know why that appened, I never bin sick like that afore."* gently patting her flushed cheeks with the palms of her hands.

Mary Prigg, standing in front of her daughter hands on hips head to one side, that old familiar worried look on her face, demanded, as if to prove her point, *"Martha, frum the day you wuz born til the day you left yer with John you was never sick at th'smell of fresh milk, what be ailin you?"*

Martha could hardly wait for Church the following Sunday when she could at last tell Mary Flower that, after more than a year, she was also expecting her first baby.

Both couples spent Christmas with their families.

After morning service Lamorock drove Mary the short distance to Kelston. It would be very quiet over at Saltford this year but everyone agreed it was best for Mary, in her advanced stage of pregnancy, not to attempt the journey, there would be plenty of time for family gatherings after their baby was born. However it would be far from dull because, this year, they were joined by Aunt Ann Tippett and her new husband John Partridge, the pair had married at St. Mary's Bitton earlier in the month.

John and Martha also attended Church before spending Christmas with the Priggs. Last year they all squashed into John and Martha's cottage and she naturally wanted to do the same again this year but there was now a good excuse for going to Swineford, apart from lack of space there was the small problem of the slaughterhouse and Martha's dreadful morning sickness!

Later that day the two families sat down to similar and yet very different festive fayre.

At Swineford everyone crammed around the old scullery table to feast on a large piece of mutton, supplied by John, cooked on a spit in front of the open range, accompanied by vegetables from the garden followed by preserved apple and plumb pudding covered with homemade cream, washed down with a choice of some very good elderberry wine or rough, very rough, cider. John glanced around the table, at his precious Martha in particular, before rising to his feet, mug in hand, to silently remember his family and John Hulburd for giving him a chance in life. He then asked everyone to join him in a toast to his present family and the new one he and Martha were about to start. Meanwhile, a mile further up the road, another family gathered for their Christmas. The Flowers sat around their large extended dining table to roast goose followed by an irresistible pudding. This veritable feast was washed down with some good wine and, of course, Flowers Ale. Mary was not enjoying this Christmas at all and faced the coming year with trepidation, in less than two months she would be a mother, with no idea or advice from anyone about how she was going to cope with the pain of childbirth, she fretted over whether the baby would be healthy, would they both survive and, most important of all, would it be the desired boy the family expected. At the beginning of February Ann Flower arrived to supervise the birth of her first grandchild having first engaged a local midwife who in turn had recommended a reliable wet nurse, should one be needed.

Mary was inconsolable when the baby was a daughter not the longed for son and heir. Lamorock, if disappointed, did not show it and a few days later, when the baby was taken to St. Mary the Virgin to be Baptised Honor, they proudly showed her to John and Martha who were amongst the congregation. Martha thought Mary looked very tired but tactfully chose to say,
*"Me n my John be s'glad you be alright, I were so pleased when he cum ome wiv thy good news."* Then, gazing at the baby dressed in her Valecienne laced muslin gown and knitted lace cap cradled in her mothers arms, Martha whispered, *"I be longin fur my babby to come but,"* walking away safely out of the earshot of both husbands she confessed, *"I be s'scared bout bringin im into th'world though."*

Mary smiled, handing Honor into the safe arms of Grandmamma Ann she led Martha gently by the arm, away from the rest of the crowd, for a quiet 'motherly' talk.

In March the Flowers gathered in Bitton for the wedding of Susannah Francis and John Huddleston, causing those not invited to imply that this was yet another fortuitous union between two influential families. Those envious of their good fortune perceived how the bride was the eldest daughter and co-heiress of a prosperous old widower who had already seen his youngest daughter make an advantageous marriage and his eldest son marry a wealthy young lady from Pucklechurch. Who would ever forget when William Francis brought his new wife, Elizabeth Nicholls, home to Bitton for the first time in a magnificent carriage and four?

Susannah's husband was the eldest son of the late John Huddleston, Rector of Kelston and grandson of the late Lawson Huddleston Arch Deacon of Bath and Wells, also a former Rector of Kelston. Through his father the groom was directly descended from Sir John and Lady Jane Huddleston of Cumbria, a Seymour by birth, whilst through his grandmother Helena Harrington he could trace his ancestry back to the eccentric Sir John Harrington of Kelston, inventor of the first flush water closet and a Godson of Elizabeth 1. John was only three when his father died so he hardly knew him. However, like Lamorock, he had known his bride and her family since childhood.

Martha, always a buxom young woman, blossomed as she waited for the birth of her first child whilst John, thanks to very hard work and long hours, had taken on a young delivery boy to give him more time to spend with her. Even those haughty wives who once snubbed her now looked to her husband to supply their households with their weekly meat order. She always planned to go home to her mother for the birth, despite pressure from Mary Flower to stay in Bitton and employ a midwife. So it was at Swineford, with Grandma Prigg in attendance, that Robert Worlock entered the world. For once John chose to care for live animals instead of the carcasses of dead ones and offered to look after his in laws animals, that way, although not actually present for the birth, he was close by and the moment Robert arrived he hastily relinquished his temporary farm labourers' duties to see his wife and new son.

John returned home to Bitton alone next day, he had a business to run, although there was small chance of that as he constantly re-assured customers and callers alike that mother and baby were fine, although very tired and would return as soon as Martha was strong enough. By mid afternoon, accepting he would never get anything done so long as he remained in Bitton, he planned his escape and told a stunned delivery boy,
*"I be takin th'orders out t'day, tell them what calls you bain't got no idea where I be."*

Harnessing up the old horse John trundled his way out of Bitton towards the tiny hamlet of Upton Cheyney, which was how he came to meet Lamorock Flower who was at the Ale House when he arrived with the last of his deliveries. Lamorock clasped John's hand warmly as he congratulated him on the birth of a son and, thrusting one of two tankards of ale into his hand, they raised a toast to 'our families'. The pair then spent what remained of the afternoon discussing their businesses over a second tankard until John realised,
*"I shud be makin fur ome else it'll be late afore I d'reach Swineford"* so, with another firm handshake, John took his leave but not before he heard himself saying, *"My Martha ould be pleased fur Mrs Flower to visit an see our Robert as zun as they do cum ome."*

The return journey was all a bit of a haze, thanks to those tankards of ale; fortunately the lumbering old horse knew his way home well enough and it was only when he was taking a cold sobering wash under the pump that John realised what he had said to Lamorock! After feeding and bedding down the horse John took a slightly staggered walk towards Swineford, desperately thinking how he was going to explain to Martha that he had invited Mary Flower to visit their cottage to see their new son after spending the afternoon drinking with her husband. As he walked so his mind cleared and he decided the best thing was to tell the truth, reasoning she was on friendly enough terms with Mary not to mind and there was no need to go into too much detail over his drinking spree because anyone with an ounce of sense could see he was far from sober and Martha of all people should know how one tankard of Flowers Ale made the strongest of legs go weak. Unfortunately in his case, it would appear two clearly did the same to brains and the power of speech as well.

Robert was just over a week old when Martha brought him home, she had spent the days since his birth cosseted and spoilt by her family but now it was time to return to Bitton and become the family for which she and John had waited so long. A few days later Martha answered a gentle tap on the door to find Mary Flower standing there. With no choice but to invite her in Martha motioned towards the front parlour but, hearing the sound of Robert gurgling, her visitor ignored her and made for the scullery where, scooping the boy into her arms, Mary turned to his proud mother,
*"Next time we shall have a son!"* as tears ran uncontrollably down her face.

Using her best china and some precious bohea, the only tea she and John could afford, Martha settled down to spend an afternoon talking about babies, husbands, households and Mary's desire for a son. In fact they completely forgot all sense of time until there came a loud knock on the door and Martha discovered a large drayman from the Mill on her doorstep. Embarrassed at being found socializing and taking tea with a butcher's wife Mary muttered,
*"Oh Mrs Worlock I really must go, thank you so much for your hospitality and for inviting me to see your beautiful son, please pass on Mr Flowers' kind regards to your husband will you?"* and with that the Mistress of Boyd Mill swept from the cottage, climbed aboard the wagon waiting outside and returned home alongside her husbands giant of a delivery man.

Christmas was tinged with sadness, John Partridge died in mid November and was laid to rest in St. Mary's Churchyard less than a year after he and Aunt Ann had married. This year the Priggs broke with tradition and joined John and Martha at Bitton where their cottage rang with laughter especially during the late afternoon when everybody was encouraged to play games by candle light. Both families looked forward to the coming year and a future of health happiness and prosperity which, for the butcher and his wife, began with the news that there was another baby on the way. This time it was the Miller's wife who watched as Martha's already ample figure blossomed with impending motherhood whilst she suffered as each passing month saw no sign of another longed for child but at least there was another family wedding to take her mind off things, Mary's youngest brother Richard Francis was to marry Mary Seldon at Bitton in June.

The Worlock's second child, another son whom they named Thomas, was born at home and as John sat on the bed next to his wife, new son in his arms Robert asleep in hers, he felt sure the future of his family business was now safe in the hands of these two little boys. The birth had not been so straight forward this time and with Martha confined to bed for a few extra days the Priggs organised a rota of aunts and sisters to look after her. Mother and son were still in bed when Mary Flower paid another unannounced visit, Honor was with her this time and the child took to Martha's sister Hannah Willis, who was busying herself in the scullery, almost immediately and soon had her playing on the floor alongside Robert, allowing her mother to slip upstairs to see Martha and the new baby. As they talked so playful sounds of Hannah and the children could be heard downstairs prompting Mary to confide,

*"I do so wish Mamma had lived to see Honor."*

As more screams and squeals drifted towards them Martha asked,
*"I thought thy mother n law ad took er place".*

Mary retorted,
*"Apart from her precious sons my mother in law allows no one to get close to her and would definitely not wish to be found sitting on any floor playing with her grandchildren. If she had her way my days would be spent at Lamorock's side and Honor would be in the care of a nursery maid. She is always saying if I did not insist on caring for my daughter myself then I might have given him a son by now!!"*

Martha, still weak from her long confinement, was not prepared for such emotions; however her visitor was not to be silenced and bemoaned the fact both her sisters in law and now her sister were expecting babies during the coming months.

*"It should be me Martha, it should be me!"*

The birth of a son, named after his father and grandpapa, for Richard and Mary Francis, a son, named after his father and grandpapa, for Susannah and John Huddleston and a daughter for William and Elizabeth Francis did nothing to lift Mary's melancholia, if anything it made her more depressed than ever, causing her to declare to those prepared to listen,
*"I am destined to be barren."*

Prompting Martha, who appeared to be the only person brave enough to dare answer her back, to remind her after Church one Sunday,
*"Don't thee be s'silly, ow cas thee be barrun wiv she,"* pointing at Honor, *"runnin bout thy feet?"*

Unaccustomed to having her word or opinions challenged, especially by the wife of a lowly butcher, however close their friendship, Mary exclaimed, *"Oh really Martha, I am barren when it comes to sons!"*

By winter everything was conveniently forgotten, Mary was pregnant, yet still she was not happy and Martha was convinced she never would be unless she had something to complain about, she should try living the lives of her 'dearest Lamorocks' workforce. Honor wanted for nothing whilst the poor labourers employed by her Papa found it a constant struggle to feed and clothe all the unplanned and, in most cases, unwanted babies arriving every year. In the years between her daughter's birth and the arrival of this new baby Martha could show the Mistress of Boyd Mill women who had given birth to at least three babies not to mention those who had lost as many to disease, malnutrition and stillbirth!

In May 1781, with the same midwife and her mother in law in attendance, Mary gave birth to a long awaited son. His father spent the day trying to work as normal whilst inside the Mill House Grandmamma Ann was asked to name the child. Everyone expected her to choose George after her husband but, gently rocking her first grandson in her arms, Ann desperately fought back her tears as she announced,
*"He is the first son of the next generation, therefore he is to be called Lamorock."*

A few days later the Flowers took their new son to St Mary the Virgin where he was given the name of his father and generations of Flowers before him. In quieter moments during the next few weeks his father would hold him and, like John Worlock, imagined the future was safe with this precious little boy.

The future, however, for the Worlocks was about to be further strengthened because, by the time baby Lamorock arrived, Martha was well into her third pregnancy and later in that year Samuel entered the world. With three babies life in their cottage was hectic, if not a touch crowded and John was working harder than ever to provide for his growing family, all the while safe in the knowledge that with three sons he had set his business on a sound footing.

The Flowers would never know what it was to go without food or to be so cold on a winter's night an entire family would cram into one room with as many as you could get into one bed, to walk barefoot to work before spending hours down a coal mine or at a grist mill grinding dusty grain. They were probably not even aware their young scullery maid had left her bed well before dawn to light the fire for their hot water before preparing their breakfast, how could they ever know real hardship cocooned as they were in their comfortable mill?

With the Worlock business flourishing their boys were also shielded from severe hardship, unlike Joseph Woodman just down the lane from them. Joseph earned less than 10/- for seventy hours at the coal face deep underground, from this Mrs Woodman had to feed a large brood, find 13/- to buy a years supply of coal on which the whole family depended for cooking, hot water and heat, pay the rent and, with what was left over, buy all the things they were unable to make, raise, grow or catch themselves.

John fully expected his boys to follow him across the yard to the slaughterhouse just as the young Woodman's would surely follow their father to the coal face. Boys of no more than eight or ten were already working underground alongside their fathers, brothers and uncles. Accidents were common place, one poor lad had his brains dashed out by falling down a mine and a thirteen year old was working at the bottom of a coal shaft when a large stone fell onto his head killing him instantly. Then there was the nine year old, employed to fill carts, who suffered a fractured skull when a large lump of coal fell off the cart he was loading, he survived but was left an imbecile for the rest of his tragic short life.

Fortunately Martha was not only married to a successful butcher but could also rely on her sewing skills whenever she chose, unlike the exhausted Mrs Woodman who, constantly pregnant, could not go out to work but spent long hours toiling at home making pins. Before he was declared bankrupt Mr Champion from Warmley Foundry delivered pins to be finished by the likes of Mrs Woodman, now most of her neighbours had their own pin blocks installed in their homes and production had developed into a thriving cottage industry with machines, often shared by several families, finishing pins at a rate of one every two seconds. When production was in full swing the noise around the quiet lanes of Oldland and Bitton was deafening.

Of course not everyone could afford, or chose, to install their own pin blocks in which case they took in filthy laundry, worked as domestic labourers or did menial jobs for which the most a woman might expect to earn from one of the big houses was no more than 6d a day but, as the implacable Mrs Newton and Mrs Brain were at pains to point out,
*"Is it not enough that we feed them with what is left from our table,"* whilst further congratulating each other by adding, as if more proof of their generosity were needed, *"and allow them to take home our wet tea leaves to dry out and re-use."*

Labour was cheap. One employer, on being censured by an Inquest Jury following an accident at his pit where five men fell to their deaths when the rope bringing them to the surface after a 12 hour shift underground proved to be nothing more than 'rotted broken old junk', rounded on the Jury to arrogantly declare,

*"I am not responsible; I concern myself so little with the works that I seldom go there."* Laying the blame on the shoulders of his unfortunate works manager he further exposed his utter contempt for his workers by circulating a poster offering a £20 reward, a small fortune to his employees, to anyone who could give him information about who had stolen some fruit trees from his garden. Tea was plentiful, especially the inferior bitter black tasting Chinese bohea, if you could afford it; beer and cheap cider was even more plentiful, poaching common with rabbits the mainstay of many a poor starving labourers family diet, occasionally there was fish from the nearby River Avon but that was fraught with danger as it was in constant use by the barges on their way to Bath and more than one stranger already lay in Bitton Churchyard having been dragged from its fast flowing waters and it was best not to get caught poaching as the local Magistrates took a dim view of this, especially should the land belong to them or their cronies.

Then there were those with no intention of doing an honest days work, preferring to rob those who did of their hard earned wages, roaming the lanes terrorising households, travellers, law abiding citizens, relieving them of anything worth stealing. Women in Bitton feared for their safety, especially after one poor lady's maid was robbed at knifepoint of 5/- and a silver thimble by two men reputedly dressed as sailors and who could forget the elderly man who was stopped on the road to Oldland, struck about the head, robbed of his money and left for dead, had he not been found he would have surely succumbed. Burglary was rife; the most common time when it was known the family would be at Church on Sunday, until householders realised there was a pattern and more criminals were caught red handed. Nowadays stealing was no longer an exclusively male activity, only recently a woman and her two sons were caught following a burglary where they had stolen a watch, money and some gold rings.

Of course there was no need for Mary Flower to find herself paid work, her days were spent being the charming hostess to her husbands' business friends, supervising her household whilst all her provisions were delivered or supplied by the likes of John Worlock or the Priggs. Lamorock would never need to go poaching to feed his brood, although he did occasionally go out coursing or shooting with his friends when their sport was mainly pigeons, pheasants or the ducks who dared to settle on his millpond. Following the birth of her son Mary took in a young girl from the Poor House as a nursery maid, giving her the freedom to be at her husbands' side. Martha, on the other hand, continued to help John support their family with her dressmaking, it was just that every time she picked up her needle and thread again she discovered she was pregnant and, unfortunately, rarely enjoyed the best of health during the early months.

Both mothers were extremely lucky to have men who cared for them, not all women were so fortunate. Unmarried mothers, abandoned by the fathers of their illegitimate children, could only hope for meagre support from the Parish; even when the alleged father was traced he always vehemently denied responsibility leaving it to the unfortunate girl to convince the Overseer of the Poor of her innocence. The accused man might find himself in Lawfords Gate House of Correction until he agreed to support his bastard by paying for the support of his child or, better still, marry the mother against his will. It was never long before violence raised its ugly head and the screams of an abused wife were heard coming from one of the hovels, the tell tale bruises next day telling the full story. Now and then violence did not stop at bruising an unloved unwanted wife, sometimes the beating was so severe she died, always by accident of course and although it was rare the residents of the little cluster of cottages along the banks of the River Boyd could still remember one such brute who was charged with killing his poor wife when, following repeated blows to her head, he killed her on the spot.

The arrival of a fourth child, a daughter at last named Elizabeth, brought a temporary halt to Martha's pregnancies, allowing her time to regain her strength and concentrate on building up a select clientele of gentlewomen eager to employ her excellent dressmaking skills. Not for her the intricate but dangerous work hammering on a pin block all day, rubbing her hands red raw in the hot soapy water of a laundry or enduring the drudgery of domestic service, despite the added perks of scraps from the table and used tea leaves.

Martha always attended Church, occasionally she walked to St. Nicholas but mostly she worshipped at St. Mary's. John on the other hand had little time for religion although he never stopped her or the children from going and, sometimes, he accompanied her but the one thing they never discussed was the vexed subject of their Christenings and whilst it did not trouble their parents it clearly concerned their Vicar. Martha was leaving Church after morning service when Charles Elwes asked to have a word with her in the Vestry where, tapping impatiently on the hard cover of the Baptismal Register, he asked,
*"Mrs Worlock there appear to be no entries for your children in here, is there a good reason for this, is it an oversight or have they been baptized elsewhere?"*

Martha was so taken aback by his question she spluttered the first thing to come into her head which was to meekly admit,
*"We bain't never got round to it Zur, owever I'll talk t'my John th'moment I do get ome, that I will,"* prompting her to remember how she longed to take her babies to St. Mary's, just like the Flowers, following their safe

arrival but, knowing how John felt, never dared raise the subject. If she had learned anything about her husband since they married it was that he could be annoyingly stubborn at times and she knew he would not take kindly at being told what to do, especially by a clergyman and she had a good idea what his answer would be and she was not disappointed,

*"Martha, next Sunday thee tell is Revrunce that when we do decide t'get em done he'll be the fust to know!"*

Naturally the Flowers always appeared the more affluent but to John's way of thinking he was just as successful, his young delivery boy was now his trusted assistant and he was considering taking on his younger brother in his place. Martha still fussed over their brood, supplementing his income with her sewing, with four growing children their cottage was cramped at times and the couple often talked of moving to a larger place but John knew that was financially impossible. The intervening years had brought mixed fortunes for Mary and her family. 1780 began with the safe arrival of a daughter, Phyllis, for William and Elizabeth Francis only to end in sadness with her tragic death two weeks after her first birthday. Two years later Susannah Huddleston gave birth to a daughter Frances but before the year was out she had buried her three year old son, John, at St. Nicholas, Kelston. Despite all their family tragedy, one Sunday as Martha knelt to say her prayers she glanced up at the Flowers, then at the people from the Dower House and Cully Hall, in their comfortable box pews and asked God was it so wrong to want just a little of what they had.

The Worlocks stayed in their cramped, overcrowded cottage, the three boys in the second bedroom, Elizabeth in with her parents. John strove to be at home on Sunday afternoons but was often obliged to visit the households who considered themselves important enough to insist he give up the only time he had to spend with his family to call for their orders or to collect his payment. Things eased slightly as the two elder boys grew older and Martha allowed them to go with him, leaving her at home with the two younger ones.

By her fifth birthday Honor was old enough to begin her lessons although her brother was still too young, however this did not stop his father from looking towards the day he could take his young son and heir with him to the Mill for his special education to begin. Like her mother before her Mary chose to teach her daughter herself, lessons were in the nursery at the top of the house with the child sitting alongside Mamma whilst Lamorock lay in the arms of his nurse. Occasionally Papa would drop in and sit for a few moments whilst Honor struggled to read to him, once she had finished he would scoop her up in his arms tell her what a clever little girl she was, kiss Mary gently on her cheek and leave.

John was so restless Martha, unable take any more, whispered,

*"What be frettin you?"*

*"Martha I got summut t'say, summut that be gonna surprise thee but tis summut I bin thinkin bout fur sum time."* Sitting bolt upright in their creaky old bed, head resting on knees grasped under his chin, he confessed,

*"Thik talk thee ad wiv Revrunt Elwes bin playin on me mind, maybe tis time we ad our little uns Chrisund but they bain't goin to ee, they be goin t'Oldland!"*

Martha was rendered temporarily speechless by this unpredictable husband of hers, the one who never had time for religion but who was now suggesting they should have their children Christened.

Everything was arranged for the first Sunday in September, all the children's names and ages were written in the Baptismal Register in descending ages. Not one of them could read or write and although John had a smattering of an education it was highly unlikely any of them would ever be taught; however as he could read and write a little Martha encouraged him to set about teaching her and the children to at least sign their name but when it came to a proper education then Martha, Robert, Thomas, Samuel and Elizabeth Worlock had none.

There was a second baby for William and Elizabeth when Ann was welcomed into their nursery, followed in January 1784 by a second daughter, Rebecca, for Lamorock and Mary Flower. Village gossip eventually reached Martha that because it had been a long, difficult birth there would be no more children and, because she was so weak, Mary had willingly handed the baby over to a wet nurse brought in from the village. Rebecca relied on her wet nurse until Mary was strong enough to leave her lying-in bed, after which she had been spoilt dreadfully. This daughter wanted for nothing, unlike her siblings she could do no wrong, if she failed to get her own way she soon learned that by misbehaving her father, desperate for peace and quiet to carry out his Parish work now he was one of the Overseers of the Poor, would tell Mary and the household servants to give into her demands. With the approach of her first birthday everyone's attention was focussed, not on Rebecca, but on Susannah Huddleston and her new son Lawson. For some unknown reason there had been no celebrations for her second birthday and, with her third birthday growing near, Mary was pregnant again and, in view of her last confinement, decreed a party too stressful. However any joy and happiness over this new baby was over shadowed by the death of Mary's brother Richard and the family joined his grieving young widow and son to say their goodbyes at St Mary's Bitton.

A month later Mary and Lamorock returned to the same Church for the Christening of their daughter Ann. Although the family lovingly welcomed this baby her grandfather saw little to celebrate, the death of his son at the age of twenty seven, coupled with the earlier deaths of two of his grandchildren, offered old Richard Francis little to live for. Not even the appointment of his son William to his old job as Surveyor of the Highways could raise his spirits and he determined to set his affairs in readiness to meet his maker and join his beloved wife, son and grandchildren. The arrival of a sister, followed a month later by another daughter for Susannah Huddleston, found Rebecca no longer the centre of attention but showing she was capable of flying into a rage should she fail to get her own way. Grandmamma Ann declared she had never known a child quite like her and suggested her mother did not to bring her to Kelston without her nurse, invitations from Saltford came with a similar hint, *"No-one will be the least bit offended if Rebecca does not come with you."*

Even the congregation at St. Mary's were becoming accustomed to having their prayers regularly disrupted with screams, stamping feet and tantrums should Miss Rebecca Flower be in attendance. Finally, following constant complaints from his congregation, the Vicar had been obliged to have a quiet word with Lamorock suggesting the nursery maid be given instructions to take the child home the moment she gave any sign of misbehaving. Naturally Rebecca revelled in such attention, all she had to do was make a scene and she immediately got her own way.

From her pew Martha watched as, once again, Rebecca caused mayhem during morning service. There was no point trying to talk to Mary any more, the child bored easily and, already agitated, took great delight in spitefully kicking out at all the other children. Lamorock rarely attended Church these days, choosing to use precious peace and quiet to catch up on his accounts.

Back home Martha helped the children out of their Sunday clothes,
*"Why do thik girl cry n shout in Church all th'time?"* Elizabeth wanted to know.
*"I don't know my pet but me n' thy father don't want thee t'be like er"*, was Martha's carefully chosen reply.

Although they were caring parents the Worlocks expected their children to behave and whilst John had shown a strict side to his nature on more than one occasion he never had cause to raise his hand to them and was proud to take them anywhere. By now there was another daughter, Hester and once she was safely tucked up in her tiny cot Martha took the other children in search of their father, eager to tell them all about what had happened at Church this morning. They found him in the orchard casting an expert eye over a fattening pig he was planning to slaughter, fed on the discarded whey from Martha's butter this particular porker must have thought he was in piggy heaven, little realising he was destined to fall under John's pole axe to become bacon and salted pork to feed the family through the winter.

Placing his strong arm around Martha's very ample waist they walked around the small paddock discussing all the latest news, especially the latest outburst of that little vixen Rebecca Flower.

*"She scream'd all drew Vicars sermon just cus she weren't able t'get from er mother or thik girl who d'look after er an when they did the readin from the bible you cussent hear what were bin said."* As her husband shook his head in disbelief Martha continued, *"Oh John t'wer awful, when they took er outside we cud still ear er screamin, nun of us could say our prayers.."*

*"Don't know why they d'take er cus they d'know ow she be gonna be'ave,"* was the best John could say as way of supporting an obviously distressed Martha.

*"They d'say Mary bain't got no choice cus Mr Flower do insist on there bein quiet when he be ome these days,"* came Martha's accusing reply.

Behind closed doors, away from young impressionable ears, the Worlocks blamed Mary for Rebecca's behaviour. Handed over to a wet nurse at birth with a father more concerned with educating his only son, happy to leave his daughters in the care of his wife and nursemaid, was it any wonder there were problems. Highly strung, Rebecca was already displaying the defiant streak everyone warned would one day cause her nothing but trouble. Bored with nursery life she wanted to be alongside Mamma when Honor took her lessons but, having got her own way, she quickly lost interest and caused such disruption the long suffering nursemaid was told to take her away, usually fighting and screaming. As a result she no longer joined in the lessons. Now, as another birthday drew near, she was a sad little girl who truly believed no one wanted or loved her. She saw her brother and sisters getting their parent's attention, Papa always managed to find time to listen as Honor read to him whilst forever boasting how Lamorock would soon be old enough to join him at the Mill and Mamma was forever in the nursery cradling Ann but each time she looked for her turn all she heard was,

*"Rebecca, why can you not sit down and be quiet?"* or, more often than not, it was, *"Why can you not be like Honor for a change?"*

Needless to say she was rapidly becoming very unhappy.

Heaving a weary sigh Charles Elwes locked the heavy oak door, grateful he had managed to placate the last of his angry parishioners. Following Rebecca's latest outburst he had been besieged by his congregation demanding something be done about her or they would join their neighbours at St. Nicholas, Kelston. Despite asking God for help none was forthcoming and, in no great hurry to return to the Vicarage but all the while still hoping for guidance, Charles decided to walk along the peaceful banks of Boyd Brook past the labourer's cottages before turning back towards the potholed track that was the excuse for the main road into Bath. He was acutely aware he could ill afford to lose any more of a flock already depleted by the enthusiastic magnetic preaching of the followers of John Wesley and George Whitefield currently drawing converts in their hundreds at their open air meetings in Kingswood. As he walked he recalled an old story he had once heard of a supposed undignified meeting between the self proclaimed 'King of Bath' Beau Nash and Methodist Motivator John Wesley when Mr Nash angrily ordered the Preacher to stop inciting the inhabitants of Bath at his open air sermons, only to be asked by the ever astute Wesley whether he had ever heard any of the aforesaid sermons, *"No, I only have your reputation to go on!"* was the reputed dismissive response.

*"Well, if it is reputations we are discussing then you are a fine one to talk"* replied the charismatic Wesley.

However, returning to his present dilemma, unless Charles Elwes addressed the problem then lose them he would. Men in his position were to be envied, living as he did in a large comfortable Vicarage with the support of a Curate in a Rectory reputed to be one of the oldest houses in the area, parts of which dated back to the 13th century. Thanks to his brother in law, King Henry V111, Thomas Seymour once owned the Rectory and it was his family who later bequeathed the magnificent blue Seymour Altar Cloth still in use at St Mary's.

Deep in thought Reverend Elwes gradually became aware of children's laughter coming from a nearby cottage.

*"Gud day to ee Revrunt"*, John Worlocks distant voice roused him from his daydreams.

Looking past the short stocky man in front of him to the orchard beyond, Charles spied the Worlock brood laughing and playing, making him realise how very different were the lives of the affluent to those with nothing of any substance but love in their hearts. Passing a few pleasantries, both men had long agreed to respect each others views when it came to religion, Charles bade his goodbyes allowing John to return to his family leaving him to continue on his slow way still desperately trying to find an answer to his dilemma.

He would be the first to admit how, in his early days here, he misguidedly paid more attention to the influential members of his congregation. Despite two flourishing Mills, some fairly large farms, pin machines, expanding collieries and the latest cottage industry to reach the village, hat making, his was a very poor Parish. Roads connecting the village with prosperous Bath, some six miles away and places further a field like Bristol were bad. Labourers and their families crammed into cottages in dire need of repair from absentee landlords very reluctant to spend money on even the most basic needs. It was not unusual to find children of poor miners or labourers running about the potholed roads bereft of shoes or warm clothes, especially during the bitter winter months when infant mortality increased dramatically because wages never covered all their needs. Overseers of the Poor, men like Lamorock Flower and his father in law, were often approached with pleas for parish relief when the best a widow or the family of man too sick to work might expect ranged from 1/- to 4/- a week with which to feed and clothe them all.

Charles knew only too well that his poor flock supplemented their meagre diets by poaching, stealing a few eggs, gathering firewood, snaring the odd rabbit or catching a fish or two from the river, how else would they survive? Self sufficiency was the norm, taking risks and bending the rules high on the agenda, which was fine so long as you did not get caught because you would be condemned by the very people from whom you were adjudged to be stealing, people who thought nothing of handing out vindictive brutal punishments as a deterrent to those caught taking game or property from their land. Over the years he had grown to understand his poor parishioners, they attended Church and came to him with their problems even though he treated them with a certain amount of unnecessary aloofness at times. Despite some who deserved to feel the weight of the law about their collar most made him welcome in their hovels unlike their 'betters' who presumed he was only after money for his Church and bitterly complained they were already paying enough through their Parish Rates. There had been many times he found himself pleading, unsuccessfully, for clemency on behalf of a labourer caught poaching only to watch helplessly as the poor man was sentenced to a long prison term with hard labour, leaving a wife and young family to starve had it not been for Parish Relief. Now he had the spoilt daughter from one such family threatening to disrupt the worship of these loyal Parishioners,

*"What to do! oh what to do indeed !!!"*

# CHAPTER THREE

Richard Francis spent the years following the death of his son preparing for the time when he would join him and his beloved wife. During those years he saw Rebecca's behaviour cause a serious rift between her parents. Lamorock expected to be left alone in his study on Sundays, happy for Mary and the young nursemaid to take the children to Church, which was fine until Rebecca threw a temper tantrum. Finally when large numbers of the congregation actually carried out their threats to worship at Kelston, (some were even seen leaving the local Methodist Hall), it left the Vicar with little option but to visit the Mill on a sacrosanct Sunday to plead with Lamorock to do something.

Old Richard was very fond of his grandchildren and made them all welcome; Richard Jnr. was nearly eight and since his father's death had grown very close to his old Grandpapa. Honor loved him dearly as did young Lamorock and, despite what everyone else said, Grandpapa Francis did not find Rebecca a problem, probably because she returned all the love and attention he gave her. He made time to sit her on his lap, or on a stool next to him, where they talked about everything or anything. In his lonely old age he often thought back to the days before his marriage and the overpowering atmosphere of his home at Northstoke, especially when the Flowers or their lawyers were there to discuss Mary's dowry or to negotiate which Flower property she would be bringing with her. Fortunately, unlike his unhappy little grand daughter, he was able to escape to the sanctuary of the small knoll on which the tiny Church of St Martins stood with Kelston Tump and the rolling hills towards Lansdown beyond. In the distance, with the sweeping valley towards Bitton at his feet, he would just make out Boyd Mill, little realising how one day his youngest daughter would marry her cousin and become its Mistress.

Richard was known to have a good eye for property and owned a share of Lower Farm with his son in law and his nephew George. There was his house in Bitton, some eighteen acres of land bought from the estate of the late John Smith of Oldland and the Keynsham property, held by him for the life of his widowed sister in law Ann Partridge, currently let to a Surgeon and Apothecary. Naturally with the early death of Richard it was William who would inherit the bulk of his estate, although his daughters and numerous grandchildren would not be forgotten.

On very rare occasions, usually following a particularly bad episode with Rebecca, Lamorock would call on Richard for advice and so it was that, following the meeting with Reverend Elwes, he was found sitting opposite the old man whilst, over a quiet talk, he revealed,

*"I assured our Vicar that whilst he and his devout flock may hold onto the misguided belief that Rebecca only misbehaves at Church her tantrums are not exclusively reserved for their ears, she is far worse at home!"* Relaxing in a large comfortable old Queen Anne chair, the warm glow from the contents of an almost empty glass of sherry, made Lamorock very reluctant to return to the mayhem his daughter caused these days. *"If she fails to get her way it is her brother and sisters who suffer, in fact we have instructed the nursemaid never to leave her alone with Ann, such is her jealousy."*

Staring intently at the intricate twisted design on the stem of his glass Richard Francis, desperate for inspiration, drew in a large breath then let out a sigh, *"So, how do you and my daughter plan to deal with the situation?"*

He was not surprised when he did not receive an answer, although he could not have known it was because his son in law was silently reliving yesterday's conversation with Reverend Elwes.

Accepting Lamorock preferred to spend his Sundays peacefully at home but acutely aware of the gamble he was taking, the Vicar had proposed,
*"Mr Flower, rather than ask Mrs Flower to leave your young daughter at home next Sunday might I humbly suggest you accompany your family then, should Miss Flower misbehave,"* which he knew she would, *"you will see the problem for yourself."*

To Mary's utter disbelief Lamorock agreed to accompany her, their three older children and as many Flowers as could be gathered, to Church next Sunday whilst the nursemaid stayed at home with Ann.

Standing with his back to the altar Charles Elwes surveyed his flock at the beginning of morning service and fancied there were several old faces he had not seen in the congregation for a while, even John Worlock was there alongside the Wilmots, the Caines and the Haynes; these last three families were not particularly known for their religious convictions....only their criminal convictions. Eventually his eyes rested on the Flower family pew and on Lamorock in particular, it had been some months since he had attended Church, always using pressure of work as an excuse whenever the Vicar chanced to meet him and enquire when they would be seeing him again. The last time Charles posed such a question suggesting,
*"The Lord's Day is a day of rest for all people,"* it brought about,
*"If I don't keep the Mill working there will be no employment for the labourers of Bitton, you and I look after our flocks in different ways,"* from an indignent Lamorock.

Turning back to face the altar the Vicar glanced up at Christ on the Cross and offered a silent prayer of thanks for moving the heart of Lamorock, despite what was by all accounts very heated arguments with his wife, to fulfil his promise to attend Church with his family. Walking towards the West door Charles stopped to politely acknowledge his presence,
*"How wonderful to see you this morning Mr Flower,"* only to notice the party had been swelled by Lamorock's mother, Mary's father and Mrs Partridge. Making his way back towards the altar the Vicar of Bitton mused, *"It only needs his brother from Saltford, William Francis and Susannah Huddleston to walk through the door and the entire family will be here!!"*

Furtively glancing at the rest of the congregation, avoiding any eye contact with those eager to witness his embarrassment but fully aware of what his daughter was capable of doing, Lamorock suddenly regretted agreeing to this morning's exhibition but there was no going back now. Rebecca, blissfully unaware she was the reason for her family gathering, sat quietly alongside Mary whilst Lamorock prayed she would, please God, behave. The congregation stood as Reverend Elwes made his way to the altar steps, welcomed everyone and announced the first hymn. Rebecca enjoyed standing to sing the hymns because it meant everyone could see her and if there was one thing she craved it was admiration from others, however sitting down again it was not long before she showed her true colours. No one had thought to warn Lamorock that she usually misbehaved during the Bible readings or the sermon and everything was fine until the Vicar climbed the steps to the pulpit where, looking down on the high sided oak pews, he could see the child already trying to escape from Mamma and Grandmamma, between whom she was sitting. The pulpit gave the best vantage point as the sides of the private family pews were so high the rest of the congregation could never see what was going on; however, this morning they did not have long to wait to find out because Reverend Elwes had barely begun his sermon when there came a piercing scream from the direction of the Flower family pew as Rebecca clambered onto the lap of a very startled Aunt Partridge, in an attempt to flee Grandmamma who was desperately trying to keep her granddaughter in her seat by holding on to her flaying legs.

Encouraged by Thomas Strange and William Atkins, his two Churchwardens sitting directly beneath him, Charles struggled to finish his Sermon against high pitched screams and, as the melee and chaos increased, Mary's voice could be heard imploring,
*"Rebecca dearest, Rebecca my pet"* or just *"Rebecca.... Please!!"*

The desperate pleas were to no avail, the child would not be pacified, dropping onto the floor she scurried on all fours between the feet of Mamma and

Grandmamma until, reaching the end of the pew and freedom she unfortunately found her father sitting straight backed and motionless blocking her exit!!. Reverend Elwes faltered again as he and his congregation waited to see what would happen next. With her screams reverberating around the high vaulted ceiling Lamorock suddenly rose to his feet and, without warning, took hold of his hysterical daughter, bowed briefly towards the altar and, glowering up at the stunned occupant in the pulpit, strode up the aisle and out through the West Door, dragging the struggling child behind him.

Inside St. Mary's as people recovered the Flowers sat motionless in their pew reluctant to look down at the congregation or up at the Vicar fearing it would bring further shame on them and wondered whether to follow Lamorock's example and leave.

Outside in the Churchyard Rebecca shook with anger, her chubby little tear stained face swollen and grotesque with rage, as her father vainly tried to calm her by gently holding her with one hand whilst caressing her mass of tangled untidy hair, bereft of its bonnet now blowing about the gravestones in the slight breeze, with the other.

As the anger subsided to a slight tremble Lamorock became genuinely concerned for his little daughter. Sadly Rebecca, not used to such affection from Papa but determined to escape him just as she did when Mamma made her do dull boring things, struggled to be free from his arms by fetching him a sharp kick on the shin after which she bit the back of the hand he had lovingly placed around her shoulder. Neither hurt, however Rebecca was once again completely uncontrollable leaving her hapless father with no choice other than to scoop the writhing hysterical child into his arms, place her on the box before climbing alongside her and urge the horse to get them home, all the while ignoring the strange looks and whispers from villagers they happened to pass on the way. Once home the nursemaid rescued the whimpering child from her father's arms and took her to the nursery where, totally exhausted, she was put to bed and soon slept. Lamorock was waiting, slightly more composed, at the foot of the nursery stairs when the nursemaid re-appeared,

*"Join me in my study, preferably before your Mistress returns, I wish to discuss certain things with Mrs Flower, however, it will help to hear your opinion of my daughter first."*

Back at St Mary's a much shortened service had ended, leaving a shocked congregation to make their silent way home. The Flowers were in utter disarray, Mary was crying already fearful of what would be said the moment they were safely behind the closed doors of the Mill. Ann Flower was mortified to discover her daughter in law had allowed the situation to reach such a point whilst

Aunt Partridge was so overcome and distraught at what people might think of her family she was presently being escorted back to her carriage so fearful were they that she might faint clean away. Mary vainly tried to defend herself, accusing Reverend Elwes of planning the whole thing. Sadly the congregation did not agree and appeared very eager to speak to their Vicar. Normally people could not wait to get away, now they waited patiently for their turn to speak to him about her precious daughter. No-one thought about talking to her, in fact they seemed to be doing their best to avoid her and rush away once they had spoken to Reverend Elwes. They claimed it was the weather and the need to get home before it turned to rain but she knew they were too embarrassed to face her. Then, as she made her way dejectedly towards the waiting carriage and her disapproving family, she heard Martha call out her name.

Prompted by Martha Mary told them to go on without her saying she preferred to walk with Honor and young Lamorock, desperate to prolong the inevitable row waiting for her at home. Martha joined her and together they strolled along the lane as their children, with the exception of Hester who tottered between them holding tight to her mother and Mary's hands, ran on ahead. Watching the youngsters running, shouting and laughing together gave Martha an idea; could Mary not suggest they be allowed to spend more time with other children, might Lamorock agree to them playing with hers now and again? Parting at the top of the lane Martha made her way back along the stream to her modest little cottage and John whilst Mary walked slowly up Golden Valley Lane towards her large, dusty, noisy Mill, unhappy daughter and angry unsympathetic husband. She knew there would be arguments and accusations as soon as she walked through the door…she was not to be disappointed.

As expected Lamorock reacted with horror at Mary's suggestion their children might mix with the ragged urchins in the village, she of all people should know the importance of giving the right impression. Choosing to bring the Worlocks into the argument by declaring,
*"Well, Martha has invited the children, especially Rebecca, to call at any time,"* was perhaps not the wisest thing with which to argue.

Meeting John Worlock as a business equal was one thing, allowing his children to enjoy a similar friendship was a completely different matter and, turning to his unfortunate wife, he asked,
*"And what makes you think I would want my children anywhere near those of Martha Worlock who is, after all, nothing but an illiterate common dressmaker?"*

*"For your information Lamorock, Martha Worlock was the only one to hold out a hand of friendship when our so called friends and neighbours turned*

*against me this morning and,"* swiftly reminding him, *"there is no need of an education for that!"* conveniently forgetting how, when in the company of her socially acceptable friends, she was usually the one who was scathing of the illiterate labourers of Bitton.

Weeks passed with neither giving way until, accepting he would never win, Lamorock finally conceded,

*"Do what ever you wish, I want nothing more to do with the whole affair, you can have your way so long as it does not interfere with the running of my business!"*

Much to John's relief, as weeks then months passed with no visit, it was clear Mary had conveniently forgotten Martha's invitation.

Unlike previous birthdays, this year Rebecca was holding a tea party; Grandmamma Flower and Grandpapa Francis were coming, Aunt Susannah was bringing Lawson, Mary and Frances; Aunt Mary promised to bring Richard but Aunt Elizabeth, whilst declining her *"sweet invitation"* had raised no objection to Ann and Susannah attending with their nursemaid. With the worrying exception of Grandpapa Francis everyone arrived by horse and carriage, cantankerous as ever he decided he needed some fresh air,

*"T'is a perfect day for a good brisk walk,"* he told a concerned Ann Flower, declining her offer of a seat in her carriage. By the time he eventually arrived, breathless and tired, everyone was anxiously waiting in the downstairs parlour.

As usual there was a huge fire blazing in the grate and, thanks to the constant noise from the Mill along with freezing temperatures outside, every window was closed, allowing no air to circulate around a room already overbearingly hot and stuffy. It was getting dark, with a flurry of snow in the air, when Grandmamma Ann decided to leave and, much to Mary's relief, this time Richard sensibly accepted the offer to join her for the short journey home.

Winter released its vice like grip, spring was returning to his garden as Richard Francis sat by his window watching his sheltered oasis yield up its rebirth. Still not fully recovered from the chill that nearly killed him, which the family blamed on his foolish decision to walk the mile up to the Mill in freezing temperatures for Rebecca's birthday tea, he searched for the appearance of tender young shoots clambering around the window frame. Glancing towards his orchard beyond, he saw the birds pairing up and knew it would not be long before the poor in the village started trapping them and any other living creature with a bounty on its head. Thinking back to his years as an Overseer of the Poor he recalled how the going rate was a farthing for the heads of every yellow hammer, greenfinch, sparrow and tit, moles were worth a penny and hedgehogs earned them a ha'penny. If nothing else this latest illness reminded him he was not immortal, he could have died and so, during the second week of April, he called in his lawyer and three chosen friends to act as witnesses.... it was time to put his affairs in order. The tragic death of his youngest son, leaving a young widow and orphaned grandson, played on his mind and he wanted to ensure they, along with his daughters, received their due. Then there were his other grandchildren, not to mention the Flower property his dear wife had brought with her as a dowry when they married.

The next time Richard was confined to his bed no one really expected him to recover, not even Mary who vainly held onto dearest Papa recovering.

The funeral, attended by his three surviving children, the cream of Bitton society and an assortment of ragged labourers, took place at St. Mary the Virgin causing those not particularly fond of the family but swift to criticise them nevertheless, to ask why he was not taken to Kelston to lie with his wife. Three weeks later his Will was proved in London and letters of Administration granted to William Francis and John Huddleston. Most of his considerable estate went to William, however unless he and Elizabeth had a son it was to be held in trust firstly for Lawson or, should he die without an heir, to the eldest Flower son. Should none of Mary or Susannah's boys live to enjoy their inheritance then everything was to go to the orphaned Richard. William was to continue the leasehold agreement on the property at Keynsham, held by his father for the life of Aunt Partridge, Susannah inherited a house along with its tenant at Highfield, Wick but, as with all the other property, should young Lawson die and there were no more sons then it was to pass to Mary and her sons on her sister's death. However if Mary or her sons died then the property reverted back to William and, ultimately his two daughters, not to Lamorock. After paying all debts, mortgages and funeral expenses Richard left detailed financial instructions; Mary received £100 and the income from various pieces of land in Bitton. All his grandchildren, with the exception of Richard, received a trust fund of £50 for when they reached their twenty first birthdays. His *"fatherless grandson"* received £100 in a similar trust fund for when he also reached twenty one. He did not forget his faithful housekeeper, Ann Chapman, to whom he bequeathed five guineas plus a week's wages, provided she was still working for him at the time of his death. William, Mary and Susannah were to share all his household goods, furniture, compliment household plate and linen along with any residue share and share alike, however his clothes, personal effects and what remained were left to William and John Huddleston, as Joint Executors, to dispose of as they thought fit.

Lamorock, fully expecting his father in law to be more generous towards Mary and the children, quietly fumed at what he considered a small inheritance compared to the others. Then towards the end of September came news that deepened Lamorock's mood even further, Elizabeth Francis gave birth to a son; William now had an heir.

# CHAPTER FOUR

**B**y the time Mary Flower eventually accepted her friend's invitation to visit it was November and far too cold for the children to play outside, instead Martha suggested they all stay indoors in the warm where an especially close eye could be kept on young Rebecca. Mary arrived clutching the youngster by the hand followed by Honor, who was frozen to the marrow and an exhausted nursemaid carrying Ann. For some unknown reason they had walked all the way from the Mill on what was possibly the coldest day of the year so far when Mary could have driven them herself or arranged for someone from the Mill to bring them, consequently the children were already tired, cold and irritable. Rescuing Ann from her nursemaid's aching arms Martha placed a welcoming arm around Rebecca's shoulders and led her freezing guests into the warmth of the scullery where Hester, Elizabeth and their two brothers Thomas and Samuel were waiting. Hopes of an immediate friendship were soon dashed, taking a swift look at the four Worlocks Rebecca scurried, not to her mother but into the sheltering arms of her nursemaid. The stand off lasted best part of the morning with Rebecca very reluctant to leave the safety of the girl's skirt, even when Martha tried to coax her with a new puppy from their old bitches' latest litter. Mary was no help whatsoever and kept harping on about how, 'Papa wouldn't want her to do this' or 'Papa wouldn't want her to do that' and, looking at the mangy mongrel wriggling in Martha's arms how, 'Papa had a fine hunting dog and would never let a dog like that into the house'.

Martha fought hard to hold her tongue, desperately wanting to say, *"S'what ould thy Papa like then?"*

With no animals for slaughter John was spending precious time with Robert out in the orchard checking on their own livestock from where he had spied Mary arrive, although he was sure she had not seen him. Around midday he dropped in, just to be sociable, with a jug of fresh milk from their old cow. The moment he appeared in the doorway Samuel and Elizabeth squealed with delight and excitedly launched themselves in his direction. Had Thomas not caught the jug of milk about to slip from his father's unsteady hands it would have surely spilled all over the floor. Gathering the children up in his empty arms John shuffled towards Hester where, placing the pair gently back on the floor, he bent down to scoop her up before turning, breathless, to face Mary, *"Well Missus Flower, ma'am, we d'certainly ave a fine brud of young uns b'tween us, bain't that a fact?"*

Mary Flower was unable to answer, she was completely lost for words because Lamorock never did such things with their children, if only he would. It was true he spent what time he could listening to Honor at her reading and he always tried to plan his very busy day around one of their meals whenever he was at home but to play with them, pick them up, laugh with them, no he would never do such things, of that she was quite sure. Finding her tongue at last she stuttered,

*"Yes...yes John, we, I mean Mr Worlock yes we both have fine sons and daughters."*

John had never been one for small talk, especially to well born ladies but he did his best,

*"We bain't sin Mister Flower fur some time, I ope e be well, th'Mill d'always look busy when I d'call."*

There was no way Mary was ready to admit, especially to the village butcher of all people that, thanks to Rebecca and her destructive ways, the atmosphere at the Mill was strained at present, so she played safe and simply replied,

*"He is quite well thank you but works far too hard of course, but I am sure you, as a fellow businessman, will appreciate he has little choice with a thriving Mill to run, a young son to train to take his place and so many people relying on him for work."*

John tactfully agreed adding,

*"I understands, we be doin the same wiv Robert bain't us Martha,"* all the while knowing all about life in the Flower household. There was little loyalty from domestic servants when it came to a bit of juicy gossip about your employer and his wife.

There were no more visits that year, Rebecca occasionally misbehaved on the rare occasions she was taken to Church and as the autumn of one year turned to the spring of the next both mothers continued to walk home from Church together. Martha continued to ask when Mary would be bringing the children to visit again even though she knew her invitations would be met with feeble excuses.

Easter was very warm, a fact not lost on Reverend Elwes as he looked at his morning congregation resplendent in their brightly coloured clothes. Gone were the drab blacks and browns of winter, spring was roaring in like the age old lion! John was with his family this morning and watched proudly as Martha and their girls sat quietly in their pew. They all had new outfits, even little Hester looked quite grown up in her first proper dress, how was she to know it was one of Elizabeth's hand me downs skilfully altered by her mother.

Whilst the three boys all wore new shirts, her husband had stubbornly refused her offer to make him one as well choosing instead to wear the familiar old jacket, breeches and shirt he usually wore on his rare attendances at Church. Martha had long since given up trying to persuade him it was time he had some new clothes.

The Flowers, of course, put on a splendid show. Father and son wore matching tailored grey jackets whilst Mary, dressed in her favourite blue with her hair tied in a topknot with matching ribbon, had chosen pale creams and yellow for her girls.

As the congregation settled Charles Elwes could not help but compare the happy babbling flock sat in the lower pews in front of him with the silent, upright coterie occupying their ornate high sided family pews and asked who were the more content, who had the most to lose, the shabbily but brightly dressed labourers or their exquisitely groomed but sombre employers looking down on them. Climbing the steps to the pulpit he made to start his sermon but not before throwing a long withering glance at Lamorock, who immediately looked down at his feet, then at Mary who simply stared straight ahead, before finally resting his eyes on Rebecca.

A few minutes into his sermon unfamiliar sounds came from the congregation, sounds that temporarily stopped him because they were not the expected shrill shouting, nor was it the normal temper tantrums or someone hastily dragging a screaming child outside. No, this sound was very different, this sound was laughter, a child's laughter, a child giggling followed by other children laughing and giggling as well. Glancing down, Charles saw Rebecca peering over the top of her pew towards the Worlock children who were waving and giggling at her from their places in the congregation. From his high vantage point she could be seen pulling faces at them whilst they made faces back at her. Lamorock moved to correct his giggling daughter only for Reverend Elwes to cough gently to attract his attention before shaking his head, the smile on his face indicating it was best to leave things alone.

As they left, the congregation commented on how short the sermon had been that morning,
*"Maybe Vicar be ill."*
*"Praps th'Good Lord ave let'n know ee do go on too long."*

Meanwhile, alone in the Vestry, the man himself was on his knees quietly thanking God for the sign he had sent during the service. Silently closing the old wooden door behind him Charles Elwes made his way out into the spring sunshine to rejoin his flock.

Mary could not be sure if it was because Lamorock was with her or if it was because their daughter had behaved herself but for some reason everybody was suddenly eager to befriend her again. Looking on from the safe distance of the churchyard gate Martha thought how fickle folk could be and how certain people, such as those now clamouring around Lamorock, had very short memories when it came to remembering how they had earlier shunned his unfortunate wife. No one appeared to be in any hurry to make their way home, even the Vicar who was always uncomfortable making small talk, was lingering longer than usual.

As the Flowers talked so their children played un-noticed until Lamorock, placing a gentle guiding hand on Mary's arm, said they should be returning home and realised they were nowhere to be seen. Mary assumed they were with Lamorock who expected them to be with her, someone suggested they were probably with their nursemaid until Mary said she had given her the day off to visit her family for Easter. Meanwhile Martha, waiting by the gate because there was no way she was going to join 'thik lot a hypocrites', was unaware of the panic ensuing by the Church door, had she known she could have told them that from where she was standing their children, even little Ann Flower, were happily playing with her ragtag brood along with a few other village children and, what was more, having the time of their lives.

Lamorock was not at all pleased to discover his children were playing with those of his own labourers, although he reluctantly agreed how happy they all seemed and how different Rebecca proved to be in Church this morning. John, who was standing next to Lamorock, decided to grab the chance by suggesting.

*"Tis such a luvly mornin would thee n Missus Flower care t'walk a while we Martha n me?"*

Not wishing to appear rude Lamorock had little choice but to agree, however he was not expecting to hear Martha add to his dilemma by proposing,

*"Why dussent thee n Missus Flower leave thy little uns wiv me n walk home fur zum preshus time on thy own?"*

Lamorock searched for an excuse for not wanting his children to stay, notwithstanding the fact he could not remember the last time he and Mary had shared any precious time on their own and forlornly blurted out the first thing to come into his desperate mind,

*"T'is very kind of you Mrs Worlock but as you can see, my son,"* placing a fatherly hand around his son's elegantly tailored shoulders, *"is not dressed for leisurely pursuits, perhaps another time might be arranged."*

Martha turned to the boy and ordered,

*"Lamruck take off thy jackut an give n t'me,"* only to fold it carefully over her arm, triumphantly turned to face his father and announced, with a touch of defiance in her voice,

*"He bain't wearin it now an,"* glancing towards her own sons, *"be just like t'others."*

That excuse having failed Lamorock tried,

*"I have arranged to take my son over to Saltford this very afternoon and,"* fearing Martha had plans for his daughters to also remain under her wing, *"my daughters do not have any coverings for their young shoulders should it turn cold."*

Martha, determined not to be beaten, assured him,

*"Dussent thee worry nun, I'll make sure thy boy gets ome in plenty o time to go wiv thee t'Saltferd an if it do turn cold yer little maids can borra one a Lizbeths shawls."*

Gazing at his perfectly groomed daughters and the simply clad Elizabeth Worlock, then back at Martha, Lamorock lamely protested,

*"They really are not dressed for playing."*

*"Nor be ours but t'is a pity t'stop um from walkin ome together,"* came Martha's swift reply.

Like a great many before him when it came to dealing with Mrs John Worlock Lamorock knew when he was beaten and, although far from convinced they were doing the right thing, he knew there was little point looking to Mary, who was secretly enjoying watching her husband suffering at the hands of this formidable woman, for support. Accepting there was no alternative he agreed, accepting it would not take long to reach the Worlock's cottage after which they could escape and go their separate ways. To Lamorock's horror John deliberately chose the long way home, instead of walking up the lane towards the village. Setting off through the churchyard in the direction of the far gate they turned, not in the expected direction of the village but down the lane towards the Dower House and Grange before circling around to the opposite side of the churchyard and then back to the High Street. Passing these two large elegant houses Lamorock prayed no one was at home to see them. Further on as a cluster of hovels, home to some of his own labourers, came into view he heard himself asking,

*"Please God, let them be away from home."*

Drawing ever closer it was obvious from the shocked expression on her face that Mary had no idea of the conditions in which these people lived, cocooned as she was in her Mill House surrounded by her family's money. John doubted whether Lamorock, who was currently an Overseer of the Poor and Mary, whose father had once held the same position, really understood the abject poverty in which their employees lived. Most of the labourers were fairly law abiding citizens unlike those a few miles away in Oldland where the only work was either on the land or down the pits in nearby Kingswood. There, thanks to greedy colliery owners demanding increased productivity for less pay from their hard pressed employees, lawlessness and protests against working conditions were common place. People blamed poverty and the attitude of the owners for the level of crime and, perhaps on a different day, John might have asked his companion if he thought better working conditions and pay would stop a similar crime wave creeping towards to Bitton, but, of course, he knew his place in the local social hierarchy and therefore held his tongue.

Luckily no one was at home; it was Easter Sunday and most labourers were using a precious day off to visit relatives. The children ran on ahead and were the first to reach the banks of the Boyd Brook; only young Lamorock stayed back preferring to be close to the father he adored. John was about to ask his companion if he could remember the last time he had walked down here when he overheard him softly telling his young son,
*"I would come here with Uncle George and Uncle William when we were boys,"*
then, not wishing his son nor wife to hear he turned and whispered to himself,
*"I had all but forgotten what it was like."*

John opened his mouth, about to say *"cluding they ovels back thur"* but thought better of it and said nothing.

Thoughts of his adored father actually playing only made young Lamorock eager to know more and the boy naively asked,
*"Papa, what did you all do when you played here?"*

Lamorock stopped and stared up at the sun shining through the sparsely covered branches of the trees and then down at the water trickling past his fine leather boots. His mind returned to his childhood days when they escaped during, what was to youngsters, a long tedious visit to Aunt Mary and Uncle Richard, to sit on the bank take off their shoes and stockings and wade into the cold water. Of course cousins Mary and Susannah, being girls, could only watch enviously from the bank…Aunt Mary would have been most displeased to have discovered her young daughters acting in such an ill bred manner,
*"Was Grandpapa angry if you returned home with wet feet and stockings like you are whenever we return home with dirt on our jackets?"* the boy innocently wanted to know.

*"Now that be a gud questun yung un,"* thought John, *"I wunder what thy father be goin t'say bout that"* as he waited for a stunned Lamorock to reply.

The answer, when it came, was for Lamorock to stride away rubbing his eye claiming,
*"A small fly has lodge itself making my eye water,"* rather than admit how, unlike his son, he never knew his father.

Continuing their walk both men discussed the present state of their businesses with Lamorock particularly eager to tell John he was considering altering the level of the weir feeding the water wheel to increase output at his Mill, a task he was considering paying William Shipp, a local Mason, 20 guineas to do.

This was, however, a family walk and as they continued their stroll so John was determined to get his companion to talk about his children instead of the state of his business and gradually brought his own brood into the conversation, pointing to each one in turn, *"We'm always bein told ow our Sam d'take after Martha's father an our Lizabeth."* Pointing in the direction of his eldest daughter happily fussing over all the others, *"be good wiv our youngest girl though our Thomas be a bit of a andful at times cus he be s'strong willed but our little Hester, bless er, makes up for it wiv her simple ways."* Pausing long enough to give Lamorock chance to join in and praise his own children before accepting none was forthcoming, John continued, *"me n Martha do hope to be blessed wiv more cus a family's appiness n future bain't complete wivout a ouseful of little uns, duss thee gree Mr Flower?"*

*"You are a fortunate man John Worlock,"* thought Lamorock, *"there is little chance of any more children whilst Mary continues to be as stubborn as she is at the moment."*

By the time the Worlock's cottage came into view Lamorock had given up on any serious conversation, how could you possibly talk profit and loss with a man as he carried his three year daughter on his shoulders whilst at the same time chase a crowd of laughing children, including Lamororck Jnr and Rebecca, around a tree. Martha took Mary and the children indoors for something to drink leaving their husbands to take a stroll and a pipe of baccie in the orchard until Lamorock reluctantly announced they must make their way back as he really was expected over at Saltford later that day and told Mary to gather the children. To cries and pleas to be allowed to stay longer John decided there was no time like the present and hinted,
*"They be getting on s'well, specially they two little maids,"* pointing towards Rebecca and Elizabeth who were happily feeding a crowd of ever hungry chickens, *"t'would be a cryin shame to stop um aving the same appiness thee*

46

*n Mr Garge shared when you wuz young, praps Missus Flower n my Martha could take um down by the brook when the weather do improve."*

With no support from Mary, Lamorock desperately searched for a reason for no such outing ever taking place, there was, after all, a limit to this morning's little escapade. Seizing the opportunity Martha added to his misery by assuring Mary,

*"You an yer little uns be welcum yer any time"* then, with that well known glint in her eye, she turned to Lamorock *"Your Becca as bin a gud little girl an really enjoyed erself t'day, dussent think,"* before moving to the children to emphasize, *"I opes yer Mamma brings ee to see us again zoon."*

To cries of,
*"Please Papa can we come again,"* *"Papa please say we can visit again"* and *"Papa, Mrs Worlock says we can milk the cow next time, please say we can come again, please! please!"* ringing in his ears, Lamorock Flower guided his reluctant but exhausted family back home to the Mill.

Martha, Mary and the children continued to meet and walk home after Church as they waited for Lamorock to agree to them spending their day by the Brook. Up at the Mill, although the couple had grown closer, the memory of the pleasant spring morning spent walking with the Worlocks was long forgotten as Lamorock concentrated on his plans to alter the weir and it was mid July before he relented and agreed to Mary and the children spending their afternoon by the Brook with the Worlocks. However, aware of how Rebecca manipulated people, especially her mother, Lamorock insisted the nursemaid went with them. He also decreed his son was to stay with him,

*"The boy has more important things to learn rather than having his young head filled with childhood fantasies like paddling, fishing or climbing trees."*

*"But what were you doing at his age Lamorock, were you not down there enjoying yourself with William and George?"* was Mary's swift sarcastic defence of her precious sons childhood.

Lamorock's stinging rebuke, *"I had taken my dead father's place or have you forgotten, considering you were there at the time!"* deeply wounded and humiliated Mary, who struggled to keep tears from welling up in her eyes, *"but if it will make you happy and avoid yet more arguments then take him, however there will be no repetition, the boy will never learn about his birthright from childish games."*

Mary, the nursemaid and the children arrived dressed in play clothes as instructed, Martha would have been happy to see her brood similarly dressed for Sundays but at least they were not in their usual finery and that was a blessing. By contrast the Worlocks wore their usual hand me downs and the rejects even she, skilled with a needle as she was, would never be able to mend. Mary also brought a picnic, as requested, to which Martha added her share of fresh baked bread and, with a twinkle in her eye, *"a jug a sommut special."*

Their time spent down by the Brook was idyllic, the boys raced to be the first to remove their shoes and stockings and wade in, leaving the girls on dry land picking bunches of buttercups and making daisy chains. With no one, especially her husband, making demands on her time Mary sat under the shade of one of the trees, keeping the damaging sun from her pale skin, in peace and tranquillity and wondered why it had taken so long to find such a haven and why she had not done this before, instead of spending her days in a dusty old house. If only Lamorock would do this once in a while she was sure they could be happy again. All too soon it was time to return home and six weary children along with two exhausted mothers and a nursemaid trundled their way back to Martha's cottage. Honor, Rebecca and Elizabeth clutched their wilting daisies whilst young Lamorock, ever the young gentleman, insisted he carry the empty picnic basket on his shoulder. Hester slept in her mother's arms, Ann was cradled in her nursemaid's arms leaving Mary and the others to carry all the discarded clothes because it was all they could do to get the boys to put their shoes and stockings back on let alone coats or jackets. Mary secretly prayed they would not be seen by anyone they knew whilst Martha earnestly hoped they would.

Approaching the cottage they spied Lamorock's new horse tied up outside and reaching the gate the raggle taggle bunch of grubby children were met with the sight of their fathers sitting in the summer sunshine sharing a jug of Martha's best cider. Catching sight of this scruffy bunch of children Lamorock's face drained of all colour as he stared accusingly, first at his long suffering wife for allowing them to be seen in public in such a state of disarray, then at the nursemaid for failing to talk her mistress out of such foolishness and finally at Martha for being responsible for the whole thing in the first place. It was only when his children swarmed all over him, eager to tell him about their adventures, Honor and Rebecca showing him their precious bunches of dead daisies, his son assuring him he had done as a gentleman should and *"Helped Mrs Worlock and Mamma by carrying the picnic basket all on my own,"* that his feelings changed and, taking the slumbering Ann from her nursemaid's tired arms, he sat down and for the first time in months listened as his excited children babbled on about their day down by the Brook.

Summer flew by, the younger children enjoyed a few more visits to Boyd Brook but they never matched that very first adventure. As expected, young

Lamorock rarely joined them preferring to spend most of his time at his father's side learning his part as the future owner of Boyd Mill and watching, through a boy's eyes, the alterations to the weir. William Ship had been specifically told not to vary, not even half an inch, from the height of the original weir and, to make absolutely sure, Lamorock and his young heir were meticulously overseeing everything. John now employed Robert as his delivery boy as he waited patiently for his apprenticeship alongside his father to begin and, when the time came, for Thomas to follow in his place. Mary and Martha still walked home after Church and Rebecca...well...Rebecca Flower was a different little girl. Rumours from Boyd Mill suggested she was behaving herself and, with fewer tantrums so warmth and happiness slowly returned to her family. There were no more picnics down by the Brook that year, Rebecca still very occasionally misbehaved during morning service but, as autumn of one year turned into spring of the next, life for both families improved. Mary's afternoon soirees were once again the talk of the village, although invitations no longer found their way to the Worlocks. Lamorock and John occasionally joined their families at Church after which they walked home together, Martha continued to ask when the children might come to see her again, all the while expecting to be given the usual lame excuses. Towards the end of the year Martha confirmed that, although Lamorock and Mary's relationship remained cool, she and John could not be closer when she announced she was pregnant again. Then, within weeks, came signs that the Master and Mistress of Boyd Mill were equally close when Mary announced that she too was expecting another baby.

Winter held its tight grip long into March but towards the end of the month, as snowdrops covered the children's special place down by Boyd Brook and catkins and pussy willows lined the lanes around the village, spring finally made her entrance. As discontented Parisians stormed the Bastille and Madame Guillotine made her horrific appearance Martha gave birth to her fourth son George closely followed by Mary who strengthened the Flower dynasty when she gave birth to her second son whom they also named George after grandpapa.

1789 found Robert and Thomas working alongside John, young Lamorock constantly at his father's side learning how to become the next owner of Boyd Mill...and Martha pregnant again.

Old Mary Prigg was always a strong woman but recently her family had noticed a change in her. Her mind and memory was as sharp as ever and, although her son had long taken over the haulage business, she was still a force to be reckoned with when it came to family decisions. With the old lady refusing

all offers of a home her daughters decided to share her care instead and whilst there had never been a problem getting up to Oldland, where she now lived, Martha reminded them she was pregnant and would be dragging four young children with her which might prove difficult unless John was able to take her there in their dilapidated old cart or someone fetched her. The arrival of another daughter Mary, named after Grandma Prigg, meant space was at a premium in their cottage, the older children shared the second bedroom, the boys crammed top to toe into one bed whilst the girls had slightly more space behind a makeshift curtain in a smaller bed. With the arrival of this latest daughter John roguishly suggested should there be any more they might need to board out the older boys, proposing, as a solution to their chronic overcrowding,
*"Course I cud always sleep in th'front parler."*

To which Martha, snuggled up next to him at the time, whispered,
*"Be you wantin t'be celibut John Worlock,"* before digging him knowingly in the ribs with her elbow!!

In a year which saw the death of John Wesley and William Wilberforce successfully place a motion before Parliament to abolish slavery, back in Bitton the alterations to the weir were diverting so much water from the River Boyd along a leat to his waterwheel and production had increased so dramatically Lamorock was currently grinding vast amounts of corn and wheat, mostly from local farmers, as well as from his own fields around the Mill. However not everyone was happy with the alterations and the interference to the flow of the river, the owner of the New Mill, for one, suffered a drastic reduction in the amount of water reaching his waterwheel and foresaw trouble.

It was Easter again before both families returned to their regular walk home after Church, causing people to suggest how they appeared to be extremely friendly these days, surely John Worlock was not anticipating full acceptance into their hallowed social circle was he? Had he forgotten how they humiliated Martha all those years ago and how strange they were no longer invited to Mary's afternoon tea parties; could they not see how nothing had changed, she was still considered the drab uneducated wife of the local butcher, an illiterate plump country woman taking in sewing and dressmaking to make ends meet. Mary had indoor servants, a scullery maid and a nursery maid to care for her perfectly groomed children, she would never need to work to support her family; in fact you only had to look at her to see she was a very elegant woman. Then there were the children, around the same age all growing up together. Honor Flower and Robert Worlock, both in their teens, lived very different lives; studious Honor, good at her lessons, accomplished both on the harpsichord and Grandmamma's little square piano in the parlour, petite pretty and demure like her mother. Robert, strong for his age, illiterate and uncouth, had already followed his father as a crude butcher's apprentice happily despatching animals brought to their slaughterhouse every day. Unlike his cultured childhood companion he would never know what a harpsichord or square piano was. Be that as it may, their friendship was causing certain envious people to shake their heads in silent disbelief, surely the Worlocks were not expecting a match between them…were they?

Next, disapproving fingers pointed to the strong bond developing between Thomas, equally as illiterate and uncouth as his older brother, a butcher's delivery boy waiting to begin his apprenticeship and Lamorock Jnr. already every inch the young gentleman, the apple of his mother's eye. Surely, the same cynics were whispering, John was not encouraging their friendship as well ….imagine how good that might be for his business. The closeness in their ages led to many people to refer to Thomas and his younger bother Samuel as *"those Worlock boys."* Elizabeth had always been something a mummy's girl and as a toddler rarely left Martha's side, preferring to hang on to her hand whenever she could. Then, of course, as the only girl in the family her brothers idolised her but, at ten years of age, she could neither read nor write and the best she might hope for was a life in domestic service, helping Martha look after her rapidly expanding family or caring for their animals all the while learning to become a seamstress at her mother's knee until she found a husband. Which Flower boy did John have in mind for her the cynics asked.

Even those with no time for the Flowers found it hard to ignore just how Rebecca had changed. The youngster who flew into a rage was gone, in its place was a large, ungainly girl content to gaze longingly from a window at her fathers' labourers rather than concentrate on her lessons or practise her chords alongside Honor. However, though she no longer gave way to childish outbursts, there could be times when she expected her own way and insiders at the Mill predicted her volatile character might make finding her a suitable husband difficult. When the time came it would rest entirely on her family name and the size of her dowry, not her personality or looks, leading to whispers that even John Worlock might be reluctant for one of his sons to marry this particular Flower

Hester was six years old and proving something of a worry to Martha, her birth had been perfectly normal but she had shown no signs of crawling or walking until she was well over a year old and did not talk properly until she was gone three, even now her speech was slow, unlike her two year old sister Mary who was happy to chatter away to anyone with time to give her.

Up at Boyd Mill Ann was the family charmer and, thanks to her mother's tuition alongside her older sisters, proving to be highly intelligent. As a baby there were times she suffered terribly at the hands of Rebecca and it needed the constant vigilance of her nursemaid; fortunately things had improved and now the sisters not only shared a bedroom but were almost inseparable. There were those who wrongly assumed because of their daughter's disruptive behaviour it was highly unlikely there would be any more children but once Mary and Lamorock were reconciled the children had joyously welcomed the arrival of their brother George, now two years later, although there was still time to spend one or two days down by Boyd Brook with Martha's brood, such outings were arranged around lessons and piano tuition. As the Flowers played their harpsichord and read their books so the Worlocks learned their different but equally important lessons in life and survival. A third son, whom they named John, arrived at Boyd Mill followed closely by a fourth daughter and eighth child, whom they named Martha, for the Worlocks.

Martha was pregnant again and as usual suffered from dreadful morning sickness, far worse this time probably because there had been barely time to fully recover from her last confinement, leading to real fears she might miscarry. Mary pressed John for news every time he delivered at the Mill and constantly advised them to see a, 'proper Doctor in Bath'. In July, came the news Martha had feared but had expected for some time, her mother died leaving brother Robert, as Sole Executor, to sort out her estate and it was only when the contents of her Will were revealed that the family realised just how astute old Mary Prigg had been with her money.

Robert, as the eldest son, inherited all his mothers' livestock, household goods and chattels. Martha and the others were each left £30 and, despite there being more than one, Mary only remembered one grandchild. Robert Worlock was left £10 which his namesake was further instructed to invest until the boy reached eighteen when he was to receive not only his ten pounds but any interest due.

It was therefore little wonder that, after learning she was to personally inherit more money in one go than she had possibly seen in her lifetime, mixed with the grief of losing her mother after caring for her for so long and a very difficult pregnancy, Martha's baby, a tiny boy, arrived early and was not expected to live. However by November the boy, whom they named John after his father, was thriving and by his first birthday he appeared as strong and bonny as his brothers and sisters.

Lamorock and Mary were happier now than they had been in years; in the nursery were three daughters and, more importantly, three healthy sons. The future looked good, especially since the earlier alterations to the weir meant their Mill continued to work at increased capacity. Meanwhile over at Saltford George was content to live his bachelor's life when, in early August, came signs that his mother's dearest wish to see him married before she died looked doubtful because she was ailing and time was running out if she was to find him a suitable wife before she joined his father in the family grave at Kelston.

In accordance with her wishes Ann Flower was laid with her husband at Kelston, she had been a widow for almost forty years.

Living so close to the slaughterhouse brought problems during the summer months, no matter where you were in the Worlock's cottage the pitiful cries of animals about to be slaughtered were never far away, nor was the constant stench from stale blood or discarded unwanted and unsavoury offal to attract flies into an already unsanitary, overcrowded household. The children regularly suffered from diarrhoea and sickness but, as they grew older and stronger, so they built up resistance to its ravages which was why, when baby John took ill with all the classic symptoms, neither John nor Martha showed any concern until he grew weaker and weaker, refusing to sleep, unable to keep any food in his stomach, reducing his distraught mother to walking helplessly around the cottage as he writhed and screamed in her arms. Finally John agreed to fetch the Doctor, no matter what the cost. Samuel Watts shook his head demanding, *"Why was I not called earlier, I am afraid there is very little I can do at this late stage."*
Martha desperately pleaded for him to *"do sommut Doctor, anything, s'long as thee saves my baby!"*
*"All I can do is make the child comfortable and give him something to reduce his fever."*

Handing his distraught mother a small packet of white powder Martha was told to give him a *"few grains mixed into warm milk and a similar dose this evening."*

Walking him to his horse in the lane alongside the cottage John asked Samuel Watts,
*"Will ee live Zur?"*
*"Highly unlikely Mr Worlock, highly unlikely, however I will return on the morrow, in the meantime I feel you should prepare your wife for the worse, your child is now in Gods hands"* was all Doctor Watts could truthfully say.

That night their baby son slept for the first time in days and his exhausted mother desperately tried to convince herself he would recover; sadly his sleep was only induced by the Doctor's sedative, in truth he was very ill and simply not strong enough to fight any infection. By morning the crying had stopped and everyone believed him to be over the worse until Martha went to pick him up when he once more screamed out in pain. Placing him on the bed beside her, all the time smoothing his head with the palm of her hand, she told John to take the younger children to one of the neighbours leaving Thomas, Robert and Elizabeth with her when Doctor Watts arrived as promised. Sadly there was nothing he could do, there was nothing anyone could do and despite a bread and water poultice to his feverish little body his mother's prayers and pleas to God to save her precious son went unheard and he died in her arms later that day.

Martha was inconsolable and clung to her baby for hours, refusing to allow anyone to touch him, until finally John was forced to prise his cold little body from her arms and watch as Hannah took her sobbing hysterically from the room. Later they all stood around his tiny cot to say goodbye to the son and brother they had barely known but who now at peace after so much suffering.

Reverend Elwes called to offer comfort and discuss the funeral only for Martha to refuse to see him blaming him, as God's man on earth, for letting her precious son be taken from her, leaving John, who had little time for religion at the best of times, to make all the arrangements instead.

The following day John carried the tiny coffin from his cottage to St Mary's as Martha and the children followed behind, even Charles Elwes was moved by their sense of loss. In poor villages like Bitton birth and death travelled together, most labourers were so poor they were barely able to feed the children who survived infancy let alone grieve for those who did not and it was rare indeed to see such outpourings as displayed by this family. It was a sad scene indeed as his mother, brothers, sisters, family and friends stood by as John lowered his son into what was now the family grave on the North side of St Mary the Virgin. In a vain attempt at comforting Martha John had used some of the money inherited from her mother to buy a burial plot, that way he ensured they would both join their beloved child when their time came. Mary Flower was only a month away from the birth of her seventh child and felt Martha's loss as though it were her own and planned to attend the funeral until Lamorock wisely suggested it might be best if she stayed away, in case her present condition caused further grief.

Martha shut herself away to grieve for her baby, refusing to attend Church or see the Vicar when he called,

*"I bain't talking to no man a God when thik God let my preshus boy be took frum me,"* she argued whenever Charles appeared on the doorstep. She

abandoned her dressmaking leaving it to John to explain the situation to all the disgruntled ladies waiting with half finished gowns and, after twenty years together, she left the bed she had eagerly shared with him, moving in with the girls whilst the boys moved in with their father. Meanwhile the safe arrival of William Wilcox Flower, fourth son and seventh child for Lamorock and Mary did little to help.

Late summer became early autumn with Martha still refusing to shed her mourning gown, choosing to sit sad and alone in the dark front parlour oblivious that John, Robert and Thomas were working longer and harder to compensate for the loss of her earnings or how the younger children felt especially neglected and looked on fourteen year old Elizabeth as their surrogate mother. Indeed, she even failed to see the pain and suffering in Johns eyes or miss him when, instead of coming home to her, he was often found standing at his sons grave praying for the day she would return to her old self again. John was at the grave one morning when Charles Elwes spied him from the Vestry and asked after Martha, not having seen her in Church for some months but when he said he was thinking of paying her a visit John had no choice but to warn him,

*"It'll be useluss Reverunt, I d'fear fur er brain so I don't think thee visitin us'll do any gud, n fact it might make things wuss cus she says twer thy God who was cruel t'take our boy from er."*

Charles knew John was not a man to confide in anyone, especially him, but suddenly everything became too much and he found himself listening to a plea from the heart.

*"We be all greevin for thik babby Zur but my Martha d'think she be th'only one who be urting!"*

All Charles could say was,
*"Give her time,"* his steady reassuring hand on John's trembling shoulder, *"Give her time my son."*

The dark curtains in the front parlour were the first to disappear, replaced by something that let sunlight in on her family again, upstairs the boys returned to their own beds, the girls were back in theirs and Martha was snuggled up alongside John. She tried to explain to John and the older children how she now realised they all missed baby John and whilst asking them to forgive she begged them to be patient. A few days later the couple talked openly about their grief, their plans, their worries and each other. The business was doing well, thanks in no small way to the efforts of their two oldest sons, whilst Samuel was bringing in extra money from any labouring work he could find and Martha said she felt strong enough to resume her dressmaking, however

John chose to wait for the right moment before telling her that whilst she had shut herself away he had been approached by one of his customers offering Elizabeth a position as live in nursemaid to their two children, including a new baby.

The following Sunday when the family attended Church the congregation welcomed Martha like the long lost friend she was and Mary Flower happily showed her baby William Wilcox for the first time. It had been a long time since the Flowers and Worlocks last walked home from Church together and although both families retraced their old steps they quickly realised it was not and probably never would be the same again, Robert, Thomas, Honor and young Lamorock now had their own circle of friends with whom they preferred to spend their time and Elizabeth was sure once she left home to take up her new job as nursemaid she would never join her family at Church on Sunday again.

# CHAPTER FIVE

Martha was very reluctant to let Elizabeth leave home and in a desperate attempt to keep her by her side she pleaded with John to allow her to stay and become her pinner up, suggesting it might help with their finances. Then when Robert and Thomas said they also planned to leave home, offering an immediate solution to the lack of space in their overcrowded cottage, Martha excitedly assumed,

*"So John, that d'mean our Lizabeth can stay ome now?"*

Never the less, within the month Elizabeth had left home and it was a sad day indeed, especially for Martha, when they took their thirteen year old daughter up to Beech to her new employers. They promised to treat her well and to give her a basic education alongside their own children, her new Mistress assured her very tearful mother she could have every Sunday afternoon off and John was free to see his daughter whenever he called to deliver their order.

With the two older boys now lodging with Widow Palmer down the lane and Elizabeth up at Beech, life in their cottage was changing. Samuel was nearly fifteen and left home, often before light, every morning taking whatever his mother could find for him to eat, to walk the roads in search of casual work. The weeks after Elizabeth's departure had been very lonely for Hester and, remembering all the heartbreak it caused, she resolved never leave home but planned to stay with her mother for ever which, when Martha heard, was music to her overprotective ears. Never a very quick witted child her mother, fearing for her future, had long decided she should be the one to learn the ways of dressmaking and stay home, leaving her more lively sisters to find suitable positions and husbands when the time came.

Just over a mile from the Worlocks, life for another family was also beginning to rely on the next generation. Since altering the weir that fed the water wheel, which in turn now supplied more power to Boyd Mill, production had increased so much Lamorock often considered leaving his fifteen year old son's special education in the capable hands of his manager, freeing him to concentrate on how to increase ale supplies to Bath, Bristol and beyond.

The Flowers had great hopes in the two eldest children and Lamorock was confident the family's future would be safe in the hands of his son, who was showing more understanding of the ways of running their mill every day, whilst it would not be long before his eldest daughter Honor, who as far as he was concerned was as pretty as her mother had been at her age, would soon have a suitable young man walking up the drive. Well, whoever he was, he would find an educated young woman able to hold her own in any kind of conversation, gifted at the piano or harpsichord and, thanks to her mother, the perfect hostess at any social gathering he may wish her to arrange.

With Christmas approaching Mary decided the three older children should join her at one of her afternoon soirees and so it was that Honor, Lamorock and Rebecca were at her side as she welcomed guests to her last tea party of the year. Light from flickering candles filled every corner with moving shadows and a fire roared away in the grate. Across the room Mary spied her young son trapped in a deep conversation with the large dull wife of their best customer, who was taking great delight in patting the side of the poor boy's face with one hand as she wrapped her other flabby arm around his shoulders completely engulfing him in her enormous bosom. Next to him stood Honor, smiling sweetly as she completely charmed the woman's buffoon of a husband. If only the same could be said for Rebecca who was making it plainly obvious she had no wish to be there at all and had only agreed on condition she be allowed to visit Martha on her own tomorrow to help Hester with the animals.

Comparing her daughters, standing side by side, the vision of a racehorse and carthorse came to mind. Honor, slim, petite, pretty, her hair neatly tied back in a pink bow to match her first grown up day dress, was every inch the blossoming sixteen year old. Beside her Rebecca was similarly dressed but looked uncomfortable and out of place in a room full of genteel ladies in their elegant gowns, probably the handiwork of the very woman the girl was insisting she visit as her reward for enduring this afternoon's gathering. A mass of tousled dark brown hair, initially so neat, now hung limply down her back and untidily hid most of her unhappy face, the piece of matching ribbon that once held it in place long since discarded.

Rebecca was never happier than when she was with Martha, if only because she was given freedom, freedom to feed the cow or the chickens, freedom to collect the eggs and to sometimes take a couple home. Despite there being chickens in abundance running around the kitchen garden at the Mill, these somehow tasted different. She also knew if she behaved her reward might be an attempt at milking the Worlock's tetchy old cow, even though Hester was the only one the animal would allow anywhere near her swollen udders. They had other animals at the Mill but Papa employed people to look after them and they never let her near them like Martha did. Being close in age Rebecca and Hester were firm friends, in many ways they mirrored each other; both were large clumsy girls content to spend their days on their own wherever and however they wanted. Neither could be considered clever nor pretty and whilst Rebecca could read and write Hester would not know what to do with a book or a quill pen if you gave her one.

In 1796 the congregation at St Mary the Virgin lost two of their old stalwarts. In March Aunt Partridge died at the advanced old age of eighty one, closely followed in July by Charles Elwes.

Everyone expected, as her Executor, for Lamorock to gain control of Aunt Partridge' share of the Flower estate denied him by his father in law and, in some way, this was true. However, Ann followed Richard Francis by remembering the younger members of the family and left a substantial estate which she sensibly set down in great detail in her Will. Conscious that her funeral would be arranged by others she stipulated she was to rest at Kelston, as close to her parents as possible, bequeathing £10 for the continuing upkeep of their graves. As promised she left two rented houses in Bristol to Lamorock and rented properties over at Keynsham jointly to him and his brother George, whom she also named as her Trustee, along with strict instructions that they collect all outstanding monies due, after which they were to, 'sell all of them, either at auction or private sale for the best price or prices that can be had'. When it came to personal bequests it was clear she had thought long and hard before deciding who was to inherit the family jewellery and silver. To Mary and Susannah she bequeathed £20 each along with some family silver and a few pieces of jewellery. To her great nephews, Lamorock and George, she left £20 each but, as he was the elder, Lamorock was to also receive her silver watch along with a small amount of family silver. Great Aunt Ann assumed Honor, as the eldest, would be the first to marry and ensured she was well prepared by leaving her most of her furniture, bed linen and china plus £50 and her three chain gold necklace. Rebecca was left £50 and, obviously a girl after the eccentric old lady's heart, her elegant gold laced scarlet petticoat, green damask gown and matching coat plus some odd bits of furniture and bed linen already stored at Boyd Mill but not destined for Honor's new home, a diamond ring with three stones and her eight day parlour clock. Young Ann was also to receive £50 along with another of Great Aunt's rings *"the one with a large stone in the middle set round with smaller ones"* and some of the family silver. The children were to receive their inheritance on reaching twenty one, should any of them die before that time then it was to be equally shared amongst the survivors, should any of them also die then everything was to go to Mary. All the young Huddlestons were given a similar amount, again on reaching twenty one and again to be shared amongst their siblings should one or more die. As with their cousins, should none survive everything was to go to Susannah, *"for her own use and benefit."*

She also left £20 to the fatherless Richard Francis, from which her Trustees were to 'educate, maintain, clothe, breed up and apprentice him'. What remained by his twenty first birthday was his to keep together with a further £20. He was also to receive her thirty hour clock.

Mary was to dispose of her clothes and linen as 'she singularly wished', that said there still remained the vexed question of a considerable amount of family silver and plate given into her care by Richard Francis which he had verbally told her to give to his orphaned grandson. Great Aunt Ann dealt with this in a codicil stating her 'desire' that her Trustees carried out these wishes and, thus, a large amount of engraved family silver found its way to young Richard Francis. There was nothing for William Francis nor his children and Lamorock and George were pressed to speedily carry out her instructions regarding the sale of her properties so that her bequests could be settled as soon as possible.

Rebecca's visits were now so regular villagers would worry should they not spot her making her lonely way from Boyd Mill down to the Worlock's cottage, her parents had long accepted it was best to let their headstrong daughter have her own way within the safety of a family they knew rather than insist she remain distant from all the labourers of Bitton. Apart from spending most of her time with Hester caring for the animals or attempting to milk one of the cows, for there was now a second younger one, Rebecca found herself drawn to her friends' older brothers and could not deny having a certain attraction for Samuel who, of them all, was the nearest to her in age. Robert and Thomas, being that bit older, frightened her, especially when they deliberately barged into the makeshift dairy, naked to the waist covered in body sweat and animal blood, pretending to look for the large jug of cider Martha always left there. Hester knew exactly what her brothers were about and would tell Rebecca,
*"They'm doin it on purpose cus they d'know ow it do upset thee s'much, take n notice of um."*

John, well aware of what his sons were doing, would gently rebuke them for acting in such a way in front of a naive thirteen year old girl and, like Hester, urge Rebecca to,
*"Take n'notice of um they be just two gert lummoxes."*

However there were times when John remembered there was only four years between Thomas and Rebecca and many local girls, not to mention their mothers, already had their lustful eyes on both his boys, he therefore eagerly waited for the day they would bring home their future wives and they found Rebecca a suitable husband from her 'own kind'.

It was only natural for Samuel, seeing the freedom his two brothers enjoyed, to want to join them and finally he persuaded his parents to let him board with

Widow Palmer as well,
*"I be old enough an she d'look after our Thomas n Robert good nough so why cassent I move in too?"*

Standing in Martha's kitchen, hands on her plump hips, in that all too familiar rebellious stance, Rebecca was showing she had lost none of her ability to fly into a rage at the merest hint of not getting her own way as she angrily demanded,
*"So what point will there be in ever coming here anymore!"* angrily stamping her foot on the flag stone floor for good measure.

*"But theese always sed you cumd t'see me Becca, not ower Sam,"* said Hester in her slow slurred speech, somewhat frightened at a side of her friend she had not seen before.

Angrily spinning round to face her, Rebecca turned on the scared girl hiding in her mothers sheltering arms,
*"Oh Hester all you ever talk about are your stupid cows and chickens, you are so dull and boring but...,"* smiling at the girl's brother standing next to his father she lowered her eyes and cooed, *"your Samuel is never boring."*

Mary had no idea why John Worlock was bringing Rebecca home himself and so early in the day, normally it was late afternoon and she walked back alone, something must be wrong. In Lamorock's absence she listened as John explained the happenings of no more than an hour ago and was left in little doubt that her daughter was not welcome back in his house unless she apologised to Hester. Partly accepting the situation Mary naturally leapt to her daughter's defence, as usual, demanding to know,
*"Mr Worlock, what exactly did my daughter mean when she said your son was never boring?"*

Incensed to be addressed as Mr Worlock when the more familiar John had always been good enough for their Sunday morning walks he courteously replied,
*"Missus Flower, my boy'll be sixteen zun an Martha n me ave raised im t'know right frum wrong, we always spect im an is brothers to be-ave proper,"* pausing to glance coolly towards Mary he continued, *"I ope theese can say the same bout thy girl,"* then, making to leave he added, *"I d'wish you a very gud day."*

Rebecca, as expected, obstinately refused to apologise even though she knew she would lose her freedom and means of escaping what she considered was unfair treatment at home. Lamorock was not well at the moment and it did not help an already bad situation to see, first her brothers and sisters and now her sick father getting all her mothers attention…instead of her. In rare quieter moments Mary continued to fret over her meeting with John, especially her daughter's implication that Samuel was never boring but, despite constantly asking the child what she meant by such a comment, nothing was forthcoming. Then, tired of her mothers incessant questions, Rebecca decided to lie,

*"He's never boring because he makes me laugh,"* whilst in truth she thought him the most wonderful exciting person in the whole world and, barely in her teens, had already decided they would marry as soon as they were old enough. Now he was moving in with his brothers who would soon entice him to mix with their sort at the White Hart Inn and she might never see him again. She refused to leave her room, even when Papa was well enough to join them for supper and asked for her. Instead she angrily accused,

*"Everything is so unfair, no one ever thinks about me and what I want, Papa is not that ill but already they are treating Lamorock as if he were dead and Honor is getting all the attention just because they think it's time to find her a stupid husband!"*

She often overheard the servants whispering about how Mamma and Papa expected problems finding her a husband, so by choosing Samuel, who naturally would agree once he learned of her plans, Rebecca truly believed she was saving her long suffering parents the trouble. Days, then weeks, passed and even though Papa was still very ill and she could see how desperately worried her poor mother was Rebecca decided there was no reason to apologise to 'the likes of Hester Worlock' consequently, until she was allowed to continue her relentless pursuit of Samuel Worlock she was content to return to the bad old days of her childhood.

Samuel, with no regular job, stubbornly refused to join the family business, *"I bain't spendin my life killin animals,"* was all he would say whenever John or his brothers suggested there might be more secure employment alongside them. Fortunately, thanks to his family name and their reputation for being hard reliable workers, he was rarely idle and in Widow Palmer, the old lady with whom his two brothers lodged, Martha had not only found a kindred spirit but someone prepared to care for them as if they were her own.

A few months later came news that the improvements to the overcrowded conditions in their little cottage had come at a very fortuitous moment when, at the age of forty two, Martha astounded everyone, none more so than John, by announcing she was expecting their tenth child. Meanwhile, further up the Golden Valley, as if to confirm Lamorock's return to health, the patter of tiny feet was also expected at the Mill when Mary, at the slightly younger age of thirty nine, announced she was expecting her eighth. However, the lives of the two expectant mothers could not have been more different.

Four Worlock boys and one simple daughter remained at home, three grown up sons lodged just down the lane and their eldest girl was in service as a live in nursery maid whilst their mother stitched gowns for the local gentry. Robert and Thomas worked alongside their father in the slaughterhouse across the yard from their old home whilst Samuel was up and out looking for work before it was light. Martha, meanwhile, was still expected to feed them all but now she was pregnant they selfishly imagined their well fed existence might possibly be interrupted by morning sickness. Taking their father to one side Robert and Thomas berated him for getting their not so young mother with child only for John, in his defence, to counter their accusations,

*"What be trublin thee th'most, thy mother's well bein or th'fact she be havin another babby an thee be all goin t'ave t'look t'thyselves fur a change?"*

They got a similar response from Martha,

*"D'ost thee think I be best pleased meself you gert lumps, I were oping theese ood ave brung ome wives an give thy father n me grandchildren be'now but tis too late an n'any case what dus spect I to do bout it?"*

Life revolved around the constant sound and smell of animals either arriving for slaughter or being killed, which was far worse because their cries were pitiful especially when one escaped and ran frantically round the yard until John or one of the boys managed to catch it and haul it back, with great cruelty, slitting its throat before even bothering to get it through the door. When the poor creatures were herded into the shed from the back of farm carts the desolate mournful look on their faces told Martha everything. Then she had to witness their mutilated headless carcases being loaded onto the cart for delivery and watch as one of the boys washed the yard clear of blood and left over animal offal. The only good thing to come from all this was having the chance to walk out into the yard and catch up on all the gossip from their customers should they call to collect their meat themselves, of course she preferred them to come into her cottage for a mug of something as the sight of the dead animals still upset her so. John was more understanding these days, especially with the arrival of all their babies but, despite a good wash down in the yard, he still came in smelling of dead animals and their bloody remains which, in her present state, worsened her morning sickness and, of course, there were the flies to bring back painful memories of the precious little son they had lost.

Mary Flower had no need to take in sewing to make ends meet, in fact she occasionally even used Martha's skills herself, although when it came to new outfits she much preferred to have her gowns and those of her daughters made by her 'excellent' dressmaker in Bath. Then there was the young maid of all work to help in the kitchen as well as a live-in nursery maid to care for the younger children and of course there was always a man free from her husband's labourers to carry in the coal or wood for the fires. Honor and Lamorock welcomed the news of another baby, Rebecca, on the other hand, was very resentful at the prospect of yet another brother or sister receiving all her mothers' attention.

Both women lived with constant noise, Martha was obliged to listen to terrified animals meeting a gruesome and not always a painless death at the hands of her husband and sons whilst Mary had to put up with the rumbling of a large water wheel, fed by the improved deeper weir, thundering all day so loud that at times, when production was in full swing, it made the floors of the house shake. Most of Lamorocks' customers were regulars and often called to either pay their account or to bring in more corn or wheat in person and Mary always took the time to invite them in for a dish of tea or a jug of ale, just like her not so close friend these days at the other end of the village.

Two babies arrived within a month of each other. Francis Flower was taken to St. Mary the Virgin whilst Sophia Worlock joined her siblings to wait for her parents to decide whether or not to do the same. Martha's age was against her this time and she took longer to recover, thankfully Elizabeth was allowed home until her mother regained her strength. Lying next to her husband a few days later

Martha urged,
*"John this un ad better be th'last, I be getting too old fur any more s'know?"*

Summer passed in a blur as Lamorock combined family life with visits to his Bristol properties, back home an increasingly worried Mary tried to encourage him to rest, then, just when she was beginning to despair for his health, a buyer was found for the Thomas Street property and it was sold for £225, not long after the Temple Street property was also sold for £200. Early in 1797 George Flower announced he had fathered a daughter called Eleanor and it was rumoured he might soon marry her mother, Ann Brewer. Closer to home the Paper Mill further up Golden Valley was sold and converted into a Cotton Mill; however Lamorock was not unduly worried about any competition, thanks to William Shipp's alterations to the weir he would always get the lion's share of the water needed to power his waterwheel. With no more travelling to and from an oppressively polluted Bristol, relief that his young bachelor brother was finally settling down to family life at Lower Farm and Boyd Mill more productive than ever, Lamorock looked to the day he could pass his business over to his sons, find suitable husbands for his daughters and spend his old age with his beloved Mary.

In December, with both families looking forward to celebrating Christmas, Mary was dealt the cruellest of blows. Despite all her tender loving care and the constant attention of the Doctor, her beloved Lamorock died. As she lay beside him on their large carved mahogany bed, bedecked with its pale curtains, she pleaded with Samuel Watts to do something to save him but all he could suggest was that he bleed him again and she had been led, crying hysterically, from the room by George whom she had thought to send for from Saltford. Using his favourite old pocket leam Samuel drew about ten ounces of blood into the cupping jar after which Lamorock appeared to rally and asked for a little warmed milk which in turn convinced Mary he was out of danger. Susannah Huddleston arrived to offer what support she could to her sister and children, who had already been called to their father's bedside to say their goodbyes, closely followed by the new inexperienced Curate of Bitton. Mary was in no fit state to make any decisions but, with George and his wife eager to take complete control, Susannah suggested they dispatch the young Curate to Kelston for her step father in law, Reverend Green, because he was sorely needed. As they waited Susannah's thoughts focused on her nieces and nephews and how she was going to explain why their father was dead at the age of forty six. Like previous generations the future once again lay in the hands of a young boy who, until he reached his majority, would have to look to his mother and no doubt his uncle for guidance.

The days leading up to the funeral passed in silent solitude, the pale hangings that once decorated their mahogany bed were replaced by sombre black drapes, the children cried, especially Rebecca, whilst young Lamorock confessed to Aunt Susannah,

*"I don't know how I will to do everything Papa taught me."*

Ann Flower arrived from Saltford full of good intentions only to swiftly make matters worse and it was not long before she fell out with both sisters in law, especially when a grieving Mary discovered she was preventing 'all and sundry from the village', as Ann chose to describe their friends and neighbours, 'from meddling in our affairs' and was turning people away when all they wanted to do was pay their respects in person. Ann then complained bitterly about her orders being undermined and disregarded once Mary let it be known,

*"Everyone is welcome, our friends were never turned away whilst my beloved Lamorock lived, why should things change now."*

Two such visitors were John and Martha.

This was only the second time in almost twenty years that Martha agreed to visit Boyd Mill; the last was the eventful afternoon not long after Lamorock and Mary returned from their honeymoon when she had been snubbed by most of the guests, however today was different. It was bad enough when John came home with the dreadful news, especially since reports from the Mill wrongly said Lamorock was gaining strength but later, when he told her how,

*"A certain lady as took it upon erself to choose who do an who don't see Mary an be already boastin ow her usband be in charge these days,"* that Martha had announced,

*"John, change thy shirt an put on thy gud jackut n breeches, we be gonna see Mary."*

Striding up Golden Valley Lane Martha muttered to herself how, *"no one, specially this yer Ann Flower frum Saltfurd be gonna stop me n John from seein Mary!!!"*

As expected Ann refused to let them in or to even ask Mary if she wished to see them, glancing at the shabby way they were dressed she decided they were not the type with whom her brother in law would have mixed and assumed they were just another pair of nosey villagers eager to gloat at the distress of their betters. However just as she was about to forcibly close the door and send them on their way Rebecca walked into the scullery at the end of the passage and, seeing them standing there, ran screaming and crying, arms outstretched, towards them,

*"Oh Mrs Worlock, Martha, Papa has died, what am I to do for I know I will never be able to live without him, I am so sorry I upset Hester, when can I come and see you again and feed the animals like I used to? Oh what are we to do without Papa, I did not realise he was so ill, oh Mrs Worlock, Martha, have you come to see Mamma she will like that, shall I go and tell her you are here"* before collapsing breathless onto Martha's reassuring shoulder. At the sight of her niece sobbing uncontrollably in the arms of this plump drab woman Ann Flower knew, like many before her, when she was beaten and stood aside. Mistakenly assuming it was highly unlikely they had ever been inside the Millhouse before, Ann made to guide them to the upstairs parlour with a tart, *"This way!"* prompting Martha, still smarting and clutching an hysterical Rebecca in her sheltering arms, to announce, equally curtly,

*"Bain't no need, we knows our way, John n me ave been guests of Mr n Mrs Flower afore!"*

However, there was no way a stunned Ann Flower could have possibly known it had only been on one occasion.

Finding Mary shut away in her darkened room, her normally beautiful face swollen from constant endless tears, brought back memories of baby John's death and, although she was determined to be strong, once the door closed behind them and they were alone all the animosity between them over Rebecca and Samuel disappeared. Martha, usually so strong, broke down and both women sobbed uncontrollably in each other's arms. Feeling helpless and out of place, John coughed gently, allowing them to part and for Mary to walk, arms outstretched, towards him. Grasping his warm rough hands in hers she whispered her thanks in between heartbreaking sobs and pleas,

*"Oh what are we to do without him John, what are we to do?"*

With Mary's blessing John left them to their grief and made his way to pay his last respects to Lamorock. As he gazed down at the man, looking at peace but old before his time, with whom he had shared family friendships, business dealings not to mention the occasional disagreement, he whispered his private goodbyes all the while knowing things would never be the same again and he found himself agreeing with his widow, indeed what were they to do without him.

The day before the funeral all the workers from the Mill, the Alehouse at Upton, business colleagues, friends and neighbours were invited to pay their last respects. A steady stream of people filed past the coffin then, with dusk falling, Lamorock was taken to St Nicholas to rest overnight in front of the altar. The next day Mary took the children to Kelston where Reverend Thomas Green laid him to rest alongside his parents. Naturally St. Nicholas was full to bursting as befitted a man of his standing in the community.

Ten days later Mary and the children tried to spend Christmas just as Papa would have wanted; even so it was a very quiet affair. George invited them over to Saltford but Mary declined, she hardly knew Ann and the old house held too many memories; instead they spent the day quietly at home. The all attended Church in the morning but left without talking to anyone, not even John and Martha.

John Worlock shook his head, as if in silent conversation with an invisible companion, spurring the old horse homewards all the while thinking about the stories he was hearing on his rounds,

*"Didn't take um long t'fall out over his money and him ardly cold in his fine family grave, all cus e bain't left no Will,"* he muttered in disbelief to his unseen, imaginary friend.

Rumours told of heated visits from George who, having already inherited a share in the Mill from his father, felt he should control its future until young Lamorock came of age. He cast doubt on whether Mary and her young son had the ability to cope, insisting his late brother would have wanted him to guide the boy into manhood.

In late March Mary, supported by her brother and Churchwarden Thomas Strange, applied for Letters of Administration for Lamorocks' Estate, two weeks later they swore an Oath before representatives of the Lord Bishop of Gloucester confirming his personal Assets, including the proceeds from the sale of Aunt Partridges' Bristol properties, did not exceed £600. Later that day Mary was granted the desired Letters of Administration for Lamorock's estate which, including the Mill but once all debts were settled, was estimated to be worth £1,200. With this document Mary became a wealthy woman and the legal mistress of Boyd Mill til her eldest son came of age. Returning home she gathered the children to her and gently explained,

*"We must now look forward to life without dearest Papa who, although he will not be here in person to see your successes, will be watching from heaven."* She ended by re-affirming, *"This will always be your home and with hard work, family love and support you can all achieve anything you want."*

The following month Mary hosted a seventeenth birthday party for her eldest son.

When their invitation arrived Martha desperately tried to persuade her family not to go, remembering how she had been treated she imagined her illiterate brood would fair no better. However the boys insisted they were going, reasoning twenty years had passed and times change, there were no problems between their families these days, in fact since his father's death young Lamorock always appeared relieved to see them whenever it was their turn to do the deliveries. Martha's pleas for John to talk to them fell on deaf ears but still she persisted until he lost patience with her and snapped,

*"Why dussent thee stop worryin bout they boys goin to zum birthday party an elp find um wives to bring us grandchildrun."*

The mention of future grandchildren reminded her of a pressing little secret she was keeping, a little secret she knew she could not hold back from her long suffering husband for much longer, at the age of forty four she was pregnant again!

When Mary heard about the baby she placed a concerned hand on her friend's arm,

*"But Martha are there not risks in having a child at your advanced age?"* before insisting, *"I will arrange for you to consult my Doctor in Bath immediately, to make sure all is well!"*

Martha had no intention of seeing any 'of them fine Dacturs in Bath' assuring everyone who expressed concern that she was fine, with the exception of John there had been no trouble with any of her other babies so why should this one

be any different? To those well meaning souls who suggested,
*"Your Robert n Thomas should be th'ones we babbies be now not you n John, "*
she would shake her head and wistfully sigh.
*"Me an John'll be in our graves afore them gert lollops finds emselves wives. "*

Mary patiently waited for Honor to attract a handsome young suitor and fill the Mill House with grandchildren and for young Lamorock to follow in the footsteps of his beloved papa and find himself a pretty little wife from her vast circle of friends. Warm May gave way to an even warmer June and plans for the children's future, under Papa's paternal celestial eye, had barely started when Mary was dealt another devastating blow when her eldest son died, six months after his father.

Like Papa, Lamorock was taken to St.Nicholas where Reverend Edward Hawkins laid him to rest with his father and grandparents but, unlike Papa, this time there were no open invitations for anyone to call to pay their respects nor for them to attend the funeral, in fact no one was sure whether Mary would even attend because she had locked herself away and was refusing to talk to anyone. When she eventually walked down the stairs on the morning of the funeral, thick veil hiding her sad tear stained face, she spoke to no-one but simply held out two gloved hands towards her heartbroken children, who were waiting in line for her.

# CHAPTER SIX

During the latter years of his life Lamorock often returned from visiting Aunt Partridge's property in Bristol with stories of how the glass, pottery, brewing and soap making industries, as well as most of the big houses, were reliant on the high quality coal from the Kingswood collieries and both he and George agreed there was money to be made from mining. Now, less than a year after his death, coal was in such demand the search for new seams had finally reached Golden Valley. It therefore came as no surprise when Aaron Brain, representing a consortium of eight local businessmen, initially approached George Flower seeking permission to sink a pit on land just up from the Mill. This was just as Lamorock had predicted however George, whilst very keen, knew they could do nothing without Mary's consent.

Mary was far from pleased when George asked her to at least listen to the proposals, she said she felt vulnerable and claimed she had not been given sufficient time to mourn her husband and son but George persisted,
*"Lamorock and I often talked about the importance coal would make to the future of the Golden Valley,"* skilfully adding, *"did he never mention it to you Mary?"* When she still refused he suggested he met Mr Brain, *"To ascertain exactly what they are planning,"* shrewdly suggesting, *"although I am sure Lamorock would have wanted you, not me, to represent his family in person."*

Eventually Mary agreed to an hours meeting on the strict understanding that should she feel unwell or at all pressured both men would leave and the subject would never be raised again. George then met with Aaron to discuss how best to get Mary to agree, stressing there might only be one chance and strongly advised him to keep emphasising how much, "dearest Lamorock" would have wanted it.

When the meeting eventually took place Mary reminded them of the Kingswood riots two years earlier when colliery owners, to whom Aaron and his partners aspired, cut their workers wages in the name of profit, only for the miners to do everything they could to prevent any coal reaching its destination in Bristol.

*"What guarantee can you give for there being no such riots in my valley, nor do I want the responsibility of such tragedies as those poor miners who drowned when Warmley Pit flooded and how can I be sure any proposed pit will not flood with an equal, if not worse, loss of life?"*

With a flourish Aaron Brain opened a map and laid out his plans before her, *"Mrs Flower, there will be a fire engine powerful enough to pump and drain the water from the coalface deep underground therefore,"* he assured her, *"there is no way our pits will flood."*

Still she was not content, *"And what will happen to all the water?"*

*"It will drain into the river, naturally"* came the confident reply.

*"But,"* turning to her brother in law, *"will that not alter the level of the river and effect our production George?"*

On July 19th 1798 Mary and George Flower signed a Twenty One Year Lease with Aaron Brain and his consortium, giving them free liberty to open pits and raise coal in six pieces of ground on the Upton side of the Brook near the Mill and to erect a fire engine to drain and carry away water, thus stopping the mines from flooding. In addition to rent they would also receive a percentage of every bag of coal brought to the surface.

John Worlock and a few smaller businessmen greeted the prospects with trepidation. Unlike Mary and George they had witnessed the aftermath of those Kingswood riots of 1795 for themselves and had no wish to see them repeated in Bitton. Colliery owners were known for their complete lack of concern for their employees, boys of no more than eight or ten years of age followed their fathers, uncles or brothers down the pits to work, stripped to the waist and bare foot, on the coalface for a twelve or fourteen hour shift. When they heard of Mary's apparent concern for the workforce, insisting future employees be treated in the same benevolent way Lamorock had cared for his labourers at the Mill, they swiftly reminded her, through George, how he was not that compassionate and only made watered down vegetable soup available to those who struggled up Golden Valley during heavy snow and freezing frost. Even then, it was suggested, he was only prompted into such kindness because he knew other employers were providing similar sustenance for their workers and he remained indifferently reluctant to allow their starving children to hunt for food and collect firewood from his land. John and his supporters also expressed concern over the number of lawless gangs and loose women already roaming the area looking for easy pickings, add drunkenness and immorality to an already increasing population and it could spell disaster for Bitton. Raising their concerns at the next Parish Meeting supporters of the plan reminded them how they could all end up gaining from the venture with increased profits and surely they all wanted to make more money, to which John and the others argued *"yes but at what cost?"*

Of course neither he nor the small group of businessmen he represented held much sway amongst those present and the plans were welcomed with open arms.

Phoebe Worlock arrived to a cottage a little less crowded than usual. Robert, Thomas and Samuel were settled in their hovel down the lane and Elizabeth was still in service up at Beech where, after four years, she was now fully accepted as part of the family. True to their word they had given her the basics of an education and she was allowed home every Sunday afternoon, in fact to save her the very long walk down the hill the family brought her with them when they attended morning service at St Mary's after which she walked home with Martha, leaving John or one of the boys to take her back in the cart before dark.

Despite all Martha's time and patience, Hester's skills with a needle would never match hers but at least the girl was capable of sewing simple seams and replacing the odd button or two; however it was in the art of husbandry that she shone and John would proudly remark, should his customers asked after his family,

*"Yes, I confess when it do cum t'lookin after animals my little Ester ave took after er Grandma Prigg, no doubt bout it!"*

Hester now had two cows, a dozen or so chickens, not to mention the odd fattening pig roaming the orchard from time to time. The small outhouse alongside the scullery, where Robert and Thomas once amused themselves by scaring their little sister and her feisty friend by appearing in front of them half naked now served as a simple dairy where Hester churned milk into cheese and butter and, on very special occasions, cream for the family. At nine George was considered too young to join his father and brothers in the slaughterhouse although he was allowed to accompany them on their deliveries; however, as all the children were expected to do their bit to support the family he was encouraged to grow vegetables in a small patch of garden at the side of the cottage, just as Grandpa Prigg had done. Young Mary and Martha helped whenever and wherever they could, leaving Sophia and baby Phoebe contentedly with their mother as she did her sewing. Then, just as the Worlocks began to enjoy financial stability and made plans to hand things over to their two older boys, Martha's freeloading cousin arrived on their doorstep looking for help.

Frances Prigg was never any good with money, even when she lived at Swineford the family were always helping her out, so everyone had breathed a sigh of relief when she moved to Twerton. Now she was back and made straight for Martha, whom she had heard was not only the wife of a successful butcher but had inherited a sizable amount from Aunt Mary, looking for some family money. This was not the first time she had appeared, last time was within weeks of leaving for Twerton when she fully expected her long suffering family to support her. Instead they had taken her to the Overseer who gave her 1/- along with the sound advice to either find work or return to Twerton. Now she was back again but, just like before, the family took her to Overseer Quarman who gave her 2/- along with the same advice as before, find work or return to Twerton, however this time she was also told not to return again because there would be no more handouts.

Despite what could be described as a conflict of opinion over the rights or wrongs of their mother agreeing to let Aaron Brain's consortium sink a pit on their land, the friendships between the young Worlocks and Flowers flourished. After her father and brother's death Rebecca, feeling even more neglected than ever at home, had mumbled enough of an apology to be allowed back at the Worlocks and was never happier than when out gathering eggs or helping Hester take a turn in the dairy. Both girls were big, slightly cumbersome creatures and, apart from the two year gap in their ages, the only difference between them was that Rebecca could read and write whilst her friend never would, not even if someone had thought it necessary to teach her in the first place. However, if Hester would never make a scholar then neither would her friend ever make a milkmaid. No matter how many times she was shown what to do Rebecca rarely collected more than half a pail for her labour before the temperamental old animal, sensing the girl's unfamiliar rough touch on her sensitive udders, would get irritable kick out and over would go the bucket along with its hard earned contents. Rebecca continued to live in a dream world most of the time; resting her head against the cows' warm backside, instead of concentrating on filling her pail, she imagined Papa and Lamorock were alive, her mother still wore light pastel coloured gowns instead of widows' weeds and interesting people were visiting the Mill again, instead there was nothing but sadness and sorrow. The only place where she was happy was here with Hester and her animals.

Thomas Worlock found it hard to accept the death of his friend, like their sisters the boys were close in ages and despite the differences in their home lives Thomas still sprang to his dead friend's defence should anyone dare besmirch his memory. Now, as the months passed, with no guiding Flower to share his days Thomas was spending more and more time with his older brother Robert in the company of the sort of unsavoury characters with whom it was wisest not to be seen.

Around the same time as Lamorock had married his Mary there was another, less auspicious, wedding at St. Mary's Bitton. The groom, Benjamin Caines, came from a local family of thieves, rogues and fraudsters with a trait for living, quite successfully, on the wrong side of the law. When he was barely six years old his parents, Benjamin Snr. and Lydia, found themselves up before the Gloucester Quarter Sessions for selling ale without a license. Young Benjamin's bride, a local girl called Ann Cool, declared herself to be totally ignorant of her in law's reputation when she agreed to marry their son, nevertheless within eleven years she had brought ten more of them into the world, all of whom were now taking an active role in the family 'business' led by the their eldest son George and his cousin Francis Britton with another son, Francis Caines, waiting patiently in the wings. Benjamin, sensibly, kept a discreet controlling hand, not wishing to follow his father and risk getting caught. Despite John Worlock's best endeavours it was inevitable his two eldest sons would find themselves drawn into their company and, much to his consternation, were often to be found alongside the Caines and Britton boys in most of the local Ale Houses.

Maybe it was because of his family's reputation or perhaps he was simply bored but, by his late teens, George Caines, already a credit to his family, was keen to try pastures new and easily convinced his cousin it was time to move on because their fortune was to be made elsewhere. The pair tried to persuade Robert and Thomas to join them,
*"Thur b'aint no future in Bitton, no money in bein a butcher workin all day fur thy father but thurs plenty t'be made vrom robbin ouses, thieving, forgry or pickin summuns pockut,"* enthused George, already a veteran of the various ways of making money dishonestly.

*"Theese just gotta make sure thee dussent get caught,"* was the best advice the less enlightened Francis Britton could think to offer.

John's boys were sorely tempted but deep down they knew it was best to remain where they were. They lived in a shared cottage just down the lane from their parents, old Mrs Palmer and Martha fed and fussed over them, they enjoyed a fairly decent life from a family business both knew would be theirs one day. Neither was stupid, they knew exactly what would happen if they got caught.

The Worlock children always knew when their father had something serious or important to tell them, especially when he found out about it at a Parish Meeting because that meant it must be true and not just a rumour. Gathering them together, making especially sure Robert and Thomas were present and displaying that smug look of 'I told you so,' they knew to expect something he clearly considered very serious. However, this evening he could barely contain his excitement, as he lectured his children so he aimed his words and frenzied finger directly towards the hapless Robert and Thomas,

*"Found out t'day that they Caines boys you d'so admire bin caught thievin in Monmouth, so t'was a gud thing theese listened to me an thy mother an didn't follow um, else theese cud've bin standing long zide um in the dock!"*

John was virtually unstoppable as he treated his wife and unfortunate children to a tirade about the entire Caines family,

*"Garge n thik cuzzon Francis ave bin up afore th'Magistrates for bein in a gang of awkers n peddlers, they were cused of passin false money n aving forged notes in their pockuts."*

*"Where be um now?"* came a quiet, almost scared, whispered question from a shocked Robert as he remembered how close he had been to following George Caines.

*"On their way t'gaol where they d'belong and where thees two"* pointing accusingly towards his two oldest sons, *"culd ave bin ad you gone wiv um,"* John replied with more than a hint of satisfaction in his voice.

What the children could not have known was that the Caines were neither friends nor strangers to their father. Back in his early days in Bitton one Ann Caines had accused John Hulburd of being the father of her expected illegitimate child and took him before the Overseers of the Poor. Churchwardens, Thomas Bush and Thomas Palmer, along with Overseers Samuel Holbin and Laurence Bush were aware the father could be any of a number of local men but, as Ann specifically named John Hulburd, they had no choice but to insist he defend himself after which they again had no choice but to order him to pay a £40 bond, should the child proved to be his and did not become a burden on the Parish. There was no way John Hulburd could find such a sum on his own, even though he was settled in Bitton and a successful butcher, so he turned to his kinsman William Hulburd and his old friend John Worlock Snr. for help and together the three agreed to pay the Bastardy Bond drawn up by the Overseers of the Poor. John never knew how the three men managed to raise the money nor how long it must have taken them to pay it back, all he knew was his father believed and trusted his friend, suspecting he was being used as a scapegoat by Ann simply because he had been seen walking out with her and, judging from the number of men seen leaving her cottage late at night, how she probably had no idea who the real father was anyway. As the years passed John continued to hold the Caines in some way responsible for his parents leaving Bitton whilst he remained as John Hulburd's apprentice. Anne Caines left the area soon after so he never knew nor did he really care what happened to her or her bastard daughter, all he cared about was ensuring his two eldest sons escaped paying a similarly high price at the hands of the same family but, as John Hulburd no longer lived locally and his brother William died back in 1780, there was no other way of making them see sense.

Naturally, Benjamin and Ann Caines vehemently defended their innocent boys, claiming they had been led astray by villains but nevertheless law abiding citizens of Bitton felt justice had been served, especially when it became known both 'innocent' boys had been sentenced to one years hard labour.

As carpenters, masons, builders and their labourers streamed into Bitton to begin work on the six pits so cracks appeared in the original consortium when two of the original lessees assigned their shares over to other people. Meanwhile at Boyd Mill, Mary Flower had taken on Peter Gerrish as her new manager whilst, on a more personal note, over at Saltford, George and Ann Flower became the proud parents of twins whom they named George and Ann.

1800 saw the inhabitants of Bitton facing a future dominated by coal. There had always been relatively secure employment at the Cotton or Grist Mills, now entire families were tempted into jobs centred on the collieries. Before long young boys, already working at the coalface alongside their fathers, uncles and older brothers, were joined by their mothers, aunts and sisters at the pit head cleaning and sorting the coal hewn hundreds of feet below. Fortunately the Worlocks had no such problems, John would never benefit from coal because no one was interested in sinking any pit in his orchard, surrounded as it was by labourer's hovels, muddy tracks, open drains and a small stream prone to flood at the merest sign of rain. Nor were their sons of the sort to attract the attention of local landowners eager to marry off their daughters, a state of affairs which often caused an exasperated John to utter,
*"Me n Martha ould settle fur wives fur them three,"* pointing to his sons, *"rather than wait fur usbands fur our little maids."*

By now a good steady woman was desperately needed, old Widow Palmer had died and, much against their fathers' advice, the three boys had taken over her tenancy thus allowing them to live in their own dilapidated old cottage, free from his restraint, drunk and out of control most of the time.

George Caines and Francis Britton had returned to their adoring followers, not as convicted criminals but as blameless innocents, eager to resume their criminal life. It was as if they had never been away; impressionable boys like the Worlocks, bored with killing animals and trekking the lanes looking for labouring jobs, welcomed them home with open arms whilst John and Martha, along with the rest of the law abiding citizens of Bitton, Oldland and further away in Kingswood, did so with trepidation. Their unwelcome return brought a further warning from John,

*"Dussent thee go gettin in wiv thik gang of villuns, they traps daft uns like thee three like moths d'fly round a candle, remember I casn't help thee if theese get into trouble, theese'll just ave to take thy chances."*

Well away from the delicate ears of their mother and sisters, John painted a much more robust picture of what would happen should they father illegitimate children, especially on any of the girls currently pursuing the Caines gang who were well known to be free with their favours....but only if you were already an accepted member. Explaining what had happened to their grandfather John warned his sons how there would be no escape should they try to avoid responsibility by moving away, never staying in one place long until the law, in the shape of the Constable with a Warrant for their arrest along with a Bastardy Order against them, found them.

Martha meanwhile warned their girls not to bring shame on the family by having a child out of wedlock, like their neighbour Ann Short.

*"Ann were left on er own after lettin Enry Smith know her, stupid girl believed im when ee sid ee ould marry er but by th'time she knowed she were aving a babby he were long gone,"* Martha told her enthralled daughters, *"course they tried to find im, even by is t'other name Black Harry but he were never sin again."*

*"What appened to her?"* little Mary wanted to know.

*"I never knowed no one called Ann Short, do she still live round yer?"* Hester asked in her slow slurred speech.

*"No my luve you on't ave knowed her, nor you our Mary,"* soothed Martha, *"but er family didn't turn er out they let er n er bastard boy stay till she found a man to take em on and move away."*

The girls gazed up at their mother, mouths and eyes wide open expecting to hear much more.

*"And dus know what appens t'girls like Ann if their family turns um out?"* Martha gently asked her captivated young audience. All three shook their heads as if spellbound by some wonderful untold story. *"Well, they goes into th'Poorhouse an you bain't endin up there,"* was Martha's final emphatic answer.

It did not take George Caines long to pick up from where he left off before his incarceration. Back at the head of his rapidly expanding gang he was soon roaming the area robbing people either by force, or other persuasive means, of anything he could lay his hands on. John miraculously managed to keep his three impetuous sons from their villainous and amorous clutches by continually reminding them how the only way to hope for a contented life was to stay out of trouble, follow his example, find a decent girl to marry and raise a family. Conveniently, all this talk about family life came at a very opportune moment because in the early days of 1800 John found himself holding something of a dubious trump card…Martha was pregnant with their twelfth child!

All her other pregnancies, with the exception of morning sickness & tiredness, had been problem free, however she was now in her mid forties and as her time grew nearer Martha sensed things were not quite as they should be. This baby was not as active as the others, nor did it feel as if it was lying in the right position but there was nothing to indicate anything was wrong until she went into labour. After an extremely painful length of time with still no sign of any baby the old midwife brought in for the delivery suddenly announced there was nothing more she could do and told John to fetch a Doctor in the vain hope he might be able to save at least one of them! Samuel Watts arrived with a desperate John at his side, a quick examination of Martha's belly told him exactly what he had suspected,
*"The baby is lying the wrong way round and will never enter the world without help, something,"* said with a cold glare and a certain amount of incredulity in the midwife's direction, *"you of all people should have noticed sooner, however there is no time to be lost laying blame if we are to save them!"*

Elizabeth was at her mother's side, in view of the serious situation Thomas had been sent to Beech to fetch her home, whilst the younger children were with a neighbour eagerly awaiting the arrival of their new brother or sister. Turning to John the Doctor suggested it might be best if he and the older ones found something to do rather than stay within earshot of their mother's distress. So, with Martha's screams ringing in their ears, John ordered the boys to make a start collecting the outstanding orders from their customers; however in the absence of Hester he announced he would be staying behind to look after the animals in the orchard, recalling how the first time he had done this was twenty two years ago when Robert was born.

With the cottage to themselves Samuel Watts and the midwife turned their attention to the matter in hand which was the delivery a very large baby determined to enter the world feet first. Having already asked John which one he was to save, 'mother or child,' he reached for his bag and carefully selected the instruments he would need. Martha was barely conscious as he inserted a fearsome pair of forceps and began trying to extricate the baby lodged firmly inside, her painful screams were such that John, standing alone in the yard, could hear and for the first time in many years he prayed, prayed he would not lose Martha, prayed Doctor Watts and the midwife would do their job and she would survive and soon be alongside him where she belonged.

Upstairs in the front bedroom the desperate struggle for Martha's baby continued, looking to grab hold of someone, or something, she held on tightly to the bed rails behind her as Doctor Watts frantically tried to shift the inert child. Suddenly he felt some movement and, using both hands, pulled with all his might until, with an almighty rush and a large quantity of blood, an enormous baby was delivered although her right leg remained caught up inside and it needed one more push from her exhausted mother before it was free. She lay still and limp next to Martha, who was haemorrhaging, until, without a word passing between them, the midwife took her away whilst the Doctor looked to her mother. When John was eventually allowed to see Martha he was shocked by the scene that met him, his wife was propped up on pillows, with little or no colour in her face, nursing their daughter, a huge baby with a large bruised odd shaped head. Taking him to one side Doctor Watts gently explained,

*"It was an extremely difficult birth and I needed to use my instruments to deliver your daughter, she is a very large baby and it took a great deal of force to have any chance of delivering her alive."*

Alarmed at what he was hearing John interrupted,
*"Did my Martha suffer Zur?"*

Samuel Watts took a deep breath between closed teeth as he answered, truthfully.

*"No, thanks to laudanum and brandy, however she has lost a great deal of blood which even ergot has not completely stemmed, she will need plenty of rest if she is to recover fully."*

*"What about our daughter Zur, what bout our Ruth, be she gonna be alright?"* was the question Samuel expected but one which he could not truthfully answer.

Guiding John well away from Martha he looked down at his hands, placed together as if at silent prayer, before pressing them to his lips as he searched for the right words,
*"Sadly the child has not emerged unscathed as her bruises show; she took a long time to start breathing and has suffered damage to one of her legs which I had to forcibly manipulate to enable her mother to deliver her and I cannot say for certain whether the child will live, nor can I say whether she will lead a normal life or even be able to walk, talk or see properly if she does."*

*"I see Zur, can I go n sit by my Martha now?"* was all John could think to say.

*"Of course, of course but,"* placing a gentle restraining hand on his arm, *"before you go there is something of which you and Martha should be aware. There must definitely be no more babies, at her age another pregnancy and especially another birth like this will surely kill her."* pausing to allow John to take in the severity of his words Samuel continued *"do I make myself absolutely clear?"*

Later, as he watched Martha nursing their new daughter, John determined there would be no more babies he simply could not run the risk of losing her.

There was a limit to how understanding Elizabeth's employers could be and they naturally needed her back to look after their children. With her older sister back at Beech, Hester took on caring for the family until Martha was fully recovered. Rebecca, who was all but living with the Worlocks these days, enjoyed helping her much slower friend about the house, however John and Martha felt Mary should be asked if she minded her daughter spending so much time away from home,
*"You be deliverin there s'afternun John, try n see Mary n ask if tis allright fer Becca t cum yer s'often"* suggested Martha.

Later that afternoon John found himself in the downstairs parlour at Boyd Mill talking to Mary Flower,
*"D'ost thee mind if thy Rebecca elps our Ester with the little uns....just till Martha be back on er feet?"*

*"Of course not"* came Mary's all too quick answer, relieved there was someone actually prepared to put up with her difficult daughter, *"she can visit as often as she likes but,"* speaking from experience, *"please do not let her have all her own way!"*

As he made to leave he could not help but feel sorry for Mary, life must be so different these days. Acting on impulse he walked over, took her smooth hands in his large, weathered palms and muttered gently,
*"I be truly sarry bout Lamrock and thy zun, they was gud friends o me n Martha, that yung zun a thine ad the makings of is father in im,"* before assuring her of a welcome at their cottage at any time, *"it'll do Martha the power o good to see thee agin an she ould love to show thee our new girl."*

Mary was lost for words, John Worlock was not a man from whom to expect such sincere kind words, he was not known for having a soft side to his nature, except maybe to his precious Martha. His was a reputation of a rough plain speaking countryman, capable of felling an animal with one mighty swing of his pole-axe, not one of passing pleasantries with a lonely widowed gentlewoman. Holding back tears Mary whispered,
*"Thank you so much, please tell Martha I will think about your kind invitation,"*

knowing she would never visit their cottage again, those days were gone, without her dearest Lamorock at her side she preferred her own company these days.

By summer villagers had accepted all the strangers walking the lanes and the steady increase, one thousand five hundred at the last count, in the number of colliers and their families desperate to secure work in the six pits Golden Valley would eventually provide. However, accepting drunkenness and dirty antisocial behaviour was a different matter and soon objectors had good cause to complain when, in August, William Lapham's entire family went down with smallpox and the finger of blame was pointed directly at the filthy itinerant labour force now streaming into Bitton from *"God knows where!!"* Fortunately, the Laphams were the only family to be seriously affected and at the next Vestry Meeting William Francis and Thomas Smallcombe made sure they receive help from the Parish and ordered James Quarman to give them 4/- immediately, provide the family with two blankets and arrange for a pair of boots to be made for their young son.

Once it was safe for Martha to be left on her own with the younger children John, mindful of the Doctor's warnings about there being no more babies, stunned his family by announcing he planned to move in with his elder sons, believing the only way to avoid any more babies was to spend his days with Martha and his nights down the lane with his sons. Bizarrely, he assumed there would be no objections whilst the boys, fearful of their father's controlling presence and his endless interrogations, thought differently.

Stubbornly refusing to join his brothers and father in the family business Samuel was now a hatter, working from the home he shared with his brothers. Hat production began as a cottage industry for those wives, unable to work but who wanted something other than pin making and had expanded at such a rate their men folk were now involved and even a factory was planned. Hats were made from felt, wool, and rabbit fur or, on occasions, imported Canadian beaver skin and although most were destined for the fashionable London market some found their way to Africa, the West Indies or America.

With Robert and Thomas returning home worse for drink most nights and Samuel already showing signs of mercury poison, cracks began to show, especially when John witnessed at first hand the depths to which his two elder sons in particular had sunk With the pair falling further and further under the influence of hardened criminals, Samuel working hard but wishing to play equally hard with more than a passing interest in the Caines himself and John believing he still had the right to control his sons, the situation was approaching breaking point. They turned to Martha but, with Ruth taking up most of her energy, for the first time ever she was unable to give the men in her life the support they needed.

Following the birth of their daughter they had been warned she might not survive infancy and even if she did she would probably be deaf and blind whilst her right leg, damaged at birth, would always be slightly shorter than the left, therefore if she managed to walk it would be with a distinctive limp. Six months on Ruth lay in her cot or in her mother's arms gazing at the ceiling, there was never a smile, no sound came from her lips except when she cried which was rare and Martha no longer needed to be told what she already knew …her baby was deaf, blind and would probably never walk. Now she centred all her love on this crippled child and promised to love her for as long as she remained with them. By her first birthday Ruth was scurrying around the stone floor on her bottom, propelled by her good left leg and, although she could hear a little bit, she made no attempt to talk but Martha was convinced there was some sight in her dull eyes, especially when the sun shone through the windows. John was now back living at home, once he accepted he *"culd take n'more of they boys"* and Martha confessed she had spent *"nuff lonely nights without thee."* however, each time that knowing glint appeared in his laughing eyes she would gently remind him,
*"I bain't gonna be like thik Ale Ouse keepers wife in Bristol, you knows the one I means…the one who as just ad er seventeenth boy an she being fifty wiv all t'other sixteen still livin!"*

With Ruth's first birthday safely behind her Martha truly believed her daughter would prove them all wrong. Sadly winter came early and proved so severe the child had no resistance against the damp cottage and bitter cold winds blowing across the meadows from the river, she developed a chill which grew into a fever leaving her parents powerless as, once again, they watched as a second baby died in Martha's arms. Two days later on October 3rd Ruth joined her brother John in the family grave at Bitton.

No one would ever know how long Mary Flower had waited for this day, her eldest daughter was sitting next to her with a nervous Coster Thompson by her side who was desperately trying to pluck up the courage to ask for permission for them to marry. His request did not come as a complete surprise however, he had been calling for some time so Mary was well aware of their plans and, like most of the business families in the district, the Thompson's, especially Coster's widowed mother, were old friends. Now her son was asking to marry her eldest daughter and, knowing how happy and proud Lamorock would have been over such a union, Mary did not hesitate in giving the couple her blessing. Just like Mary and Lamorock twenty five years earlier the betrothed couple hosted a tea party for those guests unable to attend their wedding and, also like the bride's parents, they would be married by Licence. However, when an invitation to take tea once again found its way to the Worlocks no one was at all surprised when Martha stubbornly refused to attend. John urged her accept, if only for Coster's sake who, *" be gonna need all th'support ee can git now e be joinin thik family,"* and whom, like the Flower children they had known since the day he was born. When that failed John pointed out, *"Then maybe we shouldn't ferget Honor's father n brother."*

Unfortunately Martha did not quite see it that way, reminding her altogether too conciliatory husband how it was her, not him, who had been the centre of, *"Thik families amusement, or has thee fergot what appened fust time I were there?"*

*"But Martha!"* John pleaded *"that were twenty five yer ago, things be better now an theese bin up there since. When Lamorock died we both went t'see Mary and agin after her boy died when she ouldn't see us."*

*"They weren't social visits John Worlock and well you know it!!"* retorted Martha.

When John told the family they had all been invited to Coster and Honor's party he had no choice but to add how their mother, for her own reasons, felt unable to come with them but that she fully understood if they wished to go. Eventually, after a great deal of persuasion, Martha agreed although, as they all walked up the Golden Valley to the Mill, she continued to remind them, *"Dussent spect I t'enjoy meself mind and dussent spect I t'talk t'no one neither."*

It was strange feeling indeed to be an invited guest of Mary Flower again, however things were different now, John's standing in the community was much stronger, thanks to long hours and extremely hard work his was one of many successful small businesses in the village. No one dared treat Martha as the illiterate wife of a lowly butcher these days but if they did then she would certainly know how to handle things better.

With all their guests assembled Mary announced she had chosen Honor's marriage to officially throw off her widows weeds.

*"Since the deaths of my dearest husband and our beautiful son my children have encouraged me to take more interest in life and"* looking lovingly towards her daughter and future son in law, *"with a wedding to arrange I am looking forward to returning to my old life again."*

In mid September, with only days to go before the wedding, there was a double family celebration, a small family supper party hosted by the Thompson's and the arrival of another son over at Saltford. However when George and Ann announced the boy was to be named Lamorock Mary thought she was being asked to understand and accept their choice without question or consultation.

Rebecca, at nineteen, was stubbornly refusing to choose something suitable for Mary's dressmaker to make for the wedding, insisting instead that she wear Great Aunt Ann's amorphous gold laced scarlet petticoat, green damask gown and coat. Even Martha, to whom the distraught girl turned in the vain hope she might use her sewing skills and make it fit, tried to explain it was an outdated and much older lady's choice, surely there must be something more suitable. Of all the Flower children it was this daughter who missed her father the most, without his guiding hand she had quickly returned to her old ways and was very difficult to live with at times. Preferring to mix with the common colliers and illiterate mill workers, who delighted in watching her wandering the lanes un-chaperoned with any man prepared to accompany her, rather than be at home taking tea with some more suitable young gentleman from her mother's circle of friends. Mary, reluctant to deny this daughter anything, fearful of a furious reaction if she did, desperately hoped once she saw how contented Honor was as mistress of her own household she would see sense and stop amusing herself with her current vulgar companions. Mary was constantly reminded how this would never have happened if she had been firmer with her as a child instead of allowing her to mix so freely with the likes of the Worlocks. It was also unfortunate that the new, ever alert but disapproving, young manager, Peter Gerrish, happened to be standing at Lamorock's old study window late one autumn Sunday afternoon as her dishevelled, wild, headstrong daughter ran down the drive. Knowing she had been spotted Rebecca glanced up at him, tossed her fiery untidy head in the air and raised her skirt, exposing a forbidden ankle, before scurrying through a conveniently open kitchen door. Reaching her room she slammed and locked the door before anyone could catch her. Enough was enough, Mary must be told before she brought shame and disgrace on the family and came home carrying some common labourer's bastard….

……and these days the young Manager of Boyd Mill was arrogant enough to believe he was that someone.

Everyone knew who was in charge now, all Peter Gerrish needed to do was sit next to Mary, gently take hold of her tiny hand in his firm grip and whisper the soothing words that told her he not only cared for her but that his sole purpose in life was to take all turmoil and trouble from her 'lovely' shoulders. So totally besotted was she with her young manager he now had complete control of her Mill and her endearing attention at all times, even her fatherless children did not get that! Not only did she accept his advice without question she also expected her children, family and household servants to do the same. Dissent was always met with,

*"You must understand I cannot manage without Peter by my side, he knows he is never ever to leave me."*

August and most of September passed in a frenzy of activity but, unlike her own wedding when Susannah and Aunt Ann sided with her dressmaker and tried to influence her choice of gown, Mary did not interfere and Honor's dress reflected the neo classical fashion of the day. Gone was the large skirt worn by her mother, in its place was a gown of simple lined linen, made from one piece of exquisite white lightweight material, the front was high waisted gathered just below her small bosom, with the back flowing gracefully into a short train behind. The front of the long sleeved bodice was embroidered all over with white beads thus giving it a subtle shimmering effect and, as it would be late September with no guarantee of warm weather, Honor decided against a spencer, choosing instead to have a matching pelisse of sarsenet, lined with lambs wool, made for the evening when she and Coster left for their honeymoon tour. On her head she wore a large brimmed hat tied securely with matching ribbons and, just like her younger sisters, she planned to wear her piece of Great Aunt Partridge' jewellery....the three chained gold necklace. Mary chose a gown in her favourite pale blue spotted muslin, the apron fronted bodice was lined in white linen as were the sleeves and, like the bride, it had a high waisted skirt with large box pleats underneath which Mary would be wearing her trusty stays along with a small bustle to give added fullness to the skirt. Sensibly she listened to Honor and was also ready for a change in the weather with a matching hat and sarsenet pelisse. However, be that as it may, she resolutely refused to wear flat shoes, all the rage with the genteel young ladies and their chaperones drawn to the frenetic social life of Bath, she had always worn a slight heel and saw no reason to change, nor would she entertain any Grecian hair style under her matching bonnet, preferring to dress her naturally curly hair loosely with ribbon. Lamorock loved to see her dressed that way, why change simply because he was no longer by her side.

Sitting alone in her dressing room on the wedding morning Mary thought back to Honor's birth and how the disappointment at her not being a son vanished as soon as Lamorock held her in his arms for the first time, how young Lamorock's birth a few years later had brought so much joy to the whole family. Then there was the long wait for Rebecca, together with her difficult birth, followed by another wait for Ann then George, quickly followed by three more sons to fill the nursery. Unlocking her mother's treasured velvet covered travelling box, with its exquisite silver mounting, Mary took out her precious keepsakes and laid them in front of her. The jewellery from Aunt Partridge, eight small packets containing locks of hair from each of her children and another slightly larger one containing a lock of her own hair, then there was the plain black silk pouch containing the large lock of greying brown hair she had cut from her darling's head the day he left her. With her treasures spread before her she searched back through her magical box and, unwrapping a delicate piece of muslin, held up the pale cream ribbons she had worn in her hair on her wedding day. Next she removed a small velvet covered box and, gently lifting the lid, held up her mother's necklace, the one she had worn for the first time on her wedding day and which she hoped Honor would wear for hers.

The Wedding Day, was sunny but cold. Soon the house was full of chatter and noise, a bit like Lower Farm on that lovely day in May so long ago, as Honor prepared for her big day. Rebecca and Ann did their best to help the long suffering nursemaid as she rushed hither and thither removing curling papers, dressing hair here, fixing buttons there and generally calming everyone down. Honor was nearly ready when there came a gentle tap on her bedroom door and Mary crept in,

*"I know I promised to stay away until you were ready to leave my dearest but it is impossible, I need to see you before you leave your home for the last time. I have something very precious to give to you on this, the most important day of your life."*

Honor took the ribbon from her mother's trembling hands and, with equally nervous hands, placed it in her hair thinking how she needed Papa here today of all days but when she was handed grand mamma's necklace how could she possibly tell her tearful mother she planned to wear the three gold chains Aunt Partridge had given her.

*"Never mind,"* she pondered, *"Aunt Partridge will understand if I wear her necklace when Coster and I leave later this evening instead,"* and, bending her head forward, she allowed her mother to fix the clasp.

At Mary's insistence and fully endorsed by the rest of the family, although much against his personal advice because, *"if you indulge them now they will learn to expect it,"* Peter Gerrish was told to give the entire workforce the afternoon off so that as Mr and Mrs Coster Thompson emerged from St. Mary the Virgin into the cool Autumn sunshine most of them were waiting to wish them luck. From the corner of her eye Honor glimpsed Martha with the children and waved her gloved hand in their direction, although she chose not to walk over to talk to them. However when Rebecca saw them she simply could not resist running to greet them before returning to her family as they prepared to leave for the wedding breakfast back at the Mill. No-one, not even the Worlocks, had seen or heard much of Rebecca for some time, after her sister's betrothal was announced she had been swept up in all the hustle and bustle of wedding plans. Peter Gerrish tried but failed to have her sent over to Saltford, in the meantime someone, rumoured to be Mary, had worked a transformation miracle. Gone was the large dowdy wild girl instead there was a short, though still plump, elegant young lady. Gone too was the silly notion to wear Aunt Partridge' green, red and gold damask, instead she wore pale blue linen to match Mamma.

Much to Mary's dismay Honor and Coster moved to Publow after their wedding where, thanks to her dowry and her many family heirlooms, their house was as well furnished as any in the district.

Conveniently forgetting how unwelcome her own mother in law had been at Honor's birth, but desperate to escape the prying meddlesome village busybodies, Mary descended on Publow to supervise the birth of her first grandchild, a boy, only to cause another upset by demanding to know why he was called Sumption, a Thompson family name almost as sacred as Lamorock was to the Flowers, instead of after *"dearest Papa!"*

Five months later John and Martha Worlock astounded their long suffering Vicar by taking their remaining children to be christened, this time at St. Mary's where, like their older siblings, their names and ages were entered into the Register. Later in the evening as John sat in his favourite creaky old chair by the range smoking 'a last pipe a baccie afore turning in' watching Martha patch another large tear in Robert's breeches for the umpteenth time, there came a loud knock on the door and John reluctantly went to see who it was who would want to call at this time of night.

Robert Prigg told a truly sad tale and Martha's heart immediately went out to her cousin as he explained his wife had died leaving him with a young family, which was why he had returned to the Parish of his birth hoping it might be easier to get help here rather than approach the Overseer at Twerton where they now lived. His companion on the other hand had no such sad story to tell, Betty Prigg was there to support Robert by offering, with suitable financial help from the Parish, to look after his children. There was no way Martha could turn them away at this time of night so she took them in on the understanding they go to Mr Quarman first thing tomorrow. Robert could only stay one night anyway because he desperately wanted to get back to his children who were with neighbours.

The following day Betty proved to be in the right place at the right time when, at the Vestry Meeting, William Francis and his kinsman Thomas Smallcombe ordered James Quarman to pay Robert 6/- to buy essentials for his family and recommended Betty be offered the vacant post of caring for the poor of Bitton at 2/- a week all found. William vouched for Betty,

*"She is a cousin of Mrs Worlock and comes from a God fearing and hard working local family. Miss Prigg is just what is needed for the onerous task of caring for the increasing number of poor wretches looking to us for relief."*

Naturally Betty accepted the job, especially as it came with accommodation at the rear of the Poor House and permission to take Roberts motherless children in with her.

Throughout 1803 the number of people settling in Bitton rose at an alarming rate, as did the mortality rate, until it was clear the present Churchyard was too small and permission was given to enlarge it. On July 21st the Right Reverent, Doctor Huntingford, Lord Bishop of Gloucester, consecrated an extension to the Churchyard of St. Mary the Virgin.

The following year Betty Prigg diligently carried out her duties. She applied for and received clothes for all the inmates of the Poor House, was allowed 1/- for Widow Flook to buy her daughter a new shift and secured Betty Green an extra 1/- a month on top of what she was already receiving. Henry Cook's crippled son was allowed 6/- and old William White, his labouring days over, was given 5/-. When old Chilcott and his crippled wife could no longer care for themselves and their cottage was declared unfit for habitation she took them so that the hovel could be demolished. Christian Haines and her bastard were found to be destitute and forcibly taken in, whereupon Betty swiftly arranged for her to be employed as her assistant at 2/- a week, all found. However, when John came home with rumours of favouritism and accusations of 'the lining of pockets' after Betty successfully asked for an increase of 1/- a month for Robert Priggs' children, Martha, who had become quite fond of her incorrigible cousin since her return, felt compelled to warn her,

*"Take a care or thees'll find th'self omeless an in trouble wiv th' Constable an neither my John ner Mr Francis'll be able to elp thee then!"*

# CHAPTER SEVEN

Peter Gerrish had definitely proposed to Mary Flower and, according to gossip, she had spared little time in accepting him. Rumours of a forthcoming wedding were the talk of the village, apparently he already had the Marriage Licence. Lamorocks' family and old friends shook their heads in disbelief when they heard, although their wives and daughters knew exactly why Mary, a widow of forty six, would want to marry a man twenty one years her junior. Unfortunately, like their husbands, they also knew Peter had his envious eye on her Mill, not to mention her money, why else would he possibly take a wife old enough to be his mother! However, the more astute amongst them were keen to suggest his sacrifice might all be in vain because with Lamorock's eldest son George destined to take over the Mill when he came of age, three other sons waiting to take their rightful places and two unmarried daughters expecting good dowries, control of his bride's fortune might well be limited and short lived.

Honor thought the wedding an insult to her father's memory, Rebecca was deeply hurt, not only did she think her mother was foolish to believe Peter's promises of undying love but she had also been misled by her suggestions that Peter might make her a perfect husband and she must encourage him at every opportunity. Now she was expected to accept a man, only five years her senior, not as the husband she expected but as the stepfather she did not want.

With Honor and Rebecca against her, Mary turned in vain to the others hoping for their blessing, only to find none of them wanted Peter for a stepfather either and whilst the rest of the Flowers viewed the coming nuptials with trepidation their workforce, already suffering from Peter's tyrannical behaviour, knew things would only get worse when he was in complete control. Mary, of course, refused to hear anything said against her young lover nor to understand or accept why everyone was so against their union despite, whenever she pressed Peter on her son's eventual inheritance or the size of her daughters' dowries, always receiving the same evasive reply,
*"Rest assured my dear; after we are married I will always have their best interests at heart and will honour what is legally theirs."*

Amid doubts and objections from most of the family the wedding took place on December 19th 1803 but not quite as planned because, much to Peter's chagrin, Reverend Aday Curtis conveniently found himself away from home, so 'Mary Flower, Widow aged forty years and upwards married Peter

Gerrish, Bachelor and Yeoman aged twenty five and upwards', in front of his Curate, Edward Kempe. Edward had officiated at many weddings during his Pastoral life, including those where the age gap between the bridal couple was sometimes much greater than the couple standing before him today; however, it was usually the groom who was the elder not the bride. Initially Honor and Coster refused to attend, however they changed their mind, if only for the sake of her younger siblings who had been given no such choice and used the time to visit the Thompsons at Freeman Mills in Swineford. Nor were John and Martha surprised when no invitation found its way to their address. Sadly they now belonged to a tiny band of small businesses, once so close to the Flowers, considered unimportant by the bridegroom and his grandiose plans for his new found wealth and status.

The wedding breakfast showed none of the sparkle or emotions enjoyed by Mary and Lamorock and it was something of a relief when Peter stood to his feet, tapped the bone handle of his knife on the table, not to propose a toast to his new wife but to coldly informed their guests,
*"My dear wife has had a very tiring day and I am sure your will all understand why she wishes to retire early."*

The thought of any physical union filled their family with dread but at least there was little chance of any children, or was there, it was not unknown for women to have babies well into their forties, look at Martha Worlock for example.

Two years later found the Golden Valley and Kingswood pits working at full capacity, their greedy owners only too willing to employ those no longer prepared to work for the likes of Peter Gerrish. Following his advantageous marriage he had quickly shown his plans for his widow's property which, by law, was his until the first of the Flower boys came of age. Probably because he was unable to sell what was not legally his he decided instead to lease the Mill to William Cater, one of his new banking friends from Bath and so, after almost 400 years, the Flowers' no longer held sway in Golden Valley.

At the end of September 1805 Mary was again at Publow for the birth of another grandson, this time there was no upset, as his grandmother placed him in his mother's arms she whispered, *"he is so like your dearest papa,"* to which an exhausted Honor simply replied,
*"Coster and I have already agreed, should the child be a boy he will be given the names Lamorock Flower Thompson."*

In spite of all the changes in Bitton over the past eighteen months, business had never been better for the Worlocks; they no longer depended on Martha's income from dressmaking although she continued to do occasional work for specially chosen clients and only if it was convenient to her. George, now fifteen, had joined his father and brothers as their delivery boy before starting his apprenticeship. Samuel still made hats at home but was contemplating joining the work force at the newly opened factory since it was virtually impossible to work from home when his brothers were recovering from a hard night's drinking with the likes of the Caines. Elizabeth, in her early twenties, was back living at home, her young charges up at Beech were at boarding school and although she had been offered another post within the household she chose to return to Bitton. At eighteen Hester was unmarried and likely to remain so, preferring her animals to a husband; there were two younger cows in the orchard these days so she was not only kept busy with the milking but was making and successfully selling more of her butter and cheese. Chickens still scrabbled and scratched around the yard, there was usually a fattening pig in readiness for the winter and, with John at home running the slaughterhouse, his two eldest sons now travelled the district killing animals on various farms and small holdings which, like his father before him, was how Robert met his future wife, Sophia Golding.

Sadly, whilst the Worlocks prospered there were many families who did not. Betty Prigg still cared for the poor despite being accused of lining her own pockets again when she asked for and received an increase of 1/- a month for looking after Robert Priggs' motherless children even though they were already living with her rent free on the Parish. In truth Betty did everything asked of her and the Overseers saw no reason to be rid of her even when the incorrigible Frances Prigg re-appeared in January, young son in tow this time, expecting preferential treatment. Mindful of her position and not wishing to be further accused of favouritism she followed Martha's example and wisely took her cousin straight to the Overseer. Frances asked for a new jacket and breeches for her son and expected the Overseers, one of whom was Richard Gerrish, brother of Peter, to simply hand over some money, she was therefore not at all happy when Betty was instructed to not only buy the clothes but to make sure the boy handed over his old rags and was actually seen wearing the new outfit. Frances was later overheard bitterly complaining to a friend at the White Hart Inn,

*"Thik boy baint worth all thik money, if they'd ave give it to me I ouldn't ave spent it all on im and there'd bin some left over fur other things"* raising a mug of ale in the air she chuckled *"knows what I mean !!"*

With the New Year came more changes to the Poor House. Firstly and despite any further embarrassment Frances might cause, Betty was given complete control leaving Christian Haines, who had been an inmate since she and her illegitimate son John had been forcibly taken in two years ago, in her place as 'carer of the poor' at 2/- a week. Christian was also paid 5/- for every lying-in she dealt with, such was the increase in the number of destitute and pregnant women finding their way to their door these days. In between confinements Christian slept in the lying-in room but, for decency's sake, John slept with the Poor House children in a room at the back of the building. It was also unanimously agreed to ask the Worlocks to supply the weekly order of an ox head or a piece of mutton from which Betty or one of the others made a large pot of broth, thus providing the poor with their one main meal of the day. Thanks to the dexterity of the cook, the generosity of local farmers for providing the vegetables and the Overseer for suggesting how this gourmet delight should be prepared, the broth, with its ½ a peck of peas, 2lbs of oatmeal, 4lbs of onions or leeks, one stale loaf (toasted) cooked with up to 90 pints of water (depending on how many starving mouths it had to feed) proved a very nourishing meal when the alternative was starvation.

However, despite her loyalty, questions were again asked of Betty at the February Meeting after William Francis and his colleagues agreed to provide 2 shirts and 1 shift for all the Haines and Prigg children and allow Frances Prigg 4/- for being ill for four weeks.

Sophia Golding became Mrs Robert Worlock on April 9th 1805 and swiftly added to Martha's happiness by announcing she was expecting their first grandchild. John and Martha fully expected Thomas to be next, he was very popular with all the local girls and they were sure he would soon bring home his chosen bride. So they were surprised when the second of their brood to announce he planned to walk down the aisle of St. Mary the Virgin was the independent but increasingly eccentric Samuel. Samuel Worlock and Zipporah Short's wedding on Boxing Day 1805 was followed a few months later with the birth of Robert and Sophia's son, whom they named Robert after his father.

From the day her mother remarried Rebecca spent as little time at the Mill as possible, especially when Peter was there, believing she was no longer welcome in her own home. Everyone was telling her he was only interested in Papa's money but knowing most of it, including the Mill and Alehouse at Upton, would go eventually to George she was sure it would not be long before her contemptuous stepfather turned his attention to her future and that of her sister Ann instead. Both girls assumed Honor received some of Papa's money as a dowry when she married Coster and they naturally expected the same but, with Peter's growing influence, they knew everything would depend on whom he decided they should marry, disregarding Mamma's promise that Papa would provide for them all.

Sitting alone with Mary, struggling to master the impossible stitches of her sampler, Rebecca cunningly turned the conversation to the choice of a husband,
*"Mamma, what will happen should I meet someone of whom you and Papa would have approved, am I to encourage him?"*

Taking a deep sigh Mary could only reply,
*"If he comes from a suitable family of whom your stepfather and I approve then he will be most welcome to call."*

Not content with the answer but deliberately pressing her mother to say whether she would defy her young husband Rebecca pressed,
*"But what if Mr Gerrish does not approve of my choice, what if he is the son of one of Papa's oldest friends, would you still give us your blessing Mamma?"*

Deep down Rebecca already knew the answer but, nevertheless, took great delight in seeing she was causing her mother a certain amount of discomfort,
*"That decision will be left to Mr. Gerrish,"* resigned Mary.

Things were so different from the days when a family friend would be welcomed as a suitor, now Rebecca was desperate to find anyone, just so long as he was willing to marry her and take her away from her unhappy home life. Unfortunately most of the eligible men in Bitton not only knew about her wild past but that her stepfather, should his control be threatened, would not hesitate to set the dogs on those he considered unsuitable or foolish enough to walk down the drive seeking permission to call on her. Any suitor chosen to rescue her must therefore not only want to marry her but also come from a family known and accepted by her mother so that when the rows and arguments started, as surely they would, Mary would be able to support her by insisting,
*"They are old friends of 'dearest Lamorock' and he would have readily agreed to the match."*

Following their marriage and much to Thomas' annoyance, Samuel and Zipporah assumed because Robert no longer lived with him, there would be no objection to them taking his place and they moved into the cottage, taking over the bigger of the two bedrooms and the front parlour for their use. Thomas wasted little time in expressing his opposition,
*"I dun't want no wuman living yer less she be my wife,"* and bitterly confronted his brother, *"why cassent thee n she,"* pointing to Zipporah, *"find zumwhere of thy own to live?"*

There was no point going to his parents for support, they thought it the best piece of news they had heard in months.

*"Least there'll be summun t'look after thee n curb thy wild ways,"* was all a very relieved John said when confronted by his angry son. In vain did they wait for Thomas to change his ways, in vain did they wait for him to stop drinking himself into a drunken stupor at the local Ale House every night and in vain did his mother defend her wayward son, especially to those who were noticing how he had changed, for the worse, since his brother and sister in law had moved in with him.

*"Dussent worry bout thik young curmudgeon of a son o mine, he'll see tis fer the best afore long,"* was all Martha would knowingly say, contentedly nodding her head of greying hair up and down like an old donkey.

The newlyweds, desperate for any work that came their way, left home before dawn. Samuel walked part way with Zipporah till they reached the hat factory where he left her to make her own way to her domestic labouring job at the far end of the village. Neither returned til early evening, leaving Thomas, usually nursing a sore head, to sober up on his own. Should it be his turn to work at the slaughterhouse he might manage to eventually join his father by mid morning, if, on the other hand, it was his turn to travel around the farms then he relied on George or Robert to call for him with the horse and cart whilst he slept off the previous night's excesses under some sacking in the back. However, unbeknown to anyone, Thomas was rarely alone these days. Rebecca had managed to convince him that she loved him and found her love returned with all the passion of a man who has made his first conquest. In her manic desire to escape her stepfather and the atmosphere he had created, Rebecca, having already been forced to apologise to Hester in order to return to the Worlocks, decided the only thing left was to 'sacrifice herself on their altar'!

She began by visiting Hester, deliberately arriving in the late afternoon fully aware Thomas would not be there, pretending to look for him only for the naive young girl to genuinely reply,
*"Ee's just left, why dussent thee call in,"* pointing in the direction of the cottage down the lane, *"on thy way ome....ee might be ther."*

At first Thomas dared not believe what was happening and desperately fought against temptation. She was by no means the first girl to offer him her favours, far from it but neither was she the kind he normally lay with and he was well aware of the consequences. Nor could they claim such an impressive pedigree or had grown up alongside him, like a sister, from childhood! Well, Rebecca was certainly not acting like his sister these days, in fact he had never known her so eager to please him!

With John's warning about his grandfather, the Hulburds and Ann Caines swirling about his brain, Thomas tried to restrain his strong desires but Rebecca had been a very ruthless temptress, determined to lure him into her arms and ultimately her bed at all costs. The Worlocks remained oblivious to the whole affair as Rebecca continued to disguise her contempt for Hester, enabling her to remain close to the family, until Thomas eventually succumbed and eagerly welcomed her into his passionate and lovesick arms.

Zipporah was not enjoying the best of pregnancies and, with only a month to go, she now had an increasingly eccentric husband to cope with as well. Neither she nor Samuel were very strong, in fact since starting work at the hat factory he was constantly ill and his lungs so bad Zipporah rarely had a good nights sleep thanks to his rasping and constant body tremors, what teeth he still had were rotten and moved about in swollen gums. His mood swings were so severe there was no knowing how he might treat her from one day to the next and unless she found occasional domestic labouring jobs she knew there would never be enough money for food to nourish her coming baby, nor for Samuel to build up the strength to work the long hours he did. Constantly exposed to mercury, the chemical used to soften the felt and fur for the hats, it was already in his blood stream and had been absorbed through his skin into his nervous system, causing a drastic change to his personality. The family worried but were powerless to help. It therefore did not help matters when Rebecca, resentful at all the attention the couple were getting, became more and more churlish and spiteful towards them. Refusing to accept how difficult life must be she chose to bitterly criticize and mock the couple's ignorance and, thinking back to her early teens when she had planned to marry him, to even suggest it was Samuel's fault he was forced to worked in a hat factory and be married to someone like Zipporah, when he could have had her and her Flower money.

With only weeks to go before her baby was due Zipporah should have been resting but, with Samuel rarely strong enough to spend more than a few hours a day at the factory and their desperate financial straits, she was still out scrubbing floors. Hours spent on her hands and knees, up to her arms in hot soapy water in some laundry or in a kitchen scrubbing pots and pans left her weak and tired. However, apart from her pittance of a wage, the main reason she struggled on was for the scraps of food her employer gave her, some of which she hid in order to take home to Samuel. Without these scraps and unless Martha gave them something, there was never enough to eat at home and it was little wonder their baby was a grossly under developed little boy with no chance of gaining weight from his already malnourished mother. With no immunity to the pervading chemicals brought home from the hat factory by his father he developed similar severe breathing difficulties and was plainly suffering from the effects of the same mercury poisoning. His Christening was hastily arranged but it came as no surprise when, once more, the Worlocks faced further heartache and the baby, whom they named Aaron, died before he was a month old.

Thomas and Rebecca's passion burned for the rest of the year but by the spring of 1807 it appeared to be on the wane. Despite all her planning and conniving, there had been no marriage proposal but as with everything else, unable to get her own way, she became bored. Far from being the most gentle romantic of men she now accused him of being uncouth and clumsy with no tenderness to his love making and, in a fit of pique, coldly announced,
*"Mamma has returned from Norton St. Philip and is preparing to go to Publow, Honor is expecting another child, I am to accompany her and,"* sarcastically patting the side of his rough unshaven face with her hand she mockingly added, *"who knows, I might meet someone with more of an education, breeding and money than you."*

The arrival of another son, William Francis Thompson, for Honor and Coster did nothing to raise the spirits of either his capricious aunt who, having indeed met 'someone else' realised he was totally unsuitable and that Thomas was the best chance there was of avoiding an arranged marriage and thwart any plans Peter Gerrish might have, or Grandmamma Mary who was anxious to return to her young husband of four years, fearful he was tiring of her.

Home again, Rebecca was soon back in her lover's arms although there was still no marriage proposal, not even when she hinted how,
*"Mamma and Mr Gerrish are constantly inviting agreeable young men to call and,"* warned, *"It will not be long before I am obliged to take one for a husband and who will warm your bed then Thomas Worlock?"*

Much as he desired her, she was not the first girl to find her way into his affections…nor his bed…and he was not about to relinquish that freedom just yet. Therefore if Rebecca was to be his wife she knew she would need to think up a plan to surpass her already awesome reputation for getting her own way. Finally, worn out by her intolerable nagging about when they might marry and convinced she could see no further than her wedding day, Thomas pleaded,
*"But Rebecca ow an where be us gonna live on butcher's pay?"*

*"Mamma will buy us a little house as a wedding present,"* was her naive reply, *"and I will ask her for a dowry and all my money from Grandpapa and Aunt Partridge, so you will no longer be dependent on that family of yours."*

Secretly however, Rebeccas' plans for Thomas went no further than marriage, having served his purpose he was free to return to slaughtering pathetic animals alongside his detestable family. Martha would continue to feed him, leaving her free to accompany Mamma as she travelled through Somerset visiting the family and, who knows, she might even be able to persuade her to hold her afternoon soirees again.

Lying exhausted following another passionate encounter, Rebecca pressed when they might marry and again Thomas tried to explain why it was not possible,

*"Becca I casn't marry thee an you knows it, thy mothur n Mr Gerrush ould never allow it."*

Rebecca would not to be beaten and had obviously already planned how to set her trap because the next thing Thomas heard was,

*"Well if it is only my mother and stepfather who are stopping us we can apply for a marriage licence ourselves,"* adding, *"I am over twenty one you know and no longer need their consent to marry."*

John Worlock did not wait for an invitation, he strode up to the Mill, determined to see Mary who, on this occasion, was more than willing to meet him, although her controlling young husband insisted on being present 'to offer his advice and support.' Knowing how determined their children could be, once they had set their mind on something, it was reluctantly agreed that the most sensible solution might indeed be marriage despite young Gerrish' disapproving reminder,

*"When I married my dear wife I became responsible for her fatherless children and their father, a close friend of yours I believe, would be mortified to learn one of his impressionable innocent young daughters had been seduced by your rake of a son, no I am sorry but I cannot agree to such a union!"*

*"He bain't no rake, least my boy d'want t'stand by er, weren't is fault he be the one she caught when none of t'others,"* referring to all the rumours about all the less savoury men in Rebecca's life, *"wanted er,"* John shouted back towards a very smug looking Peter.

With the two men, adversaries for so long, remaining in the same room the meeting was getting nowhere and risked deteriorating into a very bad tempered quarrel. Finally Mary, accepting the situation would probably not have reached this state had her young husband not interfered, was forced to insist,

*"Peter!, thank you but on this occasion dearest I feel this should be left to Mr Worlock and myself."*

Accepting John's assurance that Thomas truly wanted to marry her daughter Mary, in turn, agreed Rebecca appeared to be very keen to marry him but Peter, sulking behind Mary's chair and sensing control of yet another one of Lamorocks' children was about to slip from his grasp, persisted in his attempt to influence her and counselled against any union between 'a Flower and a common Worlock'.

This was the last straw, John had heard enough and angrily retorted,
*"Least we bain't gold diggers like thee!"*

Peter glowered straight at the older man and hissed,
*"Are you quite certain of that because from what I hear your family, particularly your sons, have ensured your insignificant little inheritance from old Mrs Prigg was spent in various Ale Houses. I should therefore imagine some Flower money might come in very handy at the moment!"*

The outcome of this highly charged bad tempered meeting found Mary sitting alone with her daughter late into the evening. With no interruptions from a domineering husband and controlling stepfather Rebecca convinced her mother she not only truly loved Thomas but had done so since they were children, although he had never loved her other than a brother would his sister.

*"That all changed when Honor left home and your marriage,"* she lied, hinting the real reason was the arrival of Peter Gerrish, *"and now we care deeply for each other and wish to marry."*

Unsure what thought, if any, her daughter had given to anything other than walking down the aisle on the arm of Thomas Worlock, Mary probed,
*"If you marry him where will you live?"*

Rebecca's childish reply showed just how naive she was when it came to the future and the extent to which Flower money featured in her plans,
*"You can buy us a little house, preferably in Oldland, as a wedding present from dearest Papa."*

Mary, astounded at such an assumption, continued,
*"Even if Mr Gerrish and I were mindful to use some of Papa's money in such a way do you have any idea what it will be like as a butcher's wife?"*

Throwing back an untidy head of brown unkempt and unwashed hair, Rebecca opened her large mouth and shrieked,
*"Oh Mamma of course I do, Thomas says I have spent long enough around Hester to know how to care for a few animals and his father is forever saying, thanks to old Mother Priggs' money, he and Martha will soon hand everything over to their sons, so Thomas will be part owner of his fathers business, unlike Peter who will never own Papa's Mill because it has to go to George when he is older."*

Ignoring this last deliberate hint of sarcasm aimed at her young husband Mary pressed,

*"But my dear girl, have you any idea at all how hard running a household, looking after your husband and caring for his children will be because I doubt Thomas, part owner of a business or not, will be able to afford to hire a nursery maid or indoor servants?"*

Not to be beaten Rebecca declared defiantly,

*"You and Papa took in paupers, we can do the same but until Thomas is in a position to do so and Martha's cousin finds us one from the Poor House, I have my own money."*

Slowly Mary realised her daughter had thought of everything, even down to a generous financial advance from her,

*"But Rebecca do not forget you will be expected to feed and clothe any pauper from the Poor House, Papa was in the fortunate position to be able to do such a thing, what if Thomas is unable to keep his promise?"*

Taking hold of her mother's hand she gave it a gentle squeeze saying, with a slight chuckle in her voice,

*"Oh Mamma do not worry so, when Thomas takes over the business of course we will be able to afford servants,"* adding by way of a warning to those who might choose to oppose the match, *" but I don't care what you, the Worlocks or Peter says...I will marry Thomas with or without your blessing!"*

By the time she eventually crawled into her bed later that night Mary feared her daughter had little idea about running a household but of one thing she was certain, she was determined to marry Thomas and, as usual, once her mind was made up then, by God, Rebecca Flower would have it her way!

Thomas was proving very obstinate in his determination to marry Rebecca, despite both Worlock and Flower opposition. Convinced she was using him to escape her controlling stepfather, Robert tried in vain to persuade his brother to change his mind by reminding him of all the local girls he could have had in her place. That having failed, John tried arguing that both families needed time to think about the consequences, all the while knowing his second son would marry Rebecca no matter what they or anyone else said. During one last attempt at making him see things his way Thomas turned on his father, more from frustration than anything else and angrily reminded him how his grandfather had been forced to contribute towards the £40 Bastardy Bond for his friend John Hulburd,

*"Maybe you d'want I t'go afore Mr Quarman n stir up memories of them what's old nough t'remember, cus if I d'refuse t'marry er that be what'll appen an n'any case tis too late I've already bin t'see Vicar n paid fur a Licence, we can wed whenever we d'want"* was the defiant reply.

Stunned by what he heard and fearing the worse, John demanded, *"Be you saying she be carryin thy child?"*

*"No she bain't!"* roared Thomas, *"but what ould um say if she were an we weren't wed?"*

Days passed but, try as she may, Martha found it impossible to talk to Mary. Gone were the days when they would walk home from Church together. Now she arrived in the gig Lamorock had given her as a wedding present, Peter at the reins and made straight for their family pew before leaving just as quickly at the end of the Service. Now, three weeks later, Martha finally saw her chance, young Gerrish had just ridden past her on his way out of Bitton towards Kelston and, probably, Bath….with luck her old friend might be home on her own today.

Mary saw Martha striding towards the house and was already waiting for her at the kitchen door. Although they were old friends, on this occasion few warm words of welcome were spoken as the butchers wife was shown into the downstairs parlour. Once inside and safely behind closed doors Martha wasted no time in defending her son,
*"Thy girl set out t'trap'm right frum the start an as bin tempting im fur months till she got im in er bed,"* waving a grubby crooked index finger in her companion's direction, *"now she be wantin im t'marry er when tis all round Bitton ow he bain't bin th'only one."* Mary made to reply but only got as far as opening her mouth before Martha spat, *"I bain't finished wiv all me words yet!"* hammering a chubby clenched fist onto the table she stared at her old friend as she gesticulated with that crooked accusing finger again, *"course you, bein s'crazy bout a boy young enough t'be thy son an all the pleasing he brung to thy dull life, chose t'ignore the feelings of thy poor fatherless children, specially Rebecca whose always bin a spoilt little minx even when er dear Pa were livin, God Rest is Soul. Well, she bain't nothin but a scheming hussy who as trapped my boy into a marruge no one d'want!"*

Mary knew she was only hearing what Peter and the others were also saying although she was not about to admit it. Instead she set about making the Worlocks the villains in the story, claiming it was not just Thomas who had shown an interest in Rebecca,
*"I understand two of your other sons, Robert and that simpleton Samuel, were once keen to share,"* pausing to tap an elegant lace gloved finger on her pursed lips, *"how shall I put it…a close friendship with my vulnerable daughter…or am I mistaken Mrs Worlock and it was just her dowry they sought!"*

From across the small walnut card table separating them Martha glared at the woman with whom she had shared so much but who now chose to address her as 'Mrs Worlock' and was accusing two more of her sons of having more than a passing interest in Rebecca and her family money. She could not fail to notice how old her adversary looked when she was angry and thought, *"you wuz such a beauty wunce,"* muttering silently to herself, *"but that's what thee gets fur laying wiv a young usband."*

Both women used the strained silence that followed to decide what to say and do next, had Mary shown she remained the welcoming friend of old and offered her uninvited guest some refreshment, it might have lessened some of the ill feeling between them. Martha, on the other hand, knew she was still not welcome in this house, she never had been and did not expect any kindness from *"er ladyship."* At last, thinking she had finally silenced her tormentor, Mary sat forward, hands clenched together on the table in front of her and glared at Martha, head on one side, as if silently asking,
*"Well, what else do you have to say?"*

Mary did not have long to wait because, composed again, Martha took a few deep breaths before reminding her,
*"Us Worlocks don't need thy money, we be a appy family business wiv sons to take over after me n John be in our grave which'll be zunner than we thought if thy Rebecca do carry out her evil little scheme but if that's whats bin put onto thy head then I feels sorry for thy lot Mary Flower, I really do!"*

Determined to have the last word Mary haughtily replied,
*"It is Mary Gerrish now if you don't mind Mrs Worlock."*

*"Suit thyself,"* came the dismissive response, *"but theese'll always be Mary Flower t'me, the Mary Gerrish thee claims t'be bain't no-one I d'know!"*

The wedding took place on October 7th 1807 at St Mary the Virgin before Reverend Caleb Evans. Right up until the very last minute Thomas' father and brothers tried to talk him out of making what they considered was the biggest mistake of his life but he insisted he loved Rebecca as she loved him and they intended to spend the rest of their lives together…till death did them part. Eventually accepting they were powerless to stop the marriage the Worlocks gave in and were waiting inside the Church whilst Robert, seeing the happiness on his brother's face and hoping to show he was not entirely against the match, agreed to be one of the witnesses.

Taking hold of Thomas' arm Rebecca focused her eyes on Reverend Evans waiting on the altar steps, deliberately avoiding the cold stares and glares from her future in laws as she walked past them. Standing on the large stone step in front of the altar she nonchalantly gazed about her, remembering how boring this place had been when she was a child and, apart from when she was asked to make her vows, took very little interest in the service until she heard Caleb Evans melodic voice announce, *"and I therefore pronounce you man and wife"* after which she willingly let herself to be guided into the vestry where Thomas was now endearingly calling her Mrs Worlock.

Next came the signing of the Marriage Register and even she was impressed when they passed the quill pen, first to Thomas then his brother Robert and they both signed their names, proving they were not such an illiterate bunch as some thought. At last they were legally man and wife; walking back down the aisle Thomas could not have been happier, Rebecca, on the other hand, wore the satisfying smirk Martha had seen many times before and it was clear she had, once more, got everything her own way!

Married life began in an end terrace cottage amongst a cluster of hovels in Oldland with its steep lanes descending down towards the Quarry and Oldland Bottom through which Siston Brook trickled its way towards Willsbridge Mill past the Bone Mill, where they made Sal Ammoniac, Glauber Salts and Ivory Black. From its position high on the hill the other side of the valley, Hanham and Oldland Chapel looked down majestically on the small hamlet of Coneyore, so called after all the rabbit skins used by the hat factory there. The people of Coneyore were known to keep themselves to themselves and to be fairly self sufficient with their own well, smithy, alehouse and bakery along with a collection of carpenters, boot makers and basket makers. However the one thing they appeared to lack was a butcher and, considering they were now near neighbours, Thomas planned to call on them as soon as possible.

Unlike their neighbours the newlywed's cottage opened onto a large back yard where, much to Rebecca's chagrin, there was a communal well and, hidden in the corner, a shared privy that at times was little more than a putrid bubbling sewer. Thanks to their extra space the couple enjoyed the luxury of an adjoining outhouse, complete with a stone sink and brick built oven opening directly into their scullery. Inside, Aunt Partridge's old worm-eaten bow-backed pine settle was placed long ways from the door directly into the room thus creating a dark passageway and means of preventing the bitter draughts howling through the warped ill-fitting wooden door. All their furniture was either broken, basic or sparse in the extreme. A dilapidated old table perched precariously on the uneven stone flag floor, two rickety wooden chairs lay against a crudely lime washed wall under the filthy window that overlooked the yard and an old dresser, bereft of the fine china to which Rebecca would have been accustomed, stood forlornly in a dark corner. The only sign of any comfort in this dismal room came from the flames of the fire flickering in the black range and even here the shabby armchair standing alongside, resting on one of Martha's rag rugs covering part of the cold stone floor beneath it, was ample evidence that, far from enjoying their expected affluent existence, the couple were living in a squalid cottage lacking everything except the unwanted furniture left by Aunt Partridge and Grandmamma Ann.

Naturally, living in a slightly larger cottage along with her family background, Rebecca was soon deriding her illiterate ignorant neighbours. First she objected to their children playing in the yard, then she complained because no one would draw water from the well for her, refusing to listen when Thomas tried to explain it was there for everyone to use and she must learn to get on with people. Finally she tried to prevent them from using the communal privy claiming as it was in their yard it was obviously for their exclusive use and suggested the midden at the back was good enough for the likes of them. On rare quiet moments the gentle tick of the old clock on the shelf above the range was often the only sign of contentment in what was already a strained and, at times, troubled relationship. With his friends no longer welcome and his family only making rare visits, Thomas decided it was pointless furnishing the front parlour which was in an even worse state than the scullery. Another of Martha's rag rugs adorned the floor and a pair of her curtains, made from the usual leftovers, hung at the window shielding any light that managed to trickle through the filthy glass from reaching Grandmamma Ann's day bed standing forlornly in the corner. It had earlier cluttered one of the rooms at the Mill and Mary, glad to be rid of it, had briefly relented insisting,

*"Grandmamma would have dearly wanted you to have it in your first married home."*

Upstairs the two bedrooms were little better. The slightly bigger front room boasted a simple bedstead and had it not been for the exquisite lace worked bedspread and pillowcases, inherited from Aunt Partridge, which hid the disgusting stained feather mattress given to them by a local farmer who had no need for an extra bed since he stopped providing accommodation for his labourers, there would have been further evidence of their desperate situation. In the far corner stood a weather beaten washstand, complete with a cracked marble top on which a chipped jug and wash basin vibrated noisily every time anyone climbed up the creaky wooden stairs and, if further proof of their desperate situation were needed, on the bare wooden floor underneath the washstand was an unpleasant looking stained china chamber pot, another gift from the benevolent farmer. Under the window was a worm eaten blanket box full of thin worn sheets and blankets, hand me downs from Mary. Naturally there was new linen when Peter Gerrish joined her in the large mahogany bed at the Mill and, loathed to throw anything of use away, she sent them up to the newly weds without much thought to the hurt she might cause. Underfoot another of Martha's rugs hid the worse part of the rough splintered wooden floor, whilst a pair of her colourful curtains once again hid filthy windows.

Those invited to the Worlock's first home remarked on the lack of Flower money in evidence. In fact there were those who asked why they were living in such a hovel when both families had the wherewithal to provide something more suitable. Of course those same visitors could not possibly know of all the family opposition and problems, especially from Mary Gerrish who was under extreme pressure from her young husband to prevent her daughter's inheritance from falling into the, 'grasping hands of the Worlocks!'

*"Mr Gerrish says as my daughter insisted on becoming Mrs Worlock she must make the best of her situation and accept she will only be welcome back into our arms once we are convinced her husband is not a fortune hunter,"* Mary would reply when pressed, conveniently forgetting how her family had raised similar objections when *"Mr Gerrish"* planned a similar advantageous marriage.

The decision to set the couple up in their own home, in lieu of any dowry, was supposedly Mary's. However everyone recognised another controlling hand when they saw it, especially Rebecca who fully expected her inheritance and it was not long before she realised that would never happen and, far from handing over a sizable dowry on their wedding day, her mother had effectively paid Thomas in kind by providing them with a roof over their heads. The pair had then turned to the Worlocks who, according to Rebecca, were even less generous considering their prosperity thanks to Martha's inheritance and she expected more than curtains and three pathetic rag rugs as a wedding present.

Together with the cottage, Mary also leased a small orchard further up the lane, where there were now two milking cows, some chickens scratching their way around half a dozen or so apple trees which, in early October, were laden with fruit ready for pressing into cider and, probably because of who she was, the owners of the Golden Valley Coal Works thought to send them a winter's supply of coal as a wedding present.

Oldland was surrounded by common land. However should any animal dare wander onto the lush grass without permission their owners were heavily fined and Thomas was constantly reminding his increasingly stubborn wife,
*"Dussent thee let thy cows wander off down t' Oldland Bottom, we b'aint got no shillun to pay the fine t'get um back!"*

In their present precarious situation they could ill afford such an extravagant drain on their finances but Rebecca rarely listened and never understood why he was forever pleading poverty.

The first weeks of married life were not quite what either expected, having got her man Rebecca ceased to share his enthusiasm to legally continue the passion she had eagerly shared with him and on more than one occasion Thomas, in sheer frustration, forced his attention on her. He also assumed the time spent alongside his mother and sister would have taught her how to cook but if he complained about the meagre meal put before him she would angrily retort.

*"How do you expect me to cook, it was something I never needed to do before I married you, Mamma always had a kitchen maid to do that and when are you going to employ someone to help me!"*

His answer was always the same,
*"Wi'out what's due from thy muther I casn't ford no kitchun maid, n'any case thee shuldn't need no elp, muther brung up ten of us, took in sewing, kept animals an elped father, why casn't thee be like er?"*

Unfortunately, expecting her own way she failed to see when it was sometimes better to keep quiet but, having already accused Thomas of reneging on his promise to employ a maid of all work, she continued her diatribe by taunting him,
*"I am not your mother, although it is very clear why you married me and I am glad Mamma withheld my dowry because it means you and and your accursed family will never get their filthy grabbing hands on it!"*

Knowing he had been deceived and trapped into a loveless marriage, it was not long before Thomas was the talk of the village. With their rows becoming more and more frequent he looked for but received little sympathy from his family and their pleas that he should have thought twice before marrying her, along with their reminder about poverty entering through the door so allowing love to fly out the window, were returning to haunt him! Finally, following another spectacular fiery outburst when, once again, she denied trapping him into marriage, accusing him of only wanting her for her money, he gently replied ,
*"I wed thee cus you sid thees luved me but I bain't s'sure n'more."*

Expecting the usual angry retort he paused but when none came he abruptly turned his back on her and, grabbing his battered old hat from the peg, strode out into the yard angrily threatening,
*"I be going to th'Chequers an these better be in a gud mood when I d'cum ome!"*

October gave way to November and Thomas no longer bothered Rebecca, much preferring to stay out late drinking with his bachelor brother George rather than come home to a cold unresponsive wife. Robert and Samuel were both family men and Rebecca constantly accused John and Martha of deliberately excluding her from their lives, preferring their other daughters in law and brood of grandchildren. In truth neither could afford to spend their money on drink and Thomas often wistfully dreamed what it must be like to be welcomed home by a loving wife, even if she was the fiery Sophia or feeble skeletal Zipporah.

Thomas strove to live in harmony with his neighbours, offering to help carry heavy pails of water from the communal well, giving the children a fresh egg or an apple from the orchard now and again along with an occasional bag of the meat scraps Rebecca found so offensive but from which their mothers made a rare nourishing soup and he willingly took his turn to clear out the rancid contents of the privy when the stench became too overpowering. His sullen wife, by contrast, stayed aloof wanting nothing to do with any of them, especially once she realised one or two of the older men worked for her father and remembered her as a child. As the weeks, then months, passed Rebecca became more and more convinced everything was Thomas' fault and she was not to blame for misguidedly marrying a man who was now forcing her to live amongst illiterate labourers when, as the educated daughter of Lamorock Flower, she deserved better and should be given the respect her family name deserved. The fact no one had made her marry Thomas and that she had duped him by falsely claiming to love him, when all she really wanted was a way to escape her unhappy home life, was totally lost on her.

# CHAPTER EIGHT

Robert and Thomas Worlock spent the second week of November working between Oldland, Keynsham and Hanham slaughtering animals in readiness for winter storage. Their days started and finished in darkness. Robert called for his brother around six and the pair worked till there was not one beast left standing, only then would they make their weary way home. They worked as a team, one held the unfortunate creature still with a strong rope round its neck whilst the other felled it with one swift stroke of a pole axe to the centre of its head, if that failed then a hasty slit across it's throat with a sharp knife finished the job. Thomas enjoyed working alongside his older brother, the pair were very strong and knew if they worked hard then the farmer might well reward them with a little extra on top of the rate charged for the job and fortunately for Thomas, with a wife incapable and unwilling to provide him with anything, the food and ale the farmer's wife provided was usually the only sustenance he could hope for.

Maybe it was because it had been a long day or maybe it was because they had partaken of too much of Farmer England's ale but, on the way home, Thomas found himself asking his elder brother.

*"What be it like t'be wed to a wuman who d'welcum thee to er bed, who d'look after thee an don't think she be better n you?"*

Robert sighed, Thomas and Rebecca must have quarrelled again, he could well imagine what life must be like for his younger brother these days and could say nothing but,

*"It'll get better, you bain't bin married long,"* all the while knowing it would never improve until his sister in law and one time childhood friend, stopped being selfish and started caring for his poor bewildered brother.

Returning home after a days slaughtering, Thomas was now obliged to strip off and leave his bloodstained clothes in the yard outside the scullery door, even though he always wore a leather apron and very little blood got onto his shirt and breeches, Rebecca complained they made her feel sick and refused to wash them. In the early days he understood and accepted her claims remembering how his mother was just the same, especially when she was pregnant, although she never refused to wash fathers clothes. However, after yesterdays little chat with Robert, from now on his churlish wife would have little choice, in fact he would expect a great deal more from her...or else!

Thomas had come home in a foul mood last night insisting, *"In future there bain't no reason why theese cassent wash these,"* throwing his shirt and breeches at her feet, *"cus though mother be willin't'do it she got father an t'others t'look to an you bain't doing nothin yer all day."* no longer believing her lies nor prepared to listen to her criticise Martha he continued, *"even babbies never stopped er and, whilst we be talking bout muther, she always sent us out wi summut in our pockuts n proper grub on th'table t'come ome to!"*

Rebecca felt anger surging through her entire body and spat out, *"And what do you suggest I put on the table when you never provide anything."*

These days he cared little when his wife flew into a rage at the mere sign of not getting her own way but, after two months of marriage, the ensuing rows were now no longer so one sided.

*"There be plenty a eggs from all they chickens,"* pointing in the direction of the small orchard up the lane, *"an nough milk from two gert cows to make all the butter n cheese we d'need and why cassent thee do summut wiv the bits a mutton I brings ome every week?"* He reminded Rebecca how most of the Worlock women could cook and bake bread, one of his sisters was even famed as a dairywoman, before finally accusing his vixen of a wife, *"Theese learnt nothin from all they yers wiv our Hester, thee cassent even milk a cow proper nor make us some butter n cheese."*

Enraged at being compared to the ignorant backward Worlock girls, Hester in particular, Rebecca exploded, *"How dare you compare me to that imbecile, I want a scullery maid, do you hear me ...you...you...ignorant stupid man!!!"*

Standing at the well, struggling to turn the handle as she waited for the bucket of icy water to appear from the depths Rebecca was complaining to Mrs Butler, patiently waiting her turn, about feeling violently sick from the stench of Thomas' bloodstained clothes and how her back ached from carrying buckets of water across the yard to the sink in the out house, *"Of course I was never expected to work before my marriage, my family are the Flowers from Boyd Mill....but I expect you are already aware of that."*

At last Thomas' breeches were hanging over the wall to dry and she made her weary way up the lane towards the orchard. It was all very well for Thomas to insist she did all the household chores, how could he know that was why Mamma took in young paupers from the Poor House and the reason Papa employed men to look after their animals. Resting her weary head against the warm flank of the cow she felt the first of the tears well up in her eyes. This was not how she planned things would be. Placing the heavy wooden pail underneath the animal's swollen udders she began gently squeezing the warm milk all the while dreaming she was resting on Grandmamma's old day bed, waiting for the day Mamma would send for her and she could return home to her family again. With only half a pail of milk from the first animal she moved to the other to see if she would have more success, her hands were already cold and red raw from the cold water and her fingers were turning numb as she tried to squeeze the last drop of milk from the wretched animal. If only Hester were here she would know what to do because, despite spending so much time with her, she had taken in very little of what she was shown. All she ever wanted from the Worlocks was the means of escaping Peter Gerrish. Well she had succeeded but only by swapping one kind of prison for another.

It was almost nine o'clock when a very drunk Thomas staggered home. He knew Rebecca would be furious but no longer cared about anything she said or did. The scullery was in darkness with no lighted candle on the table to guide him, even the normally welcoming fire in the range was little more than ash. Rebecca and, more to the point, his supper, were nowhere to be seen. Staggering into the old chair he stirred what remained of the dying embers into life allowing the light from its flames to guide him towards the candle on the table so that, once lit, he could search for his wife. Fumbling his way to the foot of the stairs he heard her voice calling his name!

A gullible Mary Gerrish believed everything she was told-how no-one knew her daughter was ill, that Thomas no longer cared about her, preferring to spend his time round at the Chequers whilst not even their neighbours, with whom he was rumoured to be so friendly, bothered to enquire when there had been no sign of Rebecca all day.

Martha was anxious to get to Oldland. Despite her doubts about the marriage and the way they had all been deceived, she was determined to treat Rebecca just like the others and guessed, correctly, that Mary would never think to visit her daughter.

In her younger days Martha would have thought nothing of walking the few miles across the fields up to Oldland. Now she depended on John or one of the boys to take her in the delivery cart, unfortunately they had all left before light this morning and were not due home till much later. She desperately searched amongst her neighbours and even considered walking up Golden Valley to see Mary, risking meeting Peter Gerrish, in an attempt to get up to Oldland. Finally an old farmer, calling to pay his bill, sensed something was deeply troubling her and offered to take her in his ramshackle cart.

Expecting to find Rebecca in bed Martha was taken aback to find her in the scullery and by the indifference that met her, even her offer,
*"Why dussent thee rest an let me get summut for thine n Thomas' zupper"* was met with a brusque reply,
*"Thomas says I'm not ill and I am more than capable of getting him something to eat!"*

Glancing around the drab room Martha wondered how Rebecca managed to live in such a place when she was surely accustomed to a more genteel life. Eager to use the situation in an attempt at further healing the rift between this sullen spoilt daughter in law Martha, well used to her little tantrums, gently insisted,
*"Well if theese dussent want t'rest then let I wash them sheets afore Thomas d'come back"* pointing to some bloodstained washing soaking in the sink.

*"I would rather you didn't Martha!"* was Rebecca's abrupt reply as she roughly caught hold of the older woman's arm, *"it will only give him something else to complain about because he says I am not to let you do the washing anymore, you apparently have enough to do looking after John!"*

It came as something of a relief when the Butlers young son came to the door saying Robert was waiting at the end of the lane for her. Sarah Butler was standing in the dark doorway of her dingy scullery as Martha walked by and, thinking back to her offer to wash the stained bed clothes and how Rebecca had grabbed her away from the sink she asked,
*"As thee dun any washin for er?"*

From the bland expression on Sarah's face it was clear no-one had set foot inside the house before Martha got there.

All the way home Martha thought about the morning's events, about Rebecca's strange behaviour and how the disgusting washing in the sink pointed to no more than a heavy monthly course but she knew she would be ill advised to mention such doubts to either John or her poor unfortunate son. Robert's words,
*"Theese be quiet muther"* brought Martha back from her deep thoughts.

As the old horse lurched down the rough uneven track the swaying motion of the cart aggravated every aching bone in her body but failed to take her mind from the nagging doubts troubling her, doubts she knew she could not and would never be able to share with John. There was nothing in her son's house to show that anything so traumatic as a miscarriage, which was what Mary was suggesting, had ever taken place. Sarah Butler had neither seen nor heard anything to indicate Rebecca was in distress whilst the few heavily bloodstained clothes and bed sheets simply pointed to an unusually abnormal monthly visitor.

Believing Rebecca had suffered a miscarriage and desperately trying to protect her from all the whisperings behind closed doors, Mary sent a message suggesting she arrange for Doctor Watts to call to ensure there was no permanent damage. Her conniving little hussy of a daughter, whilst willing to see her compliant mother on her own but not wanting Samuel Watts to discover her lies, assured her, through the same messenger,
*"There really is no need Mamma, the bleeding has almost stopped. However, should you wish call Thomas leaves early in the morning and does not return until late at night, so you can be assured of not having to meet him."*
Of course neither Doctor Watts nor Mary ever called.

*"Fur Gods'ake Martha what be th'matter with'ee casn't thee sleep?"* John moaned as once again Martha was out of bed, old woollen shawl about her shoulders, sitting on the blanket box gazing out of the window. From what she learned from Robert there was little chance of a baby let alone a miscarriage and Martha knew she would never be able to share her worries with anyone, especially John, for fear of how they might react or with her old 'friend' Mary Gerrish.

It was not long before Thomas, wise to Rebeccas' attention seeking little outbursts, learned there had been nothing wrong with her and he had been deceived yet again. He refused to listen to her demands that Martha 'order' Betty Prigg to find them a girl from the Poor House, instead he made it very clear she was to be up from her bed and have something ready for his pocket when he left for work, often before daybreak and for there to be a proper meal waiting on his return. He coldly ignored her cries when he forced himself on her night after night, reminding her that she was free to return to her mother whenever she wished, providing of course Mary wanted her back, *"cus theese be no use t'Gerrish now be you my sweet,"* Thomas would taunt following yet another violent hedonistic encounter.

The rows, demands and abuse worsened and continued well into December by which time, with their first family Christmas approaching, Thomas had made it perfectly clear he preferred the company of his brother George and his cronies at The Chequers Inn in Barry Road to the cold unresponsive arms of a nagging wife. At Church on the last Sunday before Christmas Martha pretended to say her prayers all the while staring at the Gerrishes in their fine pew and wondered why they ever believed the stories Rebecca told them in order to marry Thomas, especially the latest lie about a miscarriage. Rebecca's wish to join her family that first Christmas came to nothing and she was forced to stay with the Worlocks. The closest she came to seeing her family was at Church on Christmas morning, even then she was denied what she felt was her rightful place alongside them in the family pew instead of sitting in the main body of St. Mary's with her husband's family and all the rest of the village rabble. After the service she was allowed only the briefest of time to talk to them before Peter Gerrish, not wanting people to think he was losing control, intruded into their reunion and briskly led them away leaving John and Martha, with their rapidly expanding family, to return to their cottage where Robert, Sophia, Samuel and Zipporah were waiting for them.

Rebecca continued to insist there had been a miscarriage and she was not the selfish scheming woman her enemies said she was. In an attempt to quell rumours of being jealous of her sisters in law and their babies she genuinely poured all her love onto her nephews, so much so that when Samuel and Zipporah took their second child, William, to be christened at Hanham and Oldland Chapels in early February it was Rebecca who held him as the family stood around the font and it was therefore Rebecca who felt the deepest pain when, just like his brother before him, he died. Her mother's cold rejection that first Christmas stayed with Rebecca for some time, even Thomas sensed her pain and tried to be more understanding, not so demanding or insisting she match his mother or sister when it came to husbandry. In return Rebecca mellowed and, with Martha's help, concentrated on becoming a dutiful wife. With Hester at her side the milk yield from the cows increased and she sometimes had a surplus of butter which she sold, much too cheaply according to her father in law. From an abundance of eggs and milk she learned to make simple pancakes, pigeons and rabbits were plentiful and were made into stews or pies. Occasionally when customers paid in kind instead of money Thomas brought home a fish, freshly caught in the Avon. With no sign of any Flower money to make life easier, Thomas followed his father's footsteps and worked long hard hours for his pay when the only perks might be the occasional leg of mutton or piece of beef which, with Martha's help, Rebecca now knew how to cook and tide them over many days.

By late Spring Thomas and Rebecca were settled into some kind of married life, the first distressing months a thing of the past. With him working away from home all day she found contentment on her own, milking her cows, making her butter, collecting her eggs and looking to a fattening pig alongside the rest of her animals in the orchard, another payment in kind from a local farmer. Tensions between her neighbours eased slightly although there was still some way to go and she was still occasionally referred to as 'madam up the end' by one or two of them. Even John and Martha were beginning to warm to her and accept her into their family, especially once they realised she was trying to learn from her mistakes. History appeared to be repeating itself when, four months after their wedding, there was no sign of a baby. Martha, accepting she may have been wrong to doubt her, reassured her it would happen one day…

*" I were just th'same afore our Robert. "*

The birth of a third son for Samuel and Zipporah did nothing to help Rebecca's maternal instincts and, just as before, she displayed all the signs of wanting to treat him as her own however, when he was christened William, after his dead brother, this time he was held firmly in the arms of Aunt Sophia not Aunt Rebecca!

Following her supposed illness and her mothers' immediate concern for her health, especially by offering to call in Doctor Watts and pay his fee, Rebecca mistakenly believed she might soon be welcomed back into the family but after eight months of marriage there had not been a single invitation, in fact the last time she had spoken to her mother was on Easter Sunday and, although Peter had reluctantly agreed to let her and Thomas walk up Church Lane with them, there had been no indication when they might visit. However just because there was no invitation it did not mean she never saw her brothers or young sister, in fact they met quite regularly, usually in some quiet place where Peter or his spies could not necessarily find them.

As far as Rebecca was concerned her marriage to an uneducated illiterate Worlock had not been made easy because, instead of a 'the sweet little house' she expected as a wedding present from Mamma, she was forced to live in a hovel, even their furniture was used or broken. Then Thomas broke his promise to provide a domestic servant, insisting instead that she cope on her own, he even prevented Martha from helping her when he knew very well how much washing his disgusting blood stained clothes upset her so. He still occasionally complained about her ability to cook or provide him with a proper meal, choosing to compare her with his saintly mother and ignorant sisters. From childhood John and Martha never once gave the Flowers cause to doubt their affection for their children but now she was their daughter in law Rebecca imagined she saw them differently. Thomas was expected to work long hard hours for neither reward nor thanks from his father, Robert was clearly Martha's favourite whilst none of their simple minded daughters would ever find husbands so long as the domineering old crow kept them at home looking after their pathetic animals or insisted they learn how to sew instead of letting them to mix with people, especially men!

The New Year brought another severe cold spell during which many poor labourers and their families struggled to survive. Sadly many did not and the grave digger really earned his wage, up to 3/- for a grave no more than 5 foot deep, up to 7/- if it exceeded 7 foot. Following the next Vestry Meeting it was further agreed to pay the Parish Clerk 1/6 for every burial he arranged although he was expected to sweep the Church every week and keep the paths free from weeds in return. The Poor House was overflowing with poor helpless wretches unable to cope with such harsh weather or survive on their own and it was left to men like William Francis and his distant cousin Thomas Smallcombe, as two of the six Parish Representatives, to decide what help should be given to those still clamouring around its door. Buoyed by what she saw as the early beginnings of a possible reconciliation with her daughter, Mary's new found contentment was marred by the death of George Flower over at Saltford and, although they had fallen out over the sale of some jointly owned property leading to a lengthy Court Case, she was none the less saddened at his passing.

*"We were children together and were, for the most, very close, especially during dear Lamorock's lifetime,"* she was overheard telling someone after Church the following Sunday.

George Flower was taken the short distance from his Saltford Manor to lie in the sheltered St. Mary's Churchyard on February 23rd leaving Ann a widow at forty three with six children, the eldest a daughter of thirteen, the youngest a son of four. Like his brother, father and grandfather before him he left an heir too young to legally succeed him and before long rumours of a Flower curse abounded!

Fully aware of all the discontent his presence generated within the family, Peter Gerrish nevertheless expectantly waited for news from Lower Farm, confident Mary and her children would be lovingly remembered and finally receive what was due to them. When the last Will and Testament of George Flower, Yeoman of Saltford, with its many codicils added to coincide with the birth of each of his children, was eventually proved with nothing finding its way across the River to Bitton, Mary was once more treated to Peter's vitriolic opinion of her *"damn family!"*

Mary fled to Publow, ostensibly to be with Honor who was weeks away from the birth of another child but, in reality, to escape what the servants described as, *"the wrath of Mr Gerrish,"* once he learned there was little chance of gaining control of any more Flower money. Some weeks later, with the birth of another boy, came the chance for Honor to send a simple message to her young stepfather….her father, brother and Uncle George may be dead and because of him her sister was isolated from the family whilst their mother was completely in his control but she was and always would be a Flower and as if to emphasize this she called her new son George (after her grandpapa and uncle) Partridge (after her very formidable aunt) Thompson.

Returning home a month later Mary was met with the second piece of news. Rebecca, tired of waiting for an invitation to visit, had written to her, *"Dearest Mamma, I would have much preferred to tell you this in person but, fearing you will be upset to hear it from someone, other than me, I am eager for you to know that, at long last, Thomas and I are to be blessed with a child, God willing, it will arrive sometime in October. Your loving and obedient daughter, Rebecca."*

Mary decided to take no chances this time and surprised everyone, none more than Peter, by ignoring his unhelpful comments and insisted Rebecca see Doctor Watts then, content with what he had to say, pay her brother William a visit.

William Francis lived in Bitton and Mary arrived, unannounced, after driving herself there in her little gig. Sitting on her father's ancient mahogany sofa in her brother's study Mary thought back to all the other times she had been in this room. Along with the rest of the family William was far from happy when she married Peter and had told her so at the time but, once her mind was made up, he and Elizabeth had not cut her off like some and she knew she was always welcome in their home.

William listened patiently as his sister related her concerns for Rebecca and her coming baby.

*"Surely you must know of a pauper family desperate to be rid of one of their unwanted brats, of course they will pay her a small wage and provide adequate food and clothing."* When the request was met by a scornful scowl from her brother Mary continued, unmoved. *"Come now William surely you of all people must agree it is better than to expect such a child to be burdened on the Parish Rates which, I might add, Peter complains are far too high and it is about time something was done about all the paupers, vagrants and beggars streaming into Bitton expecting people like him to feed them or for the Poor House to take them in."*

William countered,
*"Mary! you would never have said such a thing in Lamorock's time. Unlike your present husband, he cared for the poor of Bitton or have you forgotten so easily?"* Unprepared for such words from her brother whom she believed, like her, must accept every single word Peter uttered, she was rendered temporary speechless giving William chance to continue because he was far from finished, *"Have you forgotten how the ale flowed following the birth of your first son, did your loyal workers not follow Lamorock's coffin such was the respect in which he was held in the district, did you not give those same workers the afternoon off for Honor's wedding and, by allowing the building of pits in our*

*Valley, are you not in someway responsible for all those beggars, paupers and vagrants that so offend your young husband!!"*

Gazing at his sister's stunned look on hearing words her normally gentle and agreeable brother would never have dared utter she heard him say, as if warning her of things to come.

*"My dear it seems your Mr Gerrish has not only allowed his foolish impressionable young head to be turned by his fine new friends in Bath but they have done a good job on yours as well!"*

Nevertheless William took his sister's request to the next Vestry Meeting where, as expected, the chance of removing another pauper from their financial responsibility was eagerly accepted, especially when the person offering to remove the said pauper was none other than Mary Gerrish.

Rebecca greeted her mother's offer with enthusiasm which was unfortunate because Mary thoughtlessly forgot to tell her petulant pregnant daughter that it would be Thomas, not her, who paid the £7 a year wages because, on Peter's advice, she decided,
*"Against using Papas money since the Worlocks are rumoured to be a successful family business these days, therefore Thomas is more than able to pay her wage himself."*

Mary and Rebecca were now meeting more regularly but only when it conveniently coincided with Peters' visits to Bath and Thomas was working away from home. On one such occasion Rebecca again pleaded for the release of a small part of her father's money to pay for some domestic help,
*"Thomas and I barely have enough to live on without having to find the means to feed another mouth."*

Sadly, reconciled or not, Mary was not to be moved, warned to expect such a request it was Peters' not her mothers' words Rebecca heard.

*"It is a great pity you gave no thought to the expense of running a household before allowing yourself to be tempted into the sorry state you now find yourself, perhaps you should have waited for Peter to find you a more suitable husband instead of expecting me to waste Papa's money on the likes of Thomas Worlock."*

So, with no place for their young daughter and no income from her meagre £7 a year wages, the pauper family remained at the mercy of the Parish, leaving Peter silently congratulating himself at having brought embarrassment onto the Worlocks by letting it be known their second son could not even find the money to pay for a pauper to help his pregnant wife around the house.

Rebecca's pregnancy was proving so trouble free she found herself actually enjoying the long hours she was spending alone. As she waited for the birth she diligently cared for their cottage, not to mention her animals and worked on improving her relationship with her neighbours. Sarah Butler, next door, was now insisting she be called, day or night, should her pains start, assuring her, *"It'll be no trouble t'send th'boy to Bitton fur thy mother."*

On hearing this Rebecca, knowing her mother would neither wish to be involved nor be allowed to be present at the birth, pleaded, *"Please Mrs Butler do not send for my mother, I would feel much happier if it was Mrs Worlock".*

Rebecca no longer saw her mother; Mr Gerrish had decreed her visits were more frequent than he wished and, fearful Mary might be tempted to offer financial help, however small, he had 'advised' his compliant wife that matters would worsen if the visits continued.

With the arrival of this baby Martha and John's surviving grandchildren would total five. Robert and Sophia had two boys, Samuel and Ziporah's sickly son William had recently been joined by another equally puny boy whom they called John and as summer grew slowly into autumn wedding bells were once again heard in the Worlock household when Elizabeth married Benjamin Robbins.

As planned, Granny Martha was present for the birth of her first granddaughter Mary Ann. The grandmother after whom it was assumed she had been named chose to wait until the following day to visit where, on taking one look at the dilapidated old box crib used quite successfully for all twelve of Martha's babies and in which her new granddaughter now slept peacefully, she declared it would not do and she would arrange for a carpenter to make a new one. Rebecca had no choice but to outwardly show her gratitude whilst inwardly thinking of all the things she could buy with the money her mother planned to waste on such an unnecessary piece of furniture.

Martha insisted Thomas was nowhere near the cottage during the birth but when he saw his daughter later it had been love at first sight, causing John to muse,
*"Always is fust time m'boy, specially when tis a little maid but theese wait til number twelve do arrive and see ow thee feels then."*

Mary Ann Worlock was christened at Hanham and Oldland Chapel on October 23rd 1809 and continued to thrive during her early weeks and well into the following year when her parents announced she was to be joined by a little

brother or sister. Mary thought it was far too soon after their first baby only for Peter to suggest,
*"What else do you expect from a Worlock, if you live like animals you breed like them."* conveniently forgetting how his fifty four year old wife had given birth to eight children, some in quick succession, during her first marriage.

Rebecca and Sophia were healthy strapping girls, completely dwarfing poor Zipporah who had never been a strong girl, even before she married Samuel. Surrounded by the highly toxic chemicals used for hat making, he brought them home to invade their cottage, the air they breathed, the food they ate, even in the dirty water thrown away after washing his clothes. Was it any wonder the couple had already lost two babies whilst the two that survived were puny, consumptive and had little or no colour in their cheeks in comparison to their bonny cousins who thrived, thanks mostly to the outdoor lives they led. Robert's two boys, at four and two, spent their days with Granny Martha or Aunt Hester in the orchard helping with the animals whilst their mother worked as a laundress. Mary Ann, who was not quite old enough to join her cousins at Bitton, stayed wrapped in an old blanket as Rebecca contentedly churned her milk into butter or cream. But, with another baby due, it would not be long before Granny Martha or Aunt Hester had another little helper.

Honor Worlock arrived with Granny Martha once again in attendance and was contentedly sleeping in the custom made cradle first used by her sister the previous year when Grandmamma Mary swept into the bedroom. Before even glancing towards her new grand daughter she deigned the room to be in dire need decorating along with the rest of the cottage and began looking for ways she might help her daughter without giving the impression she was over generous with her money or allowing Peter further reasons to criticize the way she spent it, despite it being hers to spend. Mary's determination to be less generous and keep her purse tightly shut left her when she saw Rebecca, looking very tired and pale, propped up in bed Thomas by her side, Mary Ann asleep in her arms and before long she was suggesting William Shipp send one of his men to fix the outhouse roof so Rebecca could work in a dry dairy. With two children the second bedroom was in need of proper furniture and Mary knew exactly where to find some,
*"Presumably you can arrange for someone to collect the items I have in mind Thomas?"*

Knowing every word would find its way back to Peter Gerrish and, wanting to create the right impression, Thomas suggested,
*"Well Ma-am, me n Robert ave a big job t'do t'morror but we cud call wiv the hos n cart on our way ome if that be convenyunt?"*

Trying to imagine her husband's reaction when two Worlocks drove their filthy blood stained cart and old nag of a horse, way past a visit to their slaughter house, down his fine drive Mary hastily stammered,
*"On second thoughts Thomas, Rebecca needs you here,"* looking across at her pale tired daughter as she lay against uncomfortable pillows on the stained feather mattress between well worn sheets, *"maybe it is best if I arrange for one of Mr Caters men to do it."*

Looking at Mary Ann's worn out clothes she declared,
*"Rebecca! the child is almost walking why does she not have proper shoes to wear?"*

Gazing at her mother, holding tight to her husband's hand, dark tired rings around her tearful eyes Rebecca asked,
*"Mamma where do you imagine we can find money for winter shoes when it is needed for more important things?"*

*"So what Peter says is true,"* reasoned Mary, *"nevertheless I cannot have a grandchild of mine going without warm clothing, what will people think."* Choosing to disregard what Peter would say Mary continued, *"I will see to it that a thick coat and some stout shoes are made for her and that you have a delivery of coal"* then, glancing at Thomas she could not resist asking, *"How is business at the moment Thomas, I hear you are losing customers."*

Rebecca squeezed his arm in an attempt at restraining him before he replied,
*"Things culd be better Ma'am but we bain't about to go knocking on the door of the Poor Ouse just yet."*

Releasing the clasp on the small purse hanging from her belt Mary took out a few coins and, handing them to Rebecca, advised,
*"This is for your children but remember I am still not mindful to release any of Papa's money. However as Honor received her share when she married Coster and I intend to do the same for Ann I have decided to pay for the essential repairs this place,"* looking around with some disgust on her face, *"clearly needs."*

From the pained expressions on the faces of her daughter and son in law, Mary completely misread the situation and, thinking they were stunned by her generosity, assured them,
*"I can see you are grateful but there really is no need and now I think it is best if I return to Bitton."*

Thomas escorted his mother in law back to her gig in complete silence and dutifully held out his hand to help her climb aboard, picking up the reins she turned to look down at him.

*"Take care of her Thomas, I fear she is looking most unwell,"* flicking the crop lightly across the back of the pony to urge it on. As the animal trotted away Mary called out, *"Good day to you Thomas"* without the slightest glance back.

He replied, his voice lacking any emotion,
*"An a gud day t'you Mrs Gerrush, Ma-am,"* but she would not have heard him because as he spoke he was already through the scullery heading up the steep spiral stairs towards his wife and young daughters.

Her mother may have imagined she was being more than generous but back in their bedroom Rebecca was in tears and Thomas was seething with anger at what he felt was a cruel attempt to look charitable when, on Mary's own admission, her daughter was entitled to her share of a healthy dowry just like Honor and Ann. The few coins she had given the children was nothing more than an insult when it was well known William Shipp, who would soon be mending their leaky roof, had just been paid three shillings a day plus his food to rebuild the wall of Bitton Poor House, even his young apprentice had been paid one shilling a day plus food.

With Honor's birth came a flurry of Worlock babies. Robert and Sophia had a son Gillom, Samuel and Zipporah had Hannah followed a year later by Ann. Then in 1812, following a long and difficult delivery Thomas and Rebecca, with Martha in attendance, finally had their long awaited son, John. His traumatic birth did not leave him totally unscathed, his left hand was deformed and both little fingers so crooked any plans for the boy to successfully join his father in the family business looked highly unlikely. It was Martha who first noticed his hands and reassured his exhausted mother everything would be fine in a few days, his was a long labour and he was a big baby. At one stage Mrs Butler suggested they send for Doctor Watts when it looked like Rebecca might not deliver such a big baby without his help, only for Martha to angrily retort they would do no such thing, adding,

*"I'll deliver this un, dead er live, no Doctur's gonna to butcher er"* nodding towards a screaming and near exhausted Rebecca, *"the way I were butchered with my Ruth".*

There had been no indication anything was wrong, like her previous pregnancies Rebecca blossomed especially this time because it was during the warm spring months, she even found looking after her animals and making her butter easier because the girls were now old enough to play with the other children in the lane or to be left in the care of Mrs Butler, with whom relationships were now as near perfect as they would ever be. Sometimes, especially when she spied her girls with Mrs Butler sitting on her old stool outside the scullery door mending her collier husband's breeches, her mind returned to when she would often sit next to Martha as she did the very same thing but *"life was different then, our families were friendlier, Papa was still alive and Mamma was happier"* she sighed.

Apart from his deformed hand and fingers John was a sturdy little fellow, just like his father according to Martha and was soon feeding greedily from his weary mother who was desperate for some rest. When sleep finally came Martha, who had already decided to stay for as long as she was needed this time, escaped to the scullery from where she heard the familiar sound of the rustle of material and tip tapping of expensive shoes on the uneven cobble stones in the yard and instinctively knew her 'old friend' had arrived.

Mary Gerrish was clearly not expecting to see Martha and stopped short as she emerged from the darkness of the passage behind the settle to find her by the range, large spoon in her hand.

*"Well! Martha Worlock I do declare you are the last person I expected to see, I was led to believe you were always eager to get back to John, how on earth is he managing without you?"*

Martha was prepared for some kind of derisory sarcastic comment and was swift in her reply.

*"Least thy girl d'know she can look to me when she needs elp,"* before returning to the task of stirring the large pot of rabbit and vegetables simmering on the range.

Despite the wonderful smell filling the room Mary could not resist countering,
*"So, Peter was right, times must be hard if all a butcher's son can provide for his lying-in wife and children is rabbit stew, where is the hearty loin of mutton or buttock of beef these days?"*

Martha swung round pointing the large battered ladle in her old friends' direction, shaking her head she advised,
*"Mary, t'aint a good idea t'believe all thy bigot of a usband do tell thee, specially as he be choosey over what he do want thee t'know and theese shouldn't listen to all you do ear cus, unlike thee, there be people in thy family who appen to care bout her,"* pointing upstairs to where Rebecca lay listening to every word, *"and do still come ere to see er and you'd be surprised at th'stories they brings wiv um."*

Anxious to know who was talking and, more to the point, what they were saying about her Mary moved towards the old arm chair alongside the hot

*121*

range with its glowing coals. Making to sit down she continued to ridicule her companion, her voice full of disbelief,

*"Really Mrs Worlock, why on earth would I be at all interested in what people say about my family these days?"*

Martha was no longer in awe of the likes of those who imagined themselves better than her and refused to be led, choosing to reply,

*"Frum what I yers it bain't thy family no more an"* as if offering friendly advice from the old days, *"I shouldn't sit s'close t'the fire fy was you Mary, my Thomas don't ave one of them fancy screens fur stopping flames making ladies like thee look old, but then Peter already knowed ow old theese looked when he married ee so th'damage s'probly done!"*

*"How dare you be so insulting to someone in my position, don't forget Martha Worlock I can make things very difficult for you and your unruly brood if I choose!"* was all Mary, pained beyond belief that someone so lowly dared to speak to her in such a way, could think to say.

Returning to the pot simmering gently on the range Martha turned her back on such threats muttering,

*"Doubt it, doubt it very much and fur thy information this rabbut stew be from they next door, however if tis loin a mutton you be after then why dussent thee come back t'morrow an see the gert piece my John'll be bringin um, meantime if these come to see thy new grandson he be wiv his muther an her bedroom be in the same place as afore, she bain't moved since yer last visut!"*

By the time her son reached his seventh birthday Rebecca no longer loved nor even cared for his father, in fact she loathed him more and more as each day passed and believed he no longer cared what people thought about her or her family. Miraculously there had been no more children, John was such a large baby she had taken a long time to heal, something Thomas refused to accept in the same way he refused to accept her illness during the early months of their marriage, now despite constant pleas, her torment went unheeded, especially when he was full of drink. As she suffered in silence, months then years passed until it became a cold submissive duty.

Robert now had two other daughters Martha and Sophia and a son George. Samuel had a daughter also called Martha and another son Samuel. Elizabeth and Benjamin Robbins were firmly settled back with their family in Bitton whilst Sophia had left the village to find work in Bristol where she met and married Richard Jenkins at St Philips and St Jacobs before returning to Oldland to live. George Worlock, at thirty two, remained a bachelor replacing Robert as the brother in whom Thomas now confided and it was George, with no family to support but with money to spend, whom the family blamed for turning his brother into a violent drunkard.

John and Martha could only watch, helplessly, as their second son and his wife continued to openly air their contempt for each other. Years spent sending struggling animals to their death had placed a heavy toll on John's physical well being. He no longer played such a vital role in the business, that was now in the capable hands of his three sons and Martha, with John bedridden most of the time, was unable to give her unhappy, unloved boy the sympathy he craved.

# CHAPTER NINE

Rebecca sat by the fire, mesmerised by the loud rhythmic ticking of Aunt Partridge's old clock, as she pondered over the state of her unhappy marriage. Thomas now flew into an uncontrollable rage if he came home to no food on the table, stubbornly refusing to accept there was scarcely time to care for their children, tend the animals, churn the butter, draw water from the well and prepare a meal. He refused to accept she had never known menial housework before she married him and continually ignored her demands that he employ a maid of all work. He mistook her rejection of his advances as being cold, heartless and unloving instead of realising her health and three pregnancies close together made her feel so tired and wretched. Then there were the constant cataclysmic rows over who should wash his disgusting bloodstained clothes, Martha had always understood and offered to do it but Thomas, egged on by his brothers, insisted it was her job and, no matter what anyone might otherwise say, she continued telling people that drawing up heavy pails of well water made her ill. Things briefly improved with the arrival of Mary Ann and Honor but with John's difficult labour, combined with the damage caused during his birth, came such an insensitive lack of understanding of her weak physical condition until what Thomas saw as cold rejection reached the point where she could no longer bear to have him stand next to her, let alone lie in her bed. Her differences with her mother were still not resolved and her stepfather continued to make it perfectly clear he was not prepared to accept her or her children under what was now his roof.

Samuel remained at the hat factory inhaling dangerous mercury vapours that made him act very strangely and irrational at times. Zipporah worked anywhere and for anyone willing to employ her leaving their sickly brood with Martha. Robert had all but taken John's place as head of the business whilst his wife took in other people's washing. George, with no permanent home, wandered aimlessly between his brothers and sisters as an uninvited lodger although his excessive drinking ensured he rarely had any money which to pay for his board and keep, consequently he only stayed for short spells before being asked to leave. Homeless and often hungry he invariably found his way back to the unworldly Samuel and Zipporah or Martha who naturally, despite his faults, welcomed him with open arms. Thomas rarely came home till late, usually in a foul mood and often drunk, thanks to his brother George and the regulars at The Chequers. The current Landlord, George Hook, rented the place from the executors of Mr Bryant and was to most of his clientele, except possibly

Rebecca, a popular host. Thomas chose The Chequers because of its close proximity to his cottage and the ease at which they could stagger home after closing time should George need somewhere to stay to sober up, usually in the old armchair by the fire. Mary Ann, Honor and John shared the second bedroom, the girls in one bed John in Grandpapa Flowers' old camp bed, from where all they heard these days were their parents raised voices as they constantly argued. Even at such young ages they quickly realised it was best to keep out of the way of their father until he fell into his usual alcohol induced sleep. However as time would soon tell Thomas and Rebecca's arguments were no longer exclusively reserved for their children's ears, the neighbours were now also privy to their goings on.

Rebecca awoke to a noise coming from the yard and sleepily glancing up at the old clock realised it was nearly eleven o'clock. As her eyes became more accustomed to the dim light thrown off from the single candle and dying embers she made out the shape of Thomas shuffling from behind the settle, on his own but barely able to stand. Stumbling towards her, hands outstretched as if to grab her, he tripped on the uneven flagstone floor and fell headlong landing flat on his face at her feet reeking of beer, hatless, clothes dishevelled, dirt on his hands and the knees of his breeches showing he must have literally crawled home. Glancing up all he saw was her cold sneering face looking down at him. Eventually his befuddled mind cleared and he barked the first thing to come into his mind,

*"Go n fetch zum zupper I be famished!"*

Her stinging reply, *"You are drunk again, fetch it yourself!"* brought him swiftly to his already unsteady feet and, reaching for her arm he tripped and fell again, bringing about yet more humiliation. Using the old chair by the range for support he managed to stagger to his feet as he once more demanded, *"Fetch us zum zupper, else thees'll feel this!"* waving the back of his hand in her direction.

With the chair safely between them Rebecca felt confident enough to continue,

*"You disgust me!, coming home from that place every night, spending money I can ill afford knowing your children are going hungry and in need of clothes, expecting me to be waiting here with open arms to welcome you into my bed."*

Thomas was not listening, his head was full of all the words of advice his drinking cronies had been giving him, 'Who be th'real man in thy house' and 'tis bout time theese took control of thik shrew of a wife.'

Feeling a touch steadier he once more demanded she find him some supper only to again hear, *"There is only bread and cheese and you know where that is, so you had better look there because I am going to my bed and,"* thrusting the palm of her hand into his face, *"don't think to follow me because from now on your place is down there,"* pointing to Martha's worn out rag rug in front of the range, *"where a drunkard like you belongs!"*…and with that she turned to make her way towards the stairs.

Anger surged through him as he made to grab her again. Still relying on the chair for protection Rebecca did not move allowing Thomas to catch hold of her arm and pull her across its high back and onto his lap as he sat down. Unable to escape she was powerless to stop him lifting her skirt and beating her about the backside and legs until she screamed for him to stop. Upstairs three terrified children huddled together listening to the screams of their mother, expecting their father to kill her this time and, once he was done, to be so angry he would start on them next!

Rebecca awoke to the cold light of morning barely able to move. If she needed reminding the resulting bruises across her back and legs told her about last night's beating. For the children's sake she had made light of Thomas' drunken actions when they crept silently and trembling into her bed during the night except to tell them there was nothing to worry about because it would not happen again. What she did not tell them was if it did then she was ready and quite prepared to kill their father …..before he killed her!

Thomas was still lying where she had left him, on the stone floor in front of the range, when the sound of children's voices woke him. Slowly his mind cleared and he remembered the savage events of the previous night. However if he needed any prompting the excruciating pain throbbing through his head along with the sight of his bruised and battered wife, three frightened children clinging to her skirt, left him in no doubt. With the children about their chores Rebecca wasted no time in warning him…and all their neighbours, *"Thomas, I am warning you, lay another finger on me or the children and, so help me God, I will soon put you out of this world!"*

Several weeks after the beating, although the bruises had healed, Thomas was still spending a great deal of his time and money at The Chequers leaving Rebecca to console herself that whilst he was there, coming home to sleep off its effects in the old chair by the fire, at least he was not bothering her any more. As expected, word eventually reached Mary Gerrish who was so appalled she sent a message saying she wished to see her daughter and grandchildren, adding,

*"You will be made welcome; however Mr Gerrish thinks it best if Thomas does not accompany you."*

Every time they returned from Grandmamma Gerrish the children brought home books and toys. Rebecca even mistakenly believed her rapport with her despised stepfather was improving once he began treating her civilly. Sitting next to her he would shrewdly assure her,

*"You do not deserve to suffer the way you do at the hands of that brute of a husband,"* whilst encouragingly supporting Mary when she continued to suggest,

*"Mr Gerrish and myself cannot understand why Thomas will not employ a pauper from the Poor House to help you."*

Sadly, Rebecca failed to realise how Peter Gerrish, desperate for a way in which to retaliate against what he saw as those *"damn Worlocks,"* was cunningly using the situation to encourage his moody vixen of a stepdaughter to accuse one of their sons of being an uncaring drunkard and wife beater.

Mary endured further sadness when her brother William died leaving her bereft of anyone to whom she could turn in these times of need. She still had her older sister Susannah but, thanks to Peter, she was an infrequent visitor and only called if she was staying with the Huddlestons at Kelston. With William's death Peter Gerrish again confidently anticipated his elderly wife might inherit some of their father's Bitton estate. However when his Will was finally proved in London William named his widow, the formidable Elizabeth, as his sole executrix and main beneficiary. Of their children only two daughters survived…to the twenty six year old unmarried Susannah he left five hundred pounds in the hope it would make her an 'independent wife' whilst to thirty year old Ann, wife of Thomas Cryer a Yeoman from Westbury on Trym, he left a similar amount plus an extra five guineas. Both daughters were to inherit their mother's share on her death or if she chose to remarry.

Two years later found Mary, Peter and their tenant William Cater embroiled in a legal argument with their former neighbour Thomas Bevan. The ensuing Court Case revolved around Lamorocks' alterations to the weir twenty five years ago when, by changing its height, he effectively made Bevan's water wheel tail bound. However Mary was at great pains to point out,

*"The wretched man was not even the owner then."*

Nevertheless Bevan claimed it not only damaged his mill but was affecting his paper production and expected Cater to lower the weir or he would sue him for £800. In Court William Shipp said when Lamorock employed him to rebuild his weir back in 1788 he was instructed to, *"erect it at the same height as the old one and not to vary an inch."* George Robbins, a local Millwright from Willsbridge, testified he had been employed by a Mr Bond of Bristol to make a water wheel for a Boring Mill in Bitton and confirmed it's size, working capacity and that the Mill was now occupied by William Cater. As far as Mary was concerned this completely exonerated her late husband and proved he had simply restored the weir back to its original state, furthermore, she could see no reason for either Bevan or Cater to expect her support, financial or otherwise.

Winter and spring of 1816 brought dreadful suffering to the poor and destitute of Bitton with another, more virulent, outbreak of smallpox. Martha and her neighbours did their best to nurse and feed those infected but they could do nothing to ease the pain of a grieving family when they lost one child, then another, to the disease. Reverend John Pring, served the Parish diligently; from February 1st to April 11th he buried thirteen babies and children but by July, when there were no more outbreaks, everyone thought the worst was over and he felt it safe to take a few days off leaving his colleague Reverend Thomas Hogg, Curate of Tormarton, in his place. He had not long returned home before the tale tell signs of fever, pustules and deaths reappeared and he buried fourteen more children.

The New Year began as the old one had ended and did not bode well for John Pring; in the first four months he buried Susan Lane a one year old baby who had burned to death and four young men Thomas Johnson, George Godfrey, William Gay and John White, all killed down the pits. Finally he could take no more and left the village for good, he was succeeded by Reverend Henry Ellacombe who moved into the Rectory with his new wife Ann.

Henry Ellecombe was in fine fettle this morning. During his relatively short time as Curate he had gained some notoriety for the power and passion of his sermons and the way he and Ann cared for their poor illiterate and, at times, starving flock. Henry was the second of seven boys; his father was Vicar of Clyst St. George near Exeter so it was only natural for at least two sons, Henry and Richard, to follow him into Holy Orders just as it was only natural for another to join the Army. Ellacombe's first living was as Curate of Cricklade in Wiltshire, so by the time he arrived in Bitton, at the invitation of Archdeacon MacDonald who held its patronage, he was well versed in the ways of country folk. He was also fortunate in his choice of Ann, whom he married just before coming to Bitton and with whom he founded a small Sunday School, persuading the more affluent members of the congregation to support them with regular donations or annual subscriptions. In its first year the Golden Valley Coal works supplied enough coal to keep their little schoolroom warm during the winter, the Bush family generously paid for joints of meat and puddings for the pupils dinner and, if nothing else, the Ellacombes and Smallcombes led by example encouraging not only their families but their servants to help. In that initial year alone the Rectory servants donated around £3.

If Reverend Ellacombe, or his parishioners, ever imagined those first few months as their Curate would end on a slightly quieter note than it had begun they were sadly mistaken because another member of the Caines family, having reached maturity, was causing trouble and, unfortunately, it was the Priggs who were to indirectly suffer.

Benjamin, fourth of the Caines sons and younger brother of the notorious George, constantly strove to eclipse his elder brother's reputation. Following his brush with the Monmouth Magistrates and a year's hard labour George returned to his loving family to join the infamous Cock Road Gang of thieves, cut throats and petty criminals. Gang members preferred to intermarry with like minded local families, thus developing a common bond of crime and strong family ties which, in the case of George, encouraged him to believe he was above the law and virtually untouchable. That was, however, until he tried to murder Constable Benjamin Curtis by beating him about the head with the butt of his gun. Arrested and taken to Gloster Gaol he was sentenced to hang which for some unknown reason was commuted to transportation for life and he sailed for New South Wales aboard a convict ship. Fortunately for the law abiding citizens of Oldand and Bitton, Benjamin tried, but failed, to emulate his brother; the various petty crimes he carried out never quite brought the desired financial returns til the summer of 1817 when, in the company of two fellow roughnecks, he attempted to burgle and rob Martha's elderly relative Elizabeth Prigg. The gang not only bungled the robbery but somehow Benjamin managed to lose the mask covering his face allowing Sarah and her nephew James Evans, who was lodging with her at the time, to recognise him. Transfixed to the spot by fear he could have, but did not, drawn his sword or attempted to assault them and it was not long before he was arrested and taken to the same gaol so much frequented by the rest of his family. Charged with stealing a quantity of clothes, silver teaspoons, cash, notes, Irish cloth shifts, sheets and sundry other articles to the value of £30 Benjamin was found guilty and sentenced to death; not only that but if the liverish old Magistrate had his way, he would have been hung in chains and, *"left to rot as an example to the rest of them."*

Fortunately, common sense prevailed and another Caines, denied the martyrdom he craved, saw his sentence commuted to the 'privilege' of being hanged on the scaffold above the gatehouse of Gloster Gaol.

Sadly there were those in Bitton, Peter Gerrish and understandably John Worlock amongst them, who thought common sense had not prevailed when Henry Ellacombe agreed to bury Benjamin in Bitton Churchyard and watched as the Caines set about arranging a funeral to end all funerals.

Brought home by another brother the corpse was laid out in the front parlour where neighbours and friends were invited to pay their respects…..literarily…. because the family planned to send their boy off in style by collecting a donation from everyone wishing to view his broken body….to defray the funeral expenses. Queues formed as people from miles around arrived, eager to part with their money and enough was raised to ensure such a funeral the likes of which had never been seen in the neighbourhood before. St. Mary's took on a carnival atmosphere, packed as it was by the curious and those who had paid for the privilege. The Caines planned to add some decorum to the proceedings with sufficient amounts of imported weeping and wailing whilst at the same time relied on their extended family of local criminals for suitable support. The coffin, escorted by six girls dressed from head to toe in virginal white, was carried in solemn procession from his parent's home in Cadbury Heath and received by Henry Ellacombe, after which they and the congregation, liberally aided by copious amounts of alcohol, were obliged to sit through his sermon from Ephesians *"Let him that stole steal no more."* By the time Benjamin finally joined his brother Francis, who had been committed to the same grave some thirteen years before, it was so dark candles were needed to provide sufficient light.

June 1819 saw thirty two boys and thirty seven girls attending Ellacombe's little Sunday School and thanks to continuing financial support these children, including the younger Worlocks, were not only taught the basics of reading and writing but were guaranteed at least one decent hot meal a week. The pupils were awarded annual prizes for good behaviour and good conduct whilst, in Charles Shipp, Reverend Ellacombe had found a highly qualified but firm headmaster who was not afraid to punish any pupil, boy or girl, should they misbehave.

Thomas and Rebecca gave an outward show of happy families for Christmas whilst in reality things had only worsened after that terrible night he first raised his hand to her. Spending time and money they could ill afford at The Chequers he came home always spoiling for an argument, baiting his volatile wife into losing her temper so he could claim his violent response was in self defence. When they argued the neighbours could expect a row of epic proportions, however they also noticed how Rebecca, determined to have the last word at all costs, often ended her tirades with threats to *"soon put you out of this world."*

They joined John and Martha and the rest of the family at Church on Christmas morning before returning alone to their sad little cottage. There were so many of them now neither John's health nor their cottage could cope with such a large family gathering any more.

Samuel's health was causing increasing concern, with a sickly wife and a brood of equally unhealthy children the last thing they needed was for him to fall ill but, fall ill he did. There was no need to waste money sending for Doctor Watts, it was obvious what ailed him…thanks to the mercury his mind was slowly being poisoned. From the end of April till the end of June he was so deranged he was unable to work and with no work there was no money for food, leaving Zipporah with little choice but to go to the Overseers of the Poor for help. They gave her 3/- a week whilst Martha did what she could to help by turning scraggy ends of discarded meat into some kind of meal, sending milk, eggs and butter from Hester's animals. Far from supporting Thomas, who was beginning to sicken himself, as he worried over Samuel's deteriorating health, Rebecca chose to complain bitterly,

*"Why in God's name did I allow myself to be led astray by the lies of such an impoverished weak and illiterate family without one strong man amongst them or even enough clout or a decent house large enough for at least one family gathering a year,"* after once again being forced to share a crowded wooden bench instead of her fine family pew on the rare occasion she chose to attend Church.

Although it was generally accepted they deserved each other, there were times when the couple's children and neighbours lived in fear of Thomas and Rebecca. Eventually, after one particular unforgettable outburst when the children fled to the Butlers for safety, the neighbours decided they had suffered enough and sent for the Constable which, of course, did nothing to help good neighbourly togetherness. Next day, although Thomas had been drinking heavily at The Chequers and later that night was seen staggering home extremely drunk, there were no rows, no fighting and no raised voices. In fact the only sound, if you could call it sound, was of someone or something continually shuffling back and forth across the yard towards the communal privy. Nobody saw, nor heard, anything from the Worlocks till around midday when Mary Ann hammered on the Butler's door asking what her mother could give father for an upset stomach. Sarah Butler advised,

*"Tell muther t'make up drink with zum pennyroyal,"* adding, *"that d'zumtimes elp but if he don't get no better then tell er to go to th'pothcree in Kingsood Hill or Doctur Wingrove fur a powder."*

Rebecca was later seen scurrying from the cottage muttering something about needing to pick some pennyroyal because Thomas was no better, in fact he was very much worse.

Thomas slowly recovered; he even agreed to stay away from the Chequers once Rebecca convinced him his illness was due to George Hook selling bad beer. Unfortunately, such enforced domesticity did little for his patience, temper or jealousy as he saw his educated wife teaching their children to not only read and write but to appreciate the books sent by Grandmamma Mary specifically for that purpose. As far as he was concerned there were more important things to life than reading about the adventures of Gulliver or the romantic notions of silly little love struck girls like Pamela and he wasted no time in picking fault with everything Rebecca and the children did. In particular he objected to filling his young sons head with stories from books when he should be preparing to join the family business because, despite his crippled hands, Thomas thought he might be *"useful as a delivery lad."*

With the children in their beds, Rebecca lit her candle, took down her precious copy of Clarissa from its hiding place behind the old clock and settled in the chair by the range. Straining her eyes she read the story of an innocent girl who, by refusing to marry her parent's choice of a husband, ended her life with a rake of a man who not only raped her but drove her insane. As she read so she compared her sufferings with those of her heroine and on bad days truly believed Thomas was also intent on driving her mad. Looking up she sensed his eyes glaring at her from the darkness of the room, as he thought of something sarcastic to say about her ability to read, finally his patience snapped and he spat,
*"If I'd a wanted a clever wife I could've got a decent un frum a Dame School in Bath stead of th'one I were forced t'take, one who ad already put her self bout the village like a bitch ready fur breedin!"*

The resulting row was the worse witnessed for some time, their terrified children huddled together in one bed for protection whilst they, along with all the neighbours, were treated to an exhibition of the couple's utter loathing for each other and clearly overheard Rebecca threaten to once again soon put Thomas out of this world.

Within days Thomas was so ill even copious amounts of pennyroyal failed to have much effect. Constantly wretching he was forever running to the privy after Rebecca banned him from the cottage, eventually the filth and stench was such it prevented the neighbours from going anywhere near the place as well. Reluctantly she was forced to ask Robert to take them to Keynsham to see Doctor Edwards but when he suggested it was closer and would make more sense to take his brother to Doctor Wingrove at North Common or Doctor Watts at Bitton Rebecca, being Rebecca, insisted they went to Keynsham. Roger Edwards diagnosed gastro enteritis, gave them enough stomach powders to elicit a cure and charged them a shilling they could ill afford but which Rebecca managed to find from the money put aside from selling her butter and cheese.

Thomas took weeks to fully recover but even when he was considered strong enough to rejoin his brothers it was clear this last illness had taken a dreadful toll, he had lost a great deal of weight, what teeth he still had were rotten, decaying or loose, his once fine head of hair was beginning to fall out at an alarming rate and his skin had taken on a very pale yellow hue. However it was only when an alarmed Martha saw her son out in the yard for the first time in many weeks that Robert was ordered,
*"Fur Godsake keep thy eye on thik ussy Rebecca and find owt what she be doing t'our Thomas!"*

Life was now intolerable for Rebecca and the children, she was no longer allowed to teach them once Thomas deemed, *"there bain't no point as ee,"* pointing to his son, *"be bout to earn is way same as I ad to do when I were is age an as fer they two,"* waving a filthy thumb at the dirty window towards Mary Ann and Honor sitting outside on the wall, *"summun'll want em as scullery maids afore long."* Rebecca argued that her son, with his crippled hands, would never cope with the kind of manual work expected of him in the slaughterhouse and no daughter of hers would ever be a scullery maid, however when she dared to say,
*"What will Mamma say when she learns you plan to deny her grandchildren their education and turn her granddaughters into lowly maids of all work,"* she received a sharp slap across her face from the back of a hand as a subtle reminder of, *"who d'decide things now?"*

Thomas was back drinking at the Chequers and thanks to their visit to Roger Edwards he now knew Rebecca sometimes had money from her butter and cream, so there was always the price of a pint of ale hidden somewhere in the house and if he wanted it then, by God, it was his right to have it just as it was to have his other pleasures satisfied. Despite belonging to a successful family of butchers Rebecca and the children rarely ate meat, unless it was rabbit or one of her chickens. If Thomas ever brought home the odd joint of meat and there was no money in the house, not even from Rebecca's earnings, but he was determined to have his fill of ale, he thought nothing of taking it round to Mrs Hook in exchange.

It was a fine afternoon; the children were at the Ellacombe's Sunday School and always called in on John and Martha before walking home across the fields before dark. Thomas had not returned home so, assuming he was still at The Chequers and would not be back till either his money ran out or, knowing George Hook would never refuse to serve him, he was too drunk to walk home, Rebecca felt confident enough to sit in the spring sun outside the scullery door and read. She dare not open a book in his presence anymore because he always took on so, what with her being educated and him only barely able to sign his name. Engrossed in the sufferings of poor Clarissa at the hands of Lovelace she failed to hear Thomas walking down the path until it was too late. Praying he would be too drunk to notice the offending book she was desperately trying to hide in her skirt. It was only when he lunged towards her, deftly snatching it from her grasp, turn to walk steadily but silently down the passage towards the range and toss it, with an air of defiance, onto the back of the burning coals to watch, with cold satisfaction, as it burned to ashes, that she realised he was stone cold sober! Never daring to stand up to him when he didn't have the drink in him, for the first time in their wretched thirteen years together she was scared. Desperate to avoid a argument she knew there was no chance of winning she capitulated and meekly suggested,

*"You have not taken a drink today then Thomas?"*

*"Not that tis any o thy business but father's took to is bed agin an Robert be busy in th'slaughterouse so I bin to Warmley to see thik temperance man who do live there an I've took nothin stronger than a dish of tea with im, owever I be plannin on going to Th'Chequers a bit later, meantime I've got summut better in mind!"*

Rebecca shivered as he lurched towards her all the while knowing what to expect from the leering grin on his face. She thought about shouting or screaming for help but remembered it was Sunday and everybody was away visiting relatives so there was little else but to accept her fate, submitting was an easier option to starting a fight from which she might not escape unscathed. Mercifully it was soon over and Thomas quickly disappeared to the Chequers, as if to celebrate but not before exacting further humiliation on her,

*"If theese wants thy girls t'grow up proper then get thy selfish old crow of a muther t'give I the money thy father left thee, which,"* angrily stabbing his chest with his index finger, *"be mine be rights, else I'll be sendin em t'work as fur away from ere as I can an then neither she nor thee'll ever see um agin!"*

Rebecca poured some cold water from the well bucket and splashed it onto her painfully swollen face, desperate to reduce the bruises she knew would soon appear, before washing away all the memory of the afternoon's events from her body. Although this was not the first time he had forced himself on her it had been by far the most violent and, despite the warm spring sunshine, she struggled to stop her whole body shaking from the cold as she whispered under her breath,

*"This is the last time you will ever touch me Thomas Worlock, so help me I will stop you one way or another!"*

Later that afternoon, more composed though slightly dizzy thanks to a few large swigs from bottle of gin, concealed where Thomas would never find it, she waited for the children to come home all the while planning her revenge on her brute of a husband.

The next bout of gastro enteritis to visit Thomas, two days later, nearly killed him. Everyone knew he was a drunkard. Everyone also knew how much his unhappy wife longed to return to the life she had sacrificed when she married him. Now those same people were counting the number of times he had been struck down, usually after a monumental row and always after threats to, *"soon put him out of the world."* Rebecca denied the rumours, pointing to all the times she was seen collecting pennyroyal from the hedgerows in an attempt to cure her desperately sick husband claiming the easier, more effective cure, available from a local Apothecary or Doctor Edwards was too expensive. In future when they dared accuse her again she would be ready with an answer, *"I have no money for Doctors bills, thanks to my husband drinking it away at the Chequers but, as pennyroyal worked well in the past and is free, it is not my fault he chooses to drink himself into his grave, nor is it my fault the mint herb is beginning to be less effective the more ale he consumes."*

By the beginning of March a pattern was forming. Thomas was returning home drunk most nights, forcing himself on his very unwilling wife only to be laid low a few days later with a severe bout of gastro enteritis. People such as Doctor Edwards, to whom the couple were now regular visitors, who questioned the frequency of his illnesses were hoodwinked by a very persuasive manipulative and, at all times, caring Rebecca into believing her husband was slowly drinking himself to death. Between bouts of illness Thomas tried his best to work alongside his brothers as they travelled around the local farms slaughtering animals. Sadly he had lost so much weight and strength he was no longer able to fell an animal on his own, it was as much as he could manage to butcher the dead carcass in readiness for the farmer's wife to salt down or store.

A month later and much to his father's relief, Thomas appeared to be spending less time at The Chequers. However that did not necessarily mean he had given up drinking because, unable to get there in person, he was sending Mary Ann to fetch his ale for him. Late one Sunday morning Rebecca was busy churning her latest batch of butter. Over the years she had successfully mastered the art, thanks in no small way to Hester. The outhouse, with its repaired roof, was her refuge where she could escape her husband's drunken demands and produce enough butter and cheese to support herself and the children since Thomas preferred to drink his own money away and, most important of all, it was a retreat into which no one was allowed, unless invited, just like Papa's study at The Mill. Whilst Thomas remained a regular at The Chequers, coming home so drunk he could barely stand and weakened from regular attacks of gastro enteritis, she could cope with his unwanted attentions. However, no longer spending every spare moment drinking with his cronies, he soon made it very clear how he wished to use the improvement in his health, especially on Sundays when the children attended Ellacombe's School before calling on John and Martha. With their neighbours also conveniently away from home they were left, as he constantly suggested with a squeeze to her plump waist and ample bosom, on their own with no fear of interruption!!

Rebecca was unaware Thomas was staring at her from the doorway until she turned to see him, naked to the waist, with that familiar look in his eyes. It had been many weeks since he last tried to force himself on her, that time her resistance cost her a severe thrashing. However she got her own back by watching him suffer from another excruciating attack of gastro enteritis. Well, she stopped him then and saw no reason why she could not do the same again, maybe if she ignored him and returned to her churning he would go away…. but he was having none of it, he stood there in silence seductively watching her every move, waiting for the right time to pounce. The butter was ready, there was a jug of fresh milk drawn off to take indoors and the discarded whey was waiting to be carried to the orchard for the pigs she was fattening for winter. All she needed to do was get past her husband defiantly blocking her way. Deciding on a conciliatory approach she walked towards the door and asked, in a soft appealing voice,
*"Let me pass please Thomas I need to take this up to the pigs."*

*"Only after theese do summut fur me in return,"* he sneered.

Thinking she might stand a better chance outside in the yard where she could, if necessary, make a run for it she meekly suggested,
*"Maybe if you helped with the animals a bit more we might have time for each other and,"* lowering her voice to barely a whisper she forced herself to lie through clenched teeth, *"other things but I must take this to the orchard first,"* offering up the large dirty bucket of stinking whey. Thomas stood slightly to one side as if to let her pass but as she picked up the whey and walked past him towards the door he grabbed her so hard by the back of her neck, jerking her to a stop, she dropped the bucket and its smelly contents all across the floor. With

strength and speed she had forgotten he still possessed he roughly pinioned her arms behind her with one arm whilst with the other he held onto her neck in a similar vice like grip, all the while pulling her nearer and nearer to him till his foul smelling mouth rested next to her ear and he whispered menacingly,

*"It be yer or in th'house...thee choose but, mark my words, either way you baint goin t'scape I this time!"*

Resistance was useless, Rebecca had not bargained for such strength, normally his 'illnesses' left him barely able to walk. Then he almost carried her towards the scullery door where, slamming the door behind them, he finally released his grip on her neck. Still holding her arms firmly he used his free hand to roughly rip his way into the front of her bodice until he finally found her bare breasts. There was no escape as he continued to drag her, screaming and fighting, through the scullery door along the passage towards the front parlour where, throwing her onto Grandmamma Ann's old day bed, he made to roughly put his hands beneath her skirt whilst holding her down, with his knee across her exposed breasts he began to rip at her bodice, as he did so he sarcastically snarled,

*"Doubt if this yer bed s'ever been used by a Flower fur this afore!!"*

She lay there trembling, awaiting her fate and truly believed that this time he was going to kill her. She thought about her children and what would happen to them when she heard Thomas' malevolent voice warning,

*"Do as theese bid and I won't urt thee!"*

With so much hatred between them there was no way she was ever going to do what he bid or accept his unwanted advances and, managing to free one arm, she caught him a mighty clout across the side of his face. Raging like a rampant bull he seized her by the shoulders and shook her so hard she fell back in a mild faint giving him the opportunity to return his hands under her skirt. Aware of his weight on her she desperately tried to push him away, partially succeeding she sank her teeth into his bare shoulder for good measure at which he immediately jumped to his feet, breeches undone about his knees, rubbing a very sore bite mark cursing and bellowing,

*"It'll be th'end of thee mark my wuds if theese dussent do as I bid!"* to which Rebecca, lying on her grandmothers bed, bodice ripped, skirt up about her waist breathless and desperate, silently determined,

*"Not if I finish you off first!"*

Back on her feet again she looked for a way out of this dark and dismal room but, just like the outhouse, Thomas blocked the door and, staggering towards her, he threatened,

*"I be goin to teach thee such a lesson this time theese'll never ferget who be master in this ouse agin!"*

Rebecca knew her ordeal was far from over.

Of course Thomas had his way, there was nothing she could do to defend herself from such an assault. Naturally he celebrated his new found power with an almighty drinking spree at The Chequers where, as expected, he was welcomed back with open arms by his cronies, leaving Rebecca bathing her wounds and planning how to be rid of a man she now loathed beyond belief. The children were due home soon and neither they nor their grandparents must ever learn about what had gone on in the house that afternoon….nor must they have any idea of what was going through her mind.

The following night Thomas was heard stumbling across the yard to the privy, wretching and complaining of severe stomach cramps, leaving his 'concerned and anxious wife' to explain to those neighbours worried enough to leave their beds to offer help,

*"He was doing so well and beginning to regain his strength but what can I do when he gives in to temptation, except pray my usual remedies will work and he harkens to the pleas of his family."*

# CHAPTER TEN

Rebecca paced up and down wondering if she dare approach the woman standing on the corner in front of the large rambling tenement block; she did not recognise her so assumed she was not local and therefore may not welcome a complete stranger striking up a conversation with her but she was desperate, her plight worsening by the day and she needed help from whoever and wherever she could. From her appearance, her shabby gown and shoddy shoes, it was clear the woman could use the money Rebecca was prepared to offer in return so, accepting there was no time like the present, she tentatively approached Sarah Jenkins and politely enquired,

*"Excuse me my dear, I know we have not been properly introduced but I am not from around here and I wonder if you can tell me where I might buy something for my very sick husband who is in desperate need of sleep?"*

Sarah felt sorry for the poor woman as she listened to the dreadful sufferings of her ailing husband and how she was willing to buy anything if only it would ease his pain and give him a good night's sleep. She had no idea who she was, although she claimed to come from Bitton, where Sarah and her mother also lived. Thinking of how she might help this most unfortunate woman Sarah said the first thing to come into her head.

*"Well old Missus Stephens up thur,"* pointing to a ramshackle apothecary shop halfway up the steep Kingswood Hill, *"d'sell Godfrey's Cordial which be good fur little uns who be teethin, theese could try that."*

Believing her to be as illiterate and backward as the rest of them, Rebecca imagined there would be little difficulty in persuading Sarah to help, especially if payment was mentioned and she continued,

*"I do not think a child's syrup will be strong enough, my husband suffers greatly from his stomach and cannot sleep, thank you for suggesting Mrs Stephens but I have already been there,"* jerking her untidy head in the direction of the shop, *"unfortunately, because I also require some rat poison"* using her best authoritarian voice *"the proprietor will not serve me because I am on my own."*

Assuming that was the end of the conversation Sarah made to walk away only for Rebecca to tug gently on her arm and ask, slowly and quietly,

*"I can, of course, buy a powder for my dear husband elsewhere, however I am desperate to obtain some rat poison, and living by a stream I am over run with rats and have three young children to protect. I wonder if you might consider*

*accompanying me to Mrs Stephens to enable me to buy something to rid me of one particularly big rat, of course,"* tapping her gloved hand on her purse, *"I will make it worth you while.....shall we say thrupence?"*

Sarah could not understand why, coming from Bitton, she did not recognise her companion, but as Rebecca was at pains to point out.

*"I moved away from there many years ago on my marriage to a successful businessman and although my family,"* whom she was very careful not to name, *"still live there you may not know them considering you are new in the village yourself."*

Sarah was sorely tempted by Rebecca's money and would have readily agreed had she not been scared of that particular Apothecary shop, especially its witch of an owner. But, gazing at the sad woman standing forlornly in front of her and the chance to buy a good many jugs of ale simply for helping her buy something to rid her house of a rat, she agreed and the pair made their way, like old friends, arm in arm, back to the shop. Once inside the cheerless shop they waited to be served. Closing the door behind them they were immediately hit by the pungent smells coming from bunches of dried lavender…for treating gunshot wounds burns or snake bites, lily flower…for bruises, moss…used since Roman times for healing wounds under dressings, elderflower…the much loved medicine chest of country folk and bryony which was very good for dropsy. Bunches of dried herbs and leaves dangled from every available rafter whilst on small china dishes, placed carefully on shelves behind the counter, could be seen roots of the marsh mallow…for helping the digestion, comfrey… for broken limbs, meadowsweet…for fevers and rheumatism, liquorice…long accepted as a laxative, aromatic myrrh, the cure all wormwood, and something with which Rebecca was very well acquainted… the strong minty smell of pennyroyal. With little or no light there was no way anyone could ever hope to see exactly what they were buying, let alone recognise a face.

Rebecca's companion truly believed all the thick black cobwebs made the shop into somewhere a witch really would choose to live and, having already encountered Mrs Stephens, she prayed they both knew what they were doing by coming into a place like this.

After what seemed an eternity, the anachronistic figure of Mrs Stephens shuffled, wooden clogs dragging on the flagstone floor, from the depths of her dingy shop appearing in the half light of the late March afternoon dressed from head to foot in black, her bent shoulders covered by what was once a white but now grey shawl held together by a massive rusty pin. Under her filthy cap was an equally filthy head of thinning grey hair; however it was to her black gnarled and spindly old hands that Rebecca's eyes were immediately drawn

*140*

and she wondered how many potions, powders or poisons they had prepared in their long life. It took Mrs Stephens some time to acclimatise her dull old eyes to take in the brightness of her shop and to recognise Rebecca,

*"Theese bin yer afore wantin rat poison,"* nevertheless, once she realised Rebecca was not alone, the old woman brusquely demanded, *"What's want this time then?"*

Sarah Jenkins listened intently as Mrs Stephens waited for Rebecca to reply, *"Something to kill a rat."*

Apparently satisfied with the answer, Sarah watched as the old woman wrapped two penn'oth of rat poison into a small paper cone before wagging a filthy spindly finger in their direction and warn,

*"Dussent let nun o this near childrun, dus ear what I be sayin!"*

Sarah clearly heard her companion declare, *"I have no children!"*

Outside the shop, the precious poison firmly in her grasp, Rebecca was so relieved she completely forgot all about wanting to help a very sick husband supposedly find the sleep he craved, instead she took hold of Sarah's hand and shook it warmly before, with tears of emotion mixed with relief trickling down her strained face, handing over the agreed thrupence. Sarah, happy to have earned such easy money, went to walk away only for Rebecca to take hold of her arm and excitedly confess,

*"Since you are a stranger and I know you will not tell anyone, I do not plan to kill any rats but have a hell of a man around me who is always plaguing me and will not leave me alone but I am determined to put him to sleep, possibly tonight. If not, I know there will surely be another time but, no matter when, I am determined to carry out my plan!"*

Holding tightly to Sarah's hand Rebecca pleaded,

*"Please do not betray me, please do not tell anyone about our meeting or of this conversation because you must understand it is the only way I can think of to rid myself of such a rat of a man,"* who, like her family, she was again extremely careful not to name.

*"An I bet ee be the one t'blame fur all they old bruises on thy face as s'well?"* thought Sarah as she walked away, turning just one last time to glance at her mysterious benefactress.

Martha Jenkins was frantic and about to go out and look for her daughter when she stumbled home smelling of drink. She was, if nothing else, an inquisitive, suspicious old woman and immediately demanded to know where she had been, who with and, from the state in which she had just staggered through the door, where she had come by the kind of money with which to buy the amount of ale she had obviously consumed.

*"I y'earned it onestly, doin a faver fur summun muther,"* was all a swaying Sarah could truthfully say.

Not content, Mrs Jenkins determined to discover what her daughter had been doing and was not prepared to let things rest until, unable to withstand further interrogation, Sarah succumbed and described her encounter with, *"zum desprut womun outside Moses Flooks ouse."*

Still not completely satisfied Martha insisted on knowing the woman's name.

*"Don't know Ma, onest, sh'never told I, all I d'know is she d'come from Bitton but d'live in Oldland wiv her children and do ave a sick usband who beats er bad."*

This was of no help to Martha Jenkins whatsoever; the unhappy family her daughter described could be one of any number living in the area these days.

Thomas left early that morning leaving Rebecca to wash and dress, in an attempt at hiding yet more bruises before the children woke but if she imagined for one moment they had not overheard them last night then she was very much mistaken because, as always, the three had clung together trembling at the sound of their mother once more suffering at the hands of their drunken father. He was never cruel nor mistreated them and when he was sober, which was rare these days, he was kind and caring towards them and would often prevent their mother scolding them for not doing as she ordered. If only he stayed off the drink long enough to see what was happening and what he was doing he would have been mortified to learn they were terrified of him, afraid to cross him in case they received the same treatment as their mother. Rebecca, on the other hand, was a cold selfish woman always expecting things to go her way, liable to fly into a rage if they did not. The children were expected to earn their keep helping around the house because, as their mother would constantly tell them, their liar of a father had gone back on his promise to provide them with a kitchen maid, or up in the orchard milking the cows and feeding the animals because, once again, their mother was eager to tell them they needed the money from these animals to replace what their drunken father spent at The Chequers. They rarely received any impromptu gestures of affection from her and she seldom held them in her arms except when she believed they may have overheard her threaten their father during one of their violent rows. If it was affection they craved they turned to Granny Martha not their mother, nor for that matter their other Grandmother because as far as Mary Gerrish was concerned the family were nothing but a source of embarrassment since it was common knowledge Thomas not only drank too much but was abusing her daughter who, in turn, was often heard threatening to kill him.

George and Robert did not expect Thomas to arrive for work that morning, according to the rumours filtering down from Oldland he was laid low with a bout of gastro enteritis so severe he barely had the strength to walk across his backyard, let alone be of any use killing animals but here he was on what looked like being a fine April morning saying he felt well enough to work alongside them. Pleased to have her boys with her Martha insisted they all sit down together for breakfast and, whilst George and Robert ate heartily, Thomas, although equally hungry, was unable to eat anything before rushing from the room. As they all waited patiently for him to return his distressed parents and brothers could only sit in silence and worry about what it was that constantly ailed him, only guessing why Rebecca no longer cared for him nor even showed any real concern over his deteriorating health. Later as the boys loaded the cart ready for their day's labour John, now reduced to hobbling about on two sticks, could only look on and inwardly ask himself how much longer his physically weak son could continue working and what would happen when he was unable to support his family. Catching the worried look on Martha's face John knew they would never be able to offer much financial help, especially now he was little more than a cripple himself. Thanks to her inheritance they had put enough by to allow her to give up her sewing which, for a woman of sixty six with failing eyesight, was something of a Godsend. Hester was supplementing the family income with her cheese and butter, George continued to drift aimlessly between his reluctant siblings, living with whichever one was prepared to accept his drinking and selfish assumption they were happy to put up with him. Like their older sister, Mary, Martha and Pheobe were still at home, caring in turn for their ailing father, although their mother was ever hopeful the right man might one day come along. Sadly Pheobe, at twenty two, was a very sickly girl and already showed signs of ill health making it unlikely she would live to an old age.

It was heartbreaking to watch Thomas struggling to load the cart alongside his strong brothers. They accepted he could no longer lift the heavy tools, coils of rope and sack bags needed for their day's slaughtering, instead they left him to do whatever his feeble emaciated body could manage. However it was clear, especially to those who could remember when he could fell an animal with a single blow of his pickaxe, just how very ill he was and of course the Worlocks and most of the village knew exactly who to blame and secretly pointed their accusing suspicious fingers in her direction.

The three brothers returned home after slaughtering an entire flock of spring lambs at Warmley. The temperance family, who regularly employed them, had

offered no alcohol to quench their thirst so by now not only was Thomas in particular exhausted he was also gasping for a pint of ale. Mary Ann was on her own in the scullery when he shuffled through the door, followed by the young whippet he was training to hunt alongside his ferrets and collapsed, totally drained of all energy, into the old armchair by the range. Seeing how ill he looked Mary Ann offered,
*"Shall I go n fetch muther."*

Stifling a laugh her father muttered,
*"My little maid, she be th'last person I d'want but if theese really wanna do summut fur I then,"* reaching into his waistcoat pocket he took out the last few coppers he possessed, *"theese can be a good girl n take this to Garge Hook n get I a jug of his best ale cus,"* looking at the empty table, *"there bain't nothing yer fur m'supper."*

Eager to please her tired father, Mary Ann made to leave but not before Thomas gently caught hold of her hand and, holding her back, whispered, *"kip what be left fur thee and t'other two...but don't tell thy muther."*

So with her father's coins in one hand, an empty mug in the other and the promise of some rare pocket money for herself, Honor and John, Mary Ann ran happily out of the cottage and made her way towards The Chequers in Barry Road.

George Hook, forty nine year old landlord of the Chequers was indeed a convivial host and, give or take a few minor indiscretions and one or two warning visits from Constable Gerrish, he and his wife Mary ran a good establishment. Mrs Hook kept an excellent table and its position on the main road between Kingswood and Bath meant they were never short of customers. The couple were busy with their regulars and did not see Mary Ann waiting patiently to be served; she was so small for her age she barely reached up to the counter so it was only by chance their daughter, also called Mary, saw her.

Young Mary Hook drew off a pint of ale from the barrel into a measuring jug before pouring it into the mug and, once it was paid for, Mary Ann made to return home. However, as she was walking down the path George Hook spotted her and called out,
*"Ow's thy father, we bain't sin im round yer lately?"*

*"He wer able t'work wiv Uncle Robert n Uncle Garge today an,"* raising the mug to her lips as if to drink from it she continued, *"this be fur im."*

Relieved to hear such news, George turned to his wife and suggested,
*"Zounds like things be getting better, maybe we'll see im back yer afore long."*

144

Skipping all the way home, happy to be doing something to lift her fathers' spirits, Mary Ann reached the scullery door to be met by her mother, face like thunder to discover Thomas had spent their last few coppers on beer. Snatching the mug from Mary Ann's trembling hand Rebecca angrily ordered,
*"Go and fetch your brother and sister, it is time they were here, there's work still to be done!"*

Sensing he might want his beer first Mary Ann pointed to the mug now firmly in her mother's grasp and dared to ask,
*"But on't father want that fust?"*

*"Do as you are bid or else!"* Rebecca roared adding, as if a desperate afterthought, *"if anyone is to give your father his ale tonight it will be me!"*

Relieved not to receive the usual slap across the back of her head for answering back, Mary Ann ran off to search for Honor and John, however reaching the top of the garden path she suddenly remembered the Hook's message and ran back to tell father just in time to see mother stirring some white powder into the mug of ale.

Thinking it was one from Doctor Edwards' Mary Ann paid no heed and, having passed on the message, returned to search for her brother and sister because it did not do to to disobey mother!

Alone at last, Rebecca turned from Thomas as she poured out his ale, that way he did not see as she skilfully mixed all that remained of Mrs Stephen's rat poison nor how she watched him eagerly drink it in two or three draughts!

Thomas had never known pain like it, not even during all his previous illnesses but not wanting to frighten the children, who were now gathered in the scullery, he managed to stagger out into the yard where, unable to control himself, he was violently sick and collapsed into a delirious heap on the cold stones. Recovering slightly he felt the warm body of his young whippet nuzzle against him and watched as the pup began lapping at the contents of his stomach, spread all over the doorstep. Within seconds the animal began shaking, frothing and bleeding at the mouth before dropping down dead alongside him. Deliberately ignoring her husband's body, Rebecca coldly waited for him to follow his dog into the next world and was not expecting him to find the strength to crawl back into the scullery but here he was, hands outstretched, begging her for help. Why was he not dead? With little choice but to lift her stricken, barely alive, husband into the armchair by the range she was not expecting her children, catching sight of their father, to begin screaming hysterically as they heard him demand,
*"What mischief ave thees mixed up this time, cus from where I be sittin there*

*be zum white stuff in thik ale she,"* pointing frantically at his eldest daughter, *"fetched!"*

This was not how Rebecca planned things and she knew she would need to carefully cover her tracks if she was not to be discovered. Kneeling by her husband she gently stroked his burning forehead with the back of her hand and whispered soothingly,

*"Thomas there is no white stuff in your ale, I keep telling you not to buy drink from those Hooks, you have obviously been sold bad beer again, why not let me mix you a mint drink,"* pausing before softly adding, *"you know that always works."*

Thomas refused and, roughly pushing her aside, rushed back out into the yard where he was once again very sick.

Indoors and slightly more composed he weakly ordered Mary Ann.,
*"Go n fetch Garge Hook frum th'Chequers."*

George and his wife were busy elsewhere but young Mary, seeing the breathless, hysterical Mary Ann, realised she was not there for another jug of ale and agreed to return with her. Back at the cottage they found Thomas barely conscious but desperately holding onto what was left of his mug of ale. Catching sight of Hooks daughter he rallied sufficiently to question her over the quality of the ale her father was selling and challenged,
*"Thy father's beer be still bad!"* only to change his mind when Mary firmly countered.

*"Mr Worlock there weren't nothing wrong with th'beer I sold thy Mary Ann because"* as she was at great pains to point out, *"nobody sept thee as bin took ill frum drinkin it."*

*"Well in thik case theese,"* turning on Rebecca, kneeling on the floor next to him, desperately trying to prevent him making further accusations against her by kissing his fevered brow and whispering soft endearing pleas for him to be calm and not tire himself unnecessarily anymore, *"must ave mixed summut in there when I weren't looking an theese better ave a good scuse else thees'll feel the weight of my and cross thy faaa....!"* his threats and sentence remained unfinished as agonising pain caused him to he pass out again.

Sarah Butler was nowhere to be seen, normally she would have been the first to be sent for but as the Worlocks marriage deteriorated so had the earlier improved relationships with the neighbours who Rebecca believed were siding with her violent husband. It therefore didn't help the situation when Thomas was overheard telling Mary Ann,
*"Go n fetch she frum next door... an make it quick!"*

Stepping over the still warm body of a dead dog lying in the yard Sarah Butler walked into a scene of sheer pandemonium. Honor and John were huddled together shivering, crying hysterically in a dark lonely corner of the scullery whilst Mary Ann had taken her mother's place next to her father, holding his trembling hands as he lay slumped in the chair, all the while reassuring him,
*"Everythins gonna be alright, when you bin ill afore muther always got thee better with her mixture an she be gonna do th'same agin, dussent thee worry none."*

Rebecca, meanwhile, was rushing around with no idea of what to do next. With the arrival of Sarah Butler her concern for Thomas changed to that of anger as she implored him to release his weakening grip on his mug of ale, coldly reminding him,
*"If you didn't drink so much then you wouldn't make all this disgusting mess... which no doubt I will be expected to clear up."*

Thomas, feverish and semi conscious, miraculously continued to resist Rebecca's attempts to wrestle his mug and its contents from his feeble hands, such was his determination to save 'everything fur Garge Hook t'see'. Between bouts of severe sickness, intense burning in his throat and lapses into unconsciousness Thomas gradually made out the shape of Sarah Butler and, pointing to the white powder in his mug, he demanded to know,
*"Missus, duss thee think that be bakin flour cus tis what she,"* pointing a trembling accusing finger towards his wife, *"be sayin t'is but I don't believe the lyin bitch n'more, that I don't!!"*

Everyone watched as Sarah took a good long look at the white powder in the mug before shaking her head and declaring,
*"That bain't bakin flour Mr Warlock, it be too glossy."*

Rebecca, never a woman to be denied the final word even if that word might eventually hang her, interrupted before Thomas had the chance to reply and haughtily counter,
*"Well if it's not baking flour then it must be the powder Doctor Watts gave me for the children's groin, it could easily have been mixed in by mistake."*

Convinced the white powder was poison, Thomas was more determined than ever to save it, however his cold calculating wife, fully aware of what was really floating in the beer and that it had nothing to do with any Doctor's powder, knew she must destroy everything since it would be vital incriminating evidence against her...especially should Thomas die. Suddenly and with no warning Rebecca, noticing he had once again lapsed into a deep sleep, lunged forward and snatched the mug from his weak hands before anyone could stop her. Swiftly escaping through the dark passage behind the settle out into the yard and into the outhouse she left Thomas vainly trying to stop her by desperately grabbing hold of her skirt. Even Sarah Butler and Mary Hook found themselves helpless to intervene such was their surprise at the speed with which she moved, their feet were temporarily and inextricably stuck to the stone slab floor.

Returning from the outhouse Rebecca believed she had destroyed any evidence that might condemn her and she could now focus on being the caring concerned wife once again and, searching for relief from the overpowering stench creeping into every corner of the house, she chose to talk to her neighbours gathering outside in the yard as if the tragedy unfolding a few feet away was no different from any other time,

*"I tell you Mrs Foote, I have never known him to suffer such a severe attack before,"* hinting, *"I fear this might be the end."*

With everyone's attention focused on their father, the children, more from fear and worry, were in a state of near collapse, especially young John who was beginning to show similar symptoms to those of his father. Sensing the boy was suffering Thomas found the strength to turn on Rebecca accusing her of gross stupidity for leaving dangerous powder lying about where youngsters might find it because, *"Frum where I be sittin,"* raising a trembling hand towards his eight year old son, *"looks like theese dun fur ee too!"*

Rebecca's cold callous reply, which would one day return to haunt her, was simply,

*"I never used it on their itch and I've not seen the stuff since Doctor Watts gave it to me, in fact I can remember wrapping it in some paper between two books on the shelf next to the clock for safety but when you,"* pointing to Thomas her voice rising to an hysterical scream, *"burned my copy of Clarissa out of spite I thought the powder went with it but obviously it was still there when one of those stupid girls took down Gulliver's Travels to read or,"* adding as a sudden afterthought, *"they needed the wrapping paper to curl their hair!"* Recognising her temper was starting to get the better of her and she would be well advised to calm down she finished by mumbling quietly and slowly, *"Yes, yes, that's what happened."*

Miraculously John was not suffering from whatever ailed his stricken father, the boy was simply so petrified at what he saw it brought on a panic attack, causing him to collapse in a dead faint on the floor. Meanwhile his sisters, especially Mary Ann who felt responsible for bringing home what she believed was the cause of her father's plight, were coping slightly better, although they were old enough to realise that this time his condition was much more serious.

The Worlock's cottage was becoming more and more crowded as folk gathered to offer their opinion. Two such visitors were Sophia and Richard Jenkins who arrived to find Thomas lying in the arms of his frantically worried wife. Instinctively going to her brother Sophia found her way barred by Rebecca who was leaning over his prostrate body determined no one would get near enough to hear any accusations he might make. Unable to get close to her brother, forced to watch him gasping for breath, racked with pain following spells of sickness during which he was now bringing up blood accompanied by severe burning in his throat, Sophia fixed her stony gaze on her sister in-law and demanded,

*"As anyone gone fur a Doctur?"*

Looking back, smiling sweetly, Rebecca murmured softly,
*"Sophia, why on earth should I do that, haven't I always cared for your brother myself?"*

Richard Jenkins conveniently had his own horse and wagon and, at Sophia's insistence, it was decided to take Thomas to the nearest doctor without delay. Rebecca, fearful that Doctor Watts or Doctor Wingrove, being local, might immediately see through her little scheme at first refused but relented when it was hinted Thomas might not survive the journey.

*"In that case there is little to lose,"* decided his heartless wife, *"but I will not leave his side and will only agree if I accompanied him,"* such was her fear that her sick husband might still manage to reveal her secret. In the meantime Aunt Sophia would take Honor and John back to her cottage with the understanding that Mary Ann, who was refusing to leave her father, followed as soon as they had safely left for the doctor. With Richard away harnessing the horse all eyes fixed on Thomas who, although it was the middle of a warm April, fitfully changed from shivering with the cold one minute to complaining of being 'on fire' with an insatiable thirst the next. When Rebecca eventually decided to offer him something to drink it was from her secret bottle of gin, bringing about a seizure of such ferocity some thought she had finally finished him off and there was no point finding a doctor…..just the laying out woman.

Everything was ready and Thomas, supported by his scheming wife, was propped up between two unyielding pillows and wrapped in a filthy blanket in the back of the cart. However they had barely reached Barry Road before there was a major falling out over the choice of Doctor. In view of the urgency of the situation Richard Jenkins naturally assumed they would be heading for either Doctor Watts in Bitton or Doctor Wingrove in North Common but Rebecca insisted they go all the way to Doctor Edwards at Keynsham.

*"He successfully treated Thomas in the past and there is no reason why he cannot do so again."*

Richard, not yet suspecting her of any involvement in this or any previous illness, allowed himself to be persuaded to go to Keynsham; he only hoped and prayed Thomas would still be alive by the time they got there.

With nothing else to see everyone began drifting away so that by the time George Hook and his friend William Short arrived Mary Ann, who had promised Aunt Sophie she would join her brother and sister once her parents left, was the only one left in the cottage. Both men had seen Richard's old horse trundle laboriously along Barry Road past the Chequers and, thanks to the very colourful description from young Mary Hook, they were well aware of all that had happened and knew there was every chance the place would be empty and they could at least take a good unhindered look around the outhouse, if not inside the cottage itself. In between sobs and tears Mary Ann rambled on,

*"Uncle Richard as took father t'see th'Doctur cus he were avin one of is attacks, muther said twer wuss than any ee ad afore and was brung on by thy bad beer agin. I yerd um say there were summut in it but thy Mary sid there weren't nothin in the beer she sold I, then muther sid twer baking flour but when Mrs Butler said twern't no baking flour muther sid th'only thing it cud ave bin were the powder Doctur Watts give her when we ad th'itch last yer and t'were wrapped in th'paper me an our Honor ad used fer our air."*

William and George had known all three Worlock children since they were born and in spite of the cold way their parents sometimes treated them, they found Mary Ann's concern for her father heartbreaking.

The pair searched for signs of the white powder Mary Hook and Sarah Butler claimed to have seen in the bottom of a bucket in the outhouse and in various places around the cottage. With his daughter's words, *"Missus Warlock be blamin our beer fur er husbands sickness,"* still ringing in his ears George made straight for the scullery leaving William to search the outhouse. Although the light was beginning to fade as soon as he walked into the outhouse he immediately spied an old wooden bucket barely hidden under the oven and, more importantly, its contents….at least half a teacupful of white powder which had obviously been mixed at some time with water making it thicken and swell up to look a much larger quantity than it was originally. Triumphantly grabbing the bucket he hurried towards the scullery where he was met by a jubilant George Hook who had been equally successful in his search, finding some similar wet powder in a cup as well as some dry white powder on the floor near the clock and on a small mahogany table. However, although the pair found evidence of some mysterious white powder, they were still none the wiser as to what it was so they decided the only way was for one of them to taste it to make sure. William nervously dipped his little finger into the bucket and brought out a tiny amount of the glistening powder, damp and rough from being mixed with either beer or water, cautiously placing it on the tip of his tongue he experienced an immediate sharp bitter taste accompanied by a feeling of inflammation followed by an uncontrollable urge to be sick. Fortunately, with so many rinses the powder had lost most of its potency, even so George advised his friend against swallowing any of the powder but to spit it out and make sure he rinsed his mouth with fresh water drawn from the well, not from any jug or mug found in the Worlocks house!!! At the same time George decided to scrape some of the offending powder onto a penny from his pocket, *"fur future reference."*

Back in the scullery they tried unsuccessfully to get more information from a tearful Mary Ann, the only thing she cared about was whether *"father be goin t'be alright er not,"* and both men agreed there was little point in further upsetting the child, in any case it was too dark to do much more and they decided to return home. However, they were reluctant to leave the child on her own in such dreadful surroundings and considered taking her home to Mrs Hook. Just as they were closing the door and about to walk the short distance to the Chequers, they spied Sophia Jenkins walking up the path and, after a few words with her Aunt, Mary Ann said she wanted to be with her brother and sister. Telling her niece to be a good girl and run along home, Sophia turned to George and William,
*"An what be you two doin yer?"*

George, eager to explain, simply said,
*"I understands Missus Warlock be blamin my ale fur her husband's illness an that cud be awful bad fur bisnuss so we bin lookin fur evidence Missus Jenkins that be all."*

Waiting til Mary Ann was out of earshot Sophia asked,
*"and diss find any?"*

Gently taking her arm George guided her to one side to whisper,
*"I want t'wait till they d'cum ome if theese dussent mind and I ould be grateful if theese kip our visit to thyself."*

Sophia looked at both men and shook her head before warning,
*"Theese dissent see th'state ower Thomas were in afore they took'n to find th'Doctor cus if you ad you'd doubt if he ould still be living by th'time they got thur,"* and with that she took her leave saying her nephew and nieces needed her because, *"I doubt if thik mother o theirs ave left any grub fur um."*

Roger Edwards was far from happy at having his dinner interrupted by his housekeeper telling him there were, *"certain persons,"* at the door demanding to see him. He was even less pleased to discover who the *"certain persons"* were and maybe more annoyed than perhaps he should have been, his first response was to abruptly ask Thomas,

*"Why did you not take one of the powders I gave you on your last visit?"*

Rebecca, eager to defend her reputation of a caring wife, humbly replied,

*"There are none left Doctor Edwards but, as you can see, he is far worse this time, thanks to more bad ale from that awful place run by those dreadful Hooks."*

Roger Edwards listened patiently as first Rebecca, then Richard, claimed Thomas had taken ill immediately after drinking ale from The Chequers, to which Rebecca haughtily added,

*"It is clear his present illness, along with the others, is due entirely to that ale draper and his wife."*

To everyone's amazement Thomas, whom they had chosen to ignore and assumed was far too weak to take part in any discussion about his present condition, suddenly interrupted them and said, in a languid voice,

*"She be wrong Zur, I bin poisoned with zum white powder I seen floatin in me beer. Garge Hook's girl sid tweren't there when my little maid left th'Chequers but,"* shaking a trembling accusing finger at Rebecca, *"if theese listen t'she twere th'powder Doctur Watts give er for the little uns itch...and that were poison!"*

Following a thorough examination Roger Edwards diagnosed another, more severe, attack of gastro enteritis adding,

*"And we all know the cause of that do we not,"* scornfully shaking his head, *"will you never learn?"*

Unprepared for such a rebuke, especially when he knew he was right, Thomas fumbled inside the pocket of his threadbare old jacket and stunned them all by producing the alleged poison. Looking at the filthy remains of what was once a piece of white paper, similar to that in which he often wrapped a physic for one of his patients but which now contained some disgusting sodden wet powder, Doctor Edwards cautiously asked,

*"How did you come by this?"*

*"I id it ear in me pockut an didn't tell no one Zur, specially she!,"* Thomas gasped, fixing a painful glance at Rebecca as another wave of agonizing pain racked his feeble body, *"twer in th'mug o ale she tried to be rid of but I ouldn't let er, no Zur I ouldn't let er throw nothing away!"*

Rebecca felt a surge of panic hit her and, fearful of what else he might reveal, accused her husband of being out of his mind to expect an eminent Doctor to believe such a ridiculous story about being poisoned when he had already said it was just another of his attacks. Ordering him to apologise immediately the ailing Thomas stood his ground insisting,

*"Dacter Edwards, as God be my witnuss Zur I ave bin poisoned and tweren't from no bad beer but from summut mixed behind me back by thik witch over there!"*

Roger Edwards had no choice but to let Thomas rest in one of his comfortable leather upholstered armchairs whilst he took a closer look at the damp dark brown powder he claimed was the poison, rescued from his ale. Eventually he was forced to admit,

*"Mr Worlock I really do not think this is poison, if you want my opinion it has the look of vegetable powder, maybe jalap and if this is what was mixed into your beer I cannot see how it can have caused the pain you appear to be suffering. I truly believe it is your usual trouble again."*

It was getting dark by the time they began the long tedious journey back to Oldland; thanks to another powder Thomas was very drowsy and craved peace and quiet which Rebecca resolutely denied him as she mercilessly harangued him for daring to embarrass her in front of their Doctor,

*"How dare you accuse me of trying to poison you with that disgusting white stuff you took with you when you knew all along it was vegetable powder. What* ever *will Mamma say when she finds out the next time Doctor Edwards attends her?"* adding as if to make another point, *"maybe if you stopped spending your time and my money on cheap ale you would not suffer from the kind of attacks that are now beginning to turn your brain"*

Richard Jenkins was finding it difficult enough guiding his horse through the darkness, especially as it was never a good idea to be out on the road at this time of night, now he had to listen to Rebecca tirelessly harassing a desperately sick Thomas who was pleading, *"Rebecca, PL E A S E let I be!"*

Finally Richard could take no more and shouted to his fiery sister in law, *"bide thy tongue and let the man sleep,"* only to receive a sharp side of her tongue for his trouble.

Spending the remainder of the journey in silence Richard pondered how Thomas endured living with such a harridan and, to sounds of him retching in agony, he began to question whether the allegations were true and Rebecca had indeed poisoned him but he then remembered Doctor Edward's assurances that the powder retrieved from the ale was not poison but of vegetable extract and, *"could have no injurious effect on him."* However from the sounds coming from the back of the cart it was obvious something was having an *"injurious effect on him."*

*"It is most kind of you but I am quite capable of caring for my husband myself,"* Rebecca assured Sarah Butler who was offering to stay the night, *"I have looked to him throughout all his previous illnesses and this one, although more severe, will be no different."*

Sarah, acutely aware of the earlier events that day, believed Thomas might still be in danger at the hands of his wife, considering all the times she had been overheard threatening to soon put him out of the world and insisted, *"Either I stays t'night or I be sendin my boy to Bitton for thy mothur n law."*

Sarah stayed to witness long hours of extreme agony for Thomas coupled with cruel indifference from his wife who, suspecting her neighbour would watch over him like a hawk, chose to ignore his terrible sufferings and slept soundly on a makeshift bed on the floor beside him instead. Around four o'clock Thomas woke and called out for Rebecca to fetch him a drink of water which she callously refused to do,

*"Thanks to you there was no time to bring any in from the dairy and I am not about to fetch some at this time of night,"* eager to return to her disturbed slumbers she threw a cold warning stare, first at her husband and then towards Sarah suggesting, with more than a hint of malice in her voice, *"and neither are you Mrs Butler, he must learn not to be so selfish and to think of others for a change!"*

Thomas was far worse by morning and it was decided to take him all the way back to Keynsham however, much as she tried, this time Rebecca was firmly told to stay at home with the children.

Roger Edwards was very surprised to find Thomas on his doorstep again so soon and was even more surprised, although relieved, to find him without Rebecca. This time he was more tolerant and listened intently as Thomas explained he was still being sick with a worsening burning sensation in his throat which he was sure had something to do with the white powder found floating in his beer. The Doctor once again assured him his sufferings could not be connected with the sample of powder he had showed him yesterday, patiently explaining, *"The powder is brown, whereas you told me of there being white powder in your ale, secondly it is of vegetable extract and in no way poisonous, however it is clear something is ailing you."*

Wednesday brought no respite, only further deterioration, Thomas was far worse now than throughout the previous two days, the children were allowed to spend only short spells with him and, apart from the unpleasant conditions permeating, not only the sickroom but the rest of the cottage, they could see he was in great pain and found it too upsetting to stay at his bedside for long. Doctor Edwards' new powders simply gave him sleep, they did nothing to alleviate the pain or the constant sickness. Sophia Jenkins and Sarah Butler, who were taking turns at his bedside, could not understand where John, Martha and the others were and eventually Sophia asked Rebecca if there was some reason for their absence,

*"Oh, surely it's not necessary to send for them,"* was her dismissive, almost sarcastic, reply.

Within the hour a message reached Bitton imploring the Worlocks to get to their son as soon as possible.

John and Martha arrived first, George and Robert were working down at Willsbridge but were said to be on their way, and immediately demanded to know why they had not been sent for sooner. Martha, in particular, expected some answers from Rebecca,

*"What ave you dun to 'im!"* because, despite all the lame excuses about it being just another of his attacks and how she was so accustomed to them by now she knew exactly what to do, Martha no longer believed her. Looking down at her son, lying in soiled sheets and stained clothes, she took control of the situation and ordered John to, *"go n talk to thy poor son n find out whats in God's name ave bin goin on up yer."*

Fear gripped Rebecca at the thought of what Thomas might reveal to his father once they were alone and she refused to leave, desperately trying to defend herself by making counter accusations,

*"Can you not see he is not strong enough to put up with your constant questioning, I will not allow you to bully him any more!"*

John bided his time as his son lapsed into another drug induced sleep and for Rebecca, assuming it was now safe to take the children up to the orchard to milk the cows in readiness for tomorrow's butter and cheese, to leave them on their own. Listening as the scullery door slammed behind them John grabbed the chance to sit by his son's bed in readiness should he awake and recognised him, meanwhile the rest of the Worlocks were now in no doubt they could see Rebecca's hand in all of this and were beginning to wonder if that same hand had, in some way, also been responsible for his previous illnesses.

By coincidence Roger Edwards was in Bitton visiting his colleague Samuel Watts and, learning Thomas was no better, called on the Worlocks only to discover that, despite his powders and the tender loving care of his devoted mother who had insisted his bed be moved down into the front parlour and he be laid in clean sheets and a fresh nightshirt, he had deteriorated. Roger tried to conceal his concern, especially from Martha because by now he had hoped for signs of improvement. She continued to press him to save her son.

*"He be dying bain't he Zur?"*

Taking hold of the old womans' trembling hands he had little choice but to gently admit,

*"Mrs Worlock your son is very sick and there is little more I can do save giving him something to ease his pain and help him sleep, even bleeding him will be of little help now but with rest and,"* looking kindly at her worried tear stained face, *"your wonderful care he may yet recover although I am not at all hopeful. He has been ill so many times over these past months I fear his body is so weak it may not cope with another illness. However if he is no better by Friday morning please send for Doctor Watts who is fully aware of the situation and lives at a more convenient distance."*

Mercifully Thomas slept most of the time whilst his distraught mother and sisters took turns to sit by his bed ensuring his disapproving wife came nowhere near him. Watching her sulking and stomping around the cottage, no longer the centre of attention, reminded Martha of the times she misbehaved in Church as a child. Finally, with no one taking any notice of her, Rebecca announced, *"I'd rather be doing something useful, all this sitting around is pointless I may as well be up in the orchard with my animals, at least they need me and appreciate my care,"* wrapping a light shawl around her shoulders she flounced towards the door where upon reaching for the latch she turned, as an actress at the nearby Theatre Royal in Bath might turn towards her adoring audience and announced, *"if he needs me just send one of them,"* nodding in the direction of her three distraught children, *"to find me."*

How strange that not one person gathered there made any attempt to stop her leaving.

The children were now restricted to seeing their father during rare lucid moments, in between such times they were taken away by Aunt Sophia lest his painful cries and pitiful groans further upset them. It was also decided there was no point sending for Doctor Watts or Doctor Edwards as neither could do any more, nor were the family praying for Thomas to live, they simply gathered around his bed hoping instead for a happy release. Friday morning, fearing the worse but feeling compelled to call, Roger Edwards arrived unannounced to find Reverend Ellacombe preparing a motionless, though fully conscious Thomas, to meet his maker. With Martha continually soothing her doomed son's forehead so his crippled father hobbled around the room on his sticks looking first at Robert then at George before staring back, helpless, towards his dying son. Dazed and confused he stood at the foot of the bed, clinging onto the battered old bedstead for support whilst in the scullery the rest of the family waited. Even for a warm spring day, the air and atmosphere was sombre and cold.

By mid morning everyone knew there was nothing more to be done. Thomas would not last the day, time was running out if they were to discover how he came by the powder he had taken to Keynsham. Inviting Reverend Ellacombe to join him in the yard, where at least there was still some semblance of privacy and fresh air, Doctor Edwards suggested,
*"How would it be if, during his last confession to you, Worlock was, how can I put it, encouraged to say how he came by his so called poison?"*

Whilst agreeing to what was being asked of him Henry also argued,
*"You must understand that not everything that passes between a dying man and his confessor is for others to know."*

With the room to themselves Henry sat down alongside Thomas and prepared to guide him into the arms of Jesus. However before the Chariot of the Lord arrived to take him on his last journey there remained the vexed question of the white powder and how he had obtained it.

*"No amount of prayers will ease this poor man's suffering,"* thought Henry as Thomas was again racked with indescribable pain.

*"Thomas, you know you do not have long in this life and the good Lord is waiting to protect and guide you into the next but your family deserve to know what it is that has ailed you all these months so, for the love of God, tell me how you came by the white powder you claim was poison?"*

Thomas grabbed hold of the Curate's hand so tightly Henry thought his fingers were about to break,
*"For a man so close to death you still have a vice like grip Thomas Worlock,"*
he thought but, as another violent spasm ripped through his frail fading body, Henry accepted it was simply another agonising grip of impending death..

*"The white powder,"* Thomas gasped, *"cum vrom zum dirty paper an twer mixed b'accident into the ale th'eldest maid fetched for I from Hooks place."*

The end was close now and Henry had still to find out how and by whom the mysterious white powder had been mixed into the mug so he continued,
*"But surely your child cannot be blamed for accidentally mixing poison into your beer?"*

The thought of his spiteful wife allowing his innocent daughter to take the blame for something she did not do spurred Thomas sufficiently for him to raise himself up on one arm and cry out.

*"She bain't the one t'blame, er bitch of a muther took it from er!"*

*"So,"* mused Henry, *"the ale was given to you by your wife."*

As another spasm surged through Thomas' body he managed to rasp,
*"Yes an there were summut floatin on top an some ops at th'bottom of the mug but when I asked er what twas she grabbed the cup and drew it all away. I couldn't stop er Zur, I just couldn't stop er."*

As a further wave of excruciating agony passed over the pit of his belly Henry Ellacombe decided the poor man had suffered enough and called his family to his side to say their goodbyes.

Rebecca sat next to her husband, holding his damp clammy hand against her tear stained face and gave the performance of her life as the grief stricken wife,
*"I always loved him and did everything I could during all his illnesses, this last one was no different."*

The accusing looks of utter contempt from Robert and George Worlock told her they did not believe a single word she was uttering and it was only when Robert Henderson, Church Warden and family friend, arrived to carry out Johns' instructions to draw up his son's last will and testament that, staring first at her brothers in law then at their father, Rebecca realised,
*"The cunning old fox is making sure I do not to get my hands on one penny of his precious son's paltry estate,"* such was her conviction that Thomas would be forced by his family to deny her what was her due.

# CHAPTER ELEVEN

Roger Edwards, Samuel Watts and William Wingrove had been colleagues and friends for many years, all three did their best to care for the labourers around the area and at one time William was responsible for the inmates of Bitton Poor House, a position he shared with Samuel. All three supplemented their comfortable livings from caring for the health of the wealthier families in the larger houses, however all three were very familiar with the Worlocks and Flowers, especially Roger and Samuel who were waiting for William to join them at The Chequers.

With William now present all three settled down to plan, in private and away from all the furore taking place outside, how this morning's gruesome task would ultimately unfold.. Over light refreshments, provided by Mrs Hook, they agreed they should start the Post Mortem immediately so that the cause of death would be known by the time the elderly Coroner, currently on his way from Berkeley, arrived and, should their findings prove suspicious, Constable Gerrish would be better placed to summon an Inquest Jury. In the meantime, before they began their unpleasant task, Samuel and William pressed their colleague to tell them what in heaven's name had taken place at the Worlocks!

Roger Edwards regaled his companions of the sorry tale of Thomas Worlock and his many illnesses, how he had been treating his chronic diarrhoea and sickness for some time but only after, *"his shrew of a wife had tried, unsuccessfully, to treat him with pennyroyal."* Then last Monday evening the loathsome pair arrived at his door, just as he and his wife had finished dining, with a very sick Thomas who claimed not only to have been poisoned but to have some of the so called poison on his person.

All three men agreed the couple were known around the district to be a quarrelsome pair, what with her airs of grandeur at being a Flower and his liking for a jug or two of ale, finally after years of unhappiness and abuse she complained of marrying beneath herself. She was also known to treat the rest of the Worlocks with contempt despite having never once been ill treated by them. Thomas, on the other hand, had little or no patience with her and, according to the neighbours, thought nothing of raising his fists to his volatile wife leaving their three children in fear, especially during such spectacular fights when they ran to the neighbours for protection. But, William and Samuel insisted, did he really believe the story about the so called poison?

Roger Edwards thought long and hard before answering, remembering he had already dismissed Thomas' claim he had bought poisoned ale from the same Ale House, run by the same Landlord, in which they now sat and therefore to their question *"was it poison"* he replied.

*"I assured Worlock the substance he claimed to be poison would not cause him harm, believing it to be jalap, I was therefore somewhat taken aback to find the poor wretch on my doorstep the following day demanding another physic to relieve his pain."* Ambling towards the table he cut another thick slice of meat from the hock joint laid out on a large platter in front of him, *"If you recall Samuel, I was in Bitton to visit you on Wednesday and called to see Worlock because I heard he had deteriorated and there was no way he could travel over to Keynsham again."* Placing his chosen slice of meat on his plate and tearing a chunk of bread from the crusty loaf alongside, Roger returned to his chair to continue his story, *"I found him still suffering from acute stomach pains and violent vomiting from which there was no relief, sadly I was with him when he died this morning but, until proven otherwise, I am of the opinion cause of death may not be poison but years of alcohol abuse, neglect and God knows what else judging from the state of his cottage."*

As the three Doctors talked and relished their light luncheon Thomas' lifeless body awaited them in a small downstairs room at the rear of the building.

Roger Edward's story was almost done,
*"When Worlock's body was taken from their hovel, not more than an hour since, I understand his wife became inconsolable and was dragged screaming hysterically to a neighbour's house where she remains, under strict orders from Constable Gerrish, until the Coroner arrives."* Anticipating their next question, he continued, *"She was seen trying to destroy evidence and rumour has it she is already accused by several people, specially the Worlocks, of being involved in her husband's death."*

Making his way towards the open window overlooking the yard at the back of The Chequers, Roger pointed to a small crowd gathering below and noticed three sad figures huddled in the corner. Calling to his colleagues he whispered.

*"His devoted mother has been with him since Wednesday and was by his side when he breathed his last after which, at Reverend Ellacombe's suggestion, she returned home to Bitton with Worlocks' three young children but, as you can see,"* nodding towards the three sad figures, *"his father and brothers remain here, refusing to leave until they have the answers to all their questions."*

*"What of Mrs Gerrish, has she thought to send anyone to ask after her daughter and grandchildren?"* Samuel was eager to know.

Turning towards the unlit fire laid up in a battered old cast iron grate Roger placed both hands on the mantelpiece of the cracked marble fire surround and, leaning forward, he dropped his head onto his chest before announcing slowly,
*"I fear there has been no word from Mrs Gerrish or the Flowers, although I understand Ellacombe planned to call on them once he was happy to leave old Mrs Worlock and the children on their own."*

The sound of a horse and carriage, followed by voices in the yard, told them that the Coroner had arrived and, once he had officially viewed the body and heard their individual accounts, he could now order the Constable to gather together twelve local men for an Inquest Jury after which they would also be expected to officially look at their colleague & friend in death.

The conditions under which the three men worked were far from ideal, the room was small and overbearingly hot, there was a small window which under normal circumstances might have been left opened to let in extra light and fresh air had it not been for certain villagers, including the Worlocks, lingering about outside eager to eavesdrop their every word. Thomas' naked unwashed body lay on a rough table and it was only when Roger pulled back the coarse sack cloth covering him and all three examined the emaciated body more closely that they realised he had probably been slowly dying for months. His face, once so grotesquely twisted with pain, now showed an expression of peace which was belied by the slight trickle of blood oozing from the side of his mouth. Roger Edwards stood back from the body and contemplated what was expected of him this afternoon, which was to concentrate on proving death was either due to alcoholic poisoning or gastro enteritis as he believed or arsenic poisoning as his colleagues and most of Oldland were suggesting. Removing his jacket and rolling up the long sleeves of his fine linen shirt he placed a leather dissecting apron over his head and around his elegant trousers before, supported by his colleagues, he began the onerous task of finding out what had caused a once strong, fit forty year old man to suffer such a violent, lingering and painful death. Opening his cherished box of instruments Roger Edwards approached the table and made the first incision into the chest of the still warm body.

William Joyner Ellis, His Majesty's Coroner for Gloucestershire and his clerk were partaking of the remainder of Mrs Hook's excellent boiled hock when, at his invitation, the three Doctors joined him for a tankard of Hooks best ale and the chance to update him on the happenings of the past week. Joyner Ellis, who was far more concerned with their findings following the examination of the body, listened patiently as first Samuel then William explained how there still remained a slight difference of opinion between them and Roger Edwards over the true cause of death, especially since vital evidence may have been destroyed by the widow who was regularly overheard threatening to soon put her late husband out of this world.

Draining the last drop from his mug Joyner Ellis held up his hand to stop the conversation going any further,
*"Gentlemen, I have heard enough, there is obviously something amiss here, kindly ask the Constable to join us in,"* glancing at his exquisite tortoiseshell cased pocket watch hanging from a gold chain, *"shall we say ten minutes."*

Running downstairs clutching his orders, Constable John Gerrish wasted no time in arranging an Inquest to take place that afternoon in the upstairs room of the Chequers Inn, Barry Road, Oldland Common. Richard Jenkins was charged with arranging overnight accommodation for the Coroner and, should the proceedings drag on into the evening and into the next day, refreshments for the Jury.

Twelve local men, Robert Henderson, William Short, John Long, George Rawbone, Jacob Short, Robert Short, George Short, Thomas Henderson, John Stright, Isaac Short, John Ody and James Bailey, were sitting in the Inquest Room, about to begin hearing the evidence, when a horse and rider trotted nonchalantly into yard. The excited mob, still scrambling to get in for the afternoons spectacle, fell silent as Peter Gerrish dismounted, loudly announcing,
*"I am here to represent my wife and,"* clicking his fingers towards the Landlord, *"you there....Hook, tell the Coroner I am here and will speak to him!"*

George Hook wondered at his arrogance and found it hard to suppress a wry smile when he returned with the Coroner's reply,
*"Beg pardon Zur but is Lardship says he be bout t'start an Inquest and wants t'know ow come every ones bin yer fer ours but you just got yer an, beggin y' pardon Zur, but ee sid you'll ave t'wait till ee as eard what all of um gotta say fust."*

Peter was speechless and furious at, 'Hooks damned impertinence,' and made to give him a piece of his mind, however before he was given the chance George Hook, confident with the full support of the Coroner behind him, treated him at his own game,
*"Now if thees'll scuse I Zur I be needed elsewhere,"* pointing to the upstairs supper room currently in use as a Coroner's Inquest into the suspicious death of Thomas Worlock, *"so I'll bid thee a gud day."*

162

Alone in a hostile environment Peter was forced to endure whispered comments from those who, like him, were unable to get into the Inquest, *"Who do e think he be." "Ee might be summut down Bitton but ee bain't nothing up yer."* However, the most common accusation was, *"Worlock's boy died s'mornin an is wife be blamed fer it, ow cum er muther waits til now afore sending er young errand boy to see what be goin on."*

The afternoon passed in slow tortured torment as Robert and George were forced to listen as their brother's unhappy marriage and violent death were laid bare. There was nothing they could do to shield their sick crippled father, huddled in the corner next to them enmeshed in his private grief, from learning the truth they had desperately tried to keep from him. They also knew that downstairs Peter Gerrish, unable to join them but anxious to keep the Flower name free from yet more scandal, would be doing his utmost to suggest a local Inquest Jury would know enough about their alcoholic brother to realise his wife was innocent of any crime and find he had drunk himself to death.

Two hours and five Witnesses later William Joyner Ellis knew this was no ordinary Coroners Inquest, nor would it reach its conclusion today. It was also clear from the reaction of the Jury that not only did they totally disagree with Peter Gerrish they were far from impartial. Should any witness attempt to defend Rebecca or suggest Thomas was no angel and regularly raised his fist to her, the mutterings and whispers of disbelief came, not from the multitude crammed into the room but from those who had known Thomas well....the twelve men sitting in judgement as Jurymen!

*"Constable Gerrush Zur!, is Lardship d'want she,"* pointing at Rebecca, *"t'come up now"* shouted a very breathless George Hook as he reached the bottom stair, *"an, he bain't in a gud mood neither!,"* he warned.

Concentrating on escorting her across the yard towards the back steps leading up to the Inquest Room. Neither the Constable nor Rebecca were aware they had been seen by the one person who could decide her fate. Sarah Jenkins, who had been prompted into coming forward to give evidence by her domineering mother, was waiting to be called when she recognised the woman she remembered helping to buy rat poison from Mrs Stephens only a matter of weeks ago and realised she was the widow of the poor unfortunate man whose death was the reason she had been called to give evidence today!

Of the trio of Doctors it was Roger Edwards, who had treated Thomas over many months, had been present at his death and had carried out the post mortem on his body, who was the first to take the Oath and give evidence. He told of months of suffering during which Thomas received little or no sympathy from his wife who even refused to prepare the special diet he suggested might relieve his pain. He then continued how every time Thomas fell ill Rebecca would immediately say it was his own fault and apologise because she believed her husband was not only wasting his time and her money when it was plainly obvious the cause of his illness lay in the fact he was, *"nothing but a drunkard."*

At this point the Coroner interrupted,
*"And was that the case Doctor Edwards, was Thomas Worlock nothing but a drunkard?"*

*"No more than any other of the labourers in the district,"* was the matter of fact reply.

Leaning forward to instruct his clerk to make sure to note what was said, the Coroner looked up at Roger and, waving his hand in a circular motion, indicated,
*"Pray continue Doctor Edwards."*

*"Worlock arrived at my door last Monday evening claiming to have been poisoned, causing his wife to severely chastise him for making such an outrageous accusation when it was widely known he had been drinking heavily with his brothers before coming home only to send his eldest child to buy more...'as if he had not had enough for one day' she said."*

Again the Coroner interrupted,
*"Tell me Doctor Edwards, in your opinion was the deceased drunk when he arrived upon your doorstep?"*

Roger thought for while before shaking his head,
*"No not drunk, just very ill, in fact Worock had not touched a drop of alcohol all day but I did not know that at the time, I only learned of it later...from the deceased himself."*

*"So what happened once you had ascertained the deceased was,"* glancing at his Clerks scribbled notes, *"let me see...ah yes, sober but just very ill?"* prompted the Coroner.

*"He produced some powder claiming it was poison only for his wife to immediately question his ability to recognise such a thing. Unfortunately I agreed with her and wrongly assumed he had indeed spent the day drinking."*

*"And do you now accept that was not the case Doctor Edwards,"* queried the Coroner before adding, *"for I am sure the Jury will be most interested to know why you did not think it was poison."*

*"Because the powder Worlock brought with him was brown in colour and he was claiming the powder in his beer was white."*

*"And what about his wife, how did she react to his accusations of being poisoned?"*

Taking a good long look at Rebecca, sitting uncomfortably next to Constable Gerrish, Roger Edwards turned towards the Jury and said slowly and precisely,

*"She laughed hysterically and accused him of wanting to hang her!"*

At this mutterings and mumbling filled the room, starting quietly with the Jury. Rebecca glared accusingly around the room, silently cursing everyone for doubting her word until, unable to control her temper, she stood up and screamed,

*"You know I am innocent and I expect better. You forget, without my family none of you would have work, does my father's memory mean nothing to you!"*

before she was roughly pulled back to her seat by the Constable.

This outburst earned her a stern warning from the Coroner and a reminder to everyone else in the room,

*"We may be gathered in an upstairs room of an Ale House and not a fine Court House, surrounded by lawyers or bewigged Judges, however you will be well advised to remember that I hold similar powers to a Magistrate and I shall not hesitate in instructing the Constable to remove any trouble makers from my Court!"*

Order restored, Joyner Ellis returned to the witness,

*"Can we now concentrate on the cause of death please Doctor Edwards?"*

As Roger took his hastily scribbled notes from his jacket pocket all twelve members of the Jury shuffled restlessly towards the edge of their seats eager not to miss one word of what he was about to divulge. Eventually he was ready and confessed there had been a slight difference of opinion between the three Doctors over the cause of death, a difference they had not fully resolved and which they all agreed should be left to the Members of the Jury and possibly a Higher Court to decide. However of one thing they were all agreed.

*"From the condition of Worlocks' internal organs it was clear he had been ill for some time and had probably suffered a painful, agonising death. His lungs were turgid and full of blood with considerable signs of inflammation, the stomach also showed signs of violent inflammation as did the vessels of the intestines and although this could be due to poison it could also be due to a lifetime spent drinking cheap ale but that Gentleman,"* Roger announced, looking directly at the Jury," *is for you to decide."*

Pausing to give his Clerk time to write everything down The Coroner turned back towards the witness standing alone behind the small table onto which he had placed his notes.

*"And what, Doctor Edwards, do you put as the cause of death?"*

*"Violent Inflammation, Your Honour."*

*"Violent Inflammation, is that it, not death from poison or bad ale, just violent inflammation, is that the best your knife could tell you?"* was the best the dumbfounded Coroner could think to ask, such was his utter disbelief at what he was hearing.

Calling Doctor William Wingrove the Coroner asked for his observations and William, on Oath, confirmed,
*"I was present at the opening of the body and whilst I agree with everything my colleague has already stated I am of the opinion and firmly believe death was due to poison!"*

Having finally heard one of the Doctors give the cause of death as poison William Joyner Ellis hastily returned William Wingrove to his seat next to Roger Edwards and called Samuel Watts.

Doctor Watts took the Oath and, like William before him, confirmed he was present at the opening of the body. He testified how, like Doctor Wingrove, he was also of the opinion that death was due to poison but before the Jury could hear any more of his evidence the makeshift Courtroom descended into utter turmoil until the Coroner effectively called everyone to order and motioned Samuel Watts to continue.

*"We removed between four and six ounces of brown fluid from the stomach which was put into a bottle for further analysis, there were also several livid spots of a corrosive appearance on the internal coating of the stomach and the lungs were in a putrid state although not particularly diseased."*

By now the Inquest Jury had been sitting for nearly four and a half hours and with two Doctors indicating death was due to poison and one not completely convinced it was clear they would not conclude their business today. Coroner Joyner Ellis decided to call an adjournment, warning both Jury and witnesses not to discuss their thoughts or beliefs outside the makeshift Court Room. He then closed the proceedings for the day inviting them, *"to meet again at nine of the clock on the morrow."*

William Joyner Ellis awoke the following morning to a gentle tap on the door of his room as Mrs Hook brought in his breakfast, which she placed on the table by the window; as she made to leave she asked,

*"Do e want our Mary t'come n light the fire Zur or shall she bring thee zum ot water instead?"*

He was known throughout Gloucestershire as an honest, deeply humane and fair man who would never do anything to bring his position as one of his Majesty's Coroners into question and as young Mary Hook was a witness at the Inquest over which he was currently presiding, he decided it was best if they did not meet outside the Courtroom, he therefore advised her mother, *"I have no need of a fire on such a fine day; just instruct her to leave a jug of hot water outside the door."*

With the landlady off to tell her daughter to fetch some hot water for their important guest, William rose and stood, in his favourite old linen shift for it was far too warm to be in need of his dressing gown, taking in the Hook's best room and thought it perfectly adequate…in his thirty years as Gloucestershire's Coroner he had been in far worse. The bed was old but exceedingly comfortable, there was a marble topped washstand and basin in a small recess, a tall cupboard in which his best black jacket, waistcoat and breeches now hung alongside his white over shirt and cravat. At the foot of the bed, on the bare wooden floor, stood his comfortable old leather boots and white stockings, his tricorne hat hung obliquely over the back of one of the two old chairs whilst his slightly threadbare but comfortable old wig adorned the other. Eating his breakfast as he wandered about the room William peered through the window across the field at the back of the building towards Oldland Bottom and the Hamlet of Coneyore. Despite his position in the County and his grand title William was a countryman at heart; coming from the Vale of Berkeley, with its beautiful castle, he was acutely aware of the harsh lives endured by many of the labourers appearing before him at this Inquest. There came a gentle tap on the door followed by the soft sound of a young girl's voice, *"Yer ot water Zur."*

Walking across the room William opened the door, picked up the jug and, his ablutions completed, prepared to face the adjourned Inquest into the suspicious death of Thomas Worlock.

Back in the makeshift courtroom Jury and Coroner prepared to resume their deliberations. Meanwhile outside more witnesses, including Sarah Jenkins, waited their turn whilst those called yesterday returned to join the gathering throng eager to be present for its conclusion. One person, however, was missing. Following a quick meeting between Coroner and Constable that morning it was decided it would be best for Rebecca to be secreted away in a small room until the verdict was announced.

By midday Joyner Ellis considered he had heard enough and suggested the Jury might be in a position to consider their verdict and ordered the room be cleared, leaving an apprehensive Constable Gerrish on guard outside to prevent any unwanted eavesdroppers listening in. From the very beginning John Gerrish had been reluctant to take on the job of Village Constable, being local he knew everybody and, like all government officials, he was aware he would be very unpopular, even despised, especially when called to arrest felons for trivial offences and march them before the Magistrate but most of all he hated collecting the non-payment of rates from the likes of his self advancing kinsman Peter Gerrish who believed he already paid far too much in support of the Poor. The post came with an annual salary of £3.3s plus expenses and certain perks. For instance he had recently travelled to Bath to ask the Mayor to issue an arrest warrant for a known criminal called Middlecut, returning later to arrest him, for which he earned an extra 3/6. Each time he met with the High Constable of Gloucestershire he received around 3/- over and above his salary and only last week he spent three days with him for which he received an extra guinea. Fortunately during his career, although he had sought and found many an absent father of an illegitimate child, dealt with burglaries and one or two suspicious deaths, he had never been called upon to carry anyone off to the Lunatic Asylum and the death of Thomas Worlock was his first alleged poisoning.

Everyone, none more so than Rebecca, eagerly awaited the Jury's verdict. Robert and George Worlock, along with the eccentric Samuel and Richard Jenkins remained, under strict instructions from their absent ailing father not to leave until the verdict was known. Back in Bitton Martha was frantic with worry, refusing to leave her sick husband who was unable to get from his bed following the stresses and strains of the previous day, despite knowing how much their sons needed her and that she should be with them. No longer even strong enough to climb the stairs to their bedroom John slept in a makeshift bed in the front parlour and, for the first time in her life, Martha felt so helpless as she wept softly to her sleeping husband.

*"John I d'need thee fur th'sake of they,"* as the sounds of their three young grandchildren drifting through the open window from the orchard.

Old John's absence had not gone unnoticed and whilst many were concerned enough to ask his boys what ailed him, a few chose to encourage the churlish antics of Peter Gerrish as he confidently declared,
*"Any Jury in the land can see it was death from natural causes, made worse by excessive drinking,"* adding, *"and once that is known I will be taking his long suffering widow and her fatherless children home to my wife,"* turning to

face the three Worlock boys he added with venom in his voice, *"where they belong!"*

Within half an hour Robert Henderson, appointed foreman by his fellow Jurors, sent word that they had reached a verdict and, with the news that the Inquest was drawing to it's close, Rebecca was brought into the Courtroom, whilst those unable to get in wandered aimlessly in the stable yard at the back. Anxious for a fair but swift conclusion and wishing to be home in Berkeley by night fall the Coroner ordered everyone to quickly take their places before turning to the Foreman of the Jury,

*"Have you all reached your verdict?"*

*"Yes zur we be all in agreement."*

*"In that case Mr Henderson be so good as to tell the Court."*

To a room so hushed you could hear the proverbial pin drop Foreman Henderson announced,

*"We d'say Thomus Worlock were poisoned and that twere put in is beer by er,"* pointing to Rebecca, *"an, what's more, it tweren't no accident cus she meant t'do it."*

On hearing this Rebecca fell against Constable Gerrish and cried out,

*"I am innocent! How can you sort of people have ever known what it was like to have to care for someone who was constantly ill because he drank too much!"*

This shameless exhibition brought about an angry emotional response from Robert Worlock who, up until now, had hardly said a word to anyone,

*"You bain't innocent, theese never luved Thomas, not since th'day theese trapped im into marryin thee and you know you ave cruelly used im ever since!"*

William Joyner Ellis often found himself in situations like this and, not wanting this Inquest to descend into a family battle, he ordered Constable Gerrish to clear the room by suggesting,

*"Maybe if the prisoner were speedily removed to the House of Correction others might feel more inclined to return to their homes!"* and with that Rebecca Worlock, widow and alleged murderess was escorted to her cottage to gather together a few belongings in readiness for her journey to... God knows where...but a journey that was destined to end in Gloster Gaol where, during the Summer Assize, her fate would be sealed. Meanwhile the Jury waited as the Coroner's Clerk prepared the document, to which they would all either add their signature or make their mark, confirming they had, on Oath, found

Rebecca guilty of murder. In fact the wording of the document went much further than simply finding her guilty of murder it also said she killed Thomas *"in a manner and by the poison aforesaid, feloniously, traitorously, wilfully and with malice aforethought against the peace of her said Lord The King."*

Although Rebecca was no longer present there was still uproar amongst those who remained to recall their personal dealings with her,
*"She always bin a shrew of a woman, nagging er poor usband even when he were sick."*

*"She did always think she were better n us."*

*"She do deserve all she d'get."*

*"Bet er family bain't gonna be able t'elp er this time!"*

The Flowers! suddenly all thoughts turned to Peter Gerrish and his arrogant assumption the Jury would find Thomas had hastened his own death. Turning to where he had been sitting they found his seat curiously empty with no sign of him anywhere, so much for his declarations that his wife was eager for her daughter and grandchildren to return home 'where they belong'.

His part of the proceedings over, an exhausted William Joyner Ellis told his Clerk to fetch the carriage, with luck and several changes of fresh horses they would be back in Berkeley by nightfall. Sarah was forever reminding him he would be seventy on his next birthday, far too old to be constantly travelling throughout the County even though he had long since given up riding and allowed his clerk to take him by carriage, surely it was time to hand things over to their son. It was only April but already the year was proving to be very busy and he was indeed contemplating retiring so he could spend more time at Wickselme House with her. Young William was nearly thirty, already practicing as a Lawyer and had grown up knowing he would one day succeed his father as Coroner for Gloucestershire. Old William could have had no way of knowing but by the end of 1820 he was to conduct no less than 119 Inquests.

Back in her cottage Rebecca sat on the blanket box in the empty bedroom carefully selecting the few meagre possessions she would be allowed to take with her. The place seemed eerily quiet considering all the traumatic events of the past days. Eager to impress those who dared accuse her she chose to wear the only presentable dress she possessed, a plain brown thing bought years ago from the earnings she managed to hide from her drunken husband, for the journey to Bristol. What fine gowns she had brought with her on her marriage were long gone, either sold, worn out or used to make clothes for the children. Folding the dress she had worn for the Inquest, a clean shift, a clean pair of stockings and two frayed muslin caps into a tidy bundle she was almost ready.

However there was one treasured possession she needed to find.....for her day in Court she planned to astound her accusers by wearing the elegant green, red and gold brocade gown left her by Aunt Partridge. Wrapping her precious possessions in an old shawl and tying her bonnet firmly under her chin she was almost done and made to carefully climb down the steep spiral stairs but not before she glanced into the children's bedroom one last time and wondered what would happen to them,

*"Martha can have them until I return,"* she coolly assumed.

Walking back across the narrow landing and past the open door to her own bedroom again, although sorely tempted, she chose not to gaze too long into the room or at the space where the bed had once stood, the bed she had reluctantly shared with Thomas for thirteen years, the bed in which he had died in agony that morning, supposedly by her hand, the bed that had been taken from the downstairs parlour that morning and now burned fiercely up in the orchard.

The journey to Lawfords Gate House of Correction passed in complete silence. Her escort, to whom she was securely handcuffed, was a despised Gerrish whilst her contemptible brother in law had willingly agreed to take them in his wagon. Apart from being well paid Richard Jenkins was eager to witness the further humiliation of his despised sister in law. Leaving Oldland behind them, the covered cart trundled towards Kingswood Hill, a place Rebecca knew well, past old Mrs Stephen's Apothecary shop, then down through St George towards her temporary home til arrangements were made to transfer her to Gloster Gaol and the Summer Assize where, with the lawyer she expected Mamma to provide, she would be declared innocent.

No one could have prepared her for what awaited her at Lawfords Gate. Once safely behind its doors she encountered the Governor, Isaac Cowley, from whom she expected some courtesy, instead he chose to completely ignore her, making no attempt to help her down from the carriage preferring to talk to his friend Constable Gerrish and Richard Jenkins. Things did not improve, in fact they deteriorated, when she was given into the care of the Prison Matron who took malevolent pleasure in further adding to her discomfort by refusing to give her similar respect and insisted on calling her 'Worlock,'

*"She forgets her place,"* fumed Rebecca, *"how dare she talk to me in such a way, well, like my family and the pathetic creature I married, she must learn otherwise or I simply will not co-operate."*

But Matron knew her place well enough because she was, after all, employed to ensure female prisoners did exactly as they were bid...a position for which she was well paid to do!

Rebecca did not take kindly at having to share a cell and swiftly made her objections known to the hapless Cowley,

*"If I am to go to Gloster within the next few days why should I be expected to spend my time with the likes of, of...that?"* pointing to the filthy, syphilitic prostitute sitting forlornly on her straw mattress in the corner the cell. Governor Cowley, for reasons best known to himself, gave into her demands and allowed her a cell on her own. Unfortunately, thinking she was receiving preferential treatment because of her family name prompted Rebecca to expect the same when she reached Gloster.

Two days later, fulfilling his promise to the John and Martha, Reverend Ellacombe officiated at their son's funeral at St. Mary's when, on the beautiful Spring day of April 23$^{rd}$, Saint George's Day and Shakespeare's birthday, the family and most of Bitton stood around the family grave as his mutilated body was laid with his baby brother and sister. Back in Lawfords Gate Rebecca remained blissfully unaware the funeral had even taken place, nor was she of a mind to ask when it was or if she might be allowed to attend...despite her claim to have 'loved Thomas so much' in fact when the Prison Chaplain asked if she wished to, *"pray for the deliverance of his soul as it ascends unto heaven."* he received the swift insolent reply,

*"Are there not already enough hypocrites in Bitton to do that!"*

Come Monday morning everyone, from the lowliest of prisoner to the Governor himself, heaved a sigh of relief, at long last Rebecca was off to Gloster. Cowley entered her cell at first light brandishing a set of hand cuffs and leg irons, impassively explaining,

*"You will be obliged to wear these,"* rattling the heavy chains in front of her, *"for the entire journey."* Matron, standing beside him, could barely disguise her euphoric sadistic delight at what she knew the Governor was going to say next, *"Due to the Magistrates sitting today I am unable to escort you personally however, Matron and Constable Gerrish will accompany you in my place."*

With the arrival of a small covered wagon, unknown driver on the box and the despised John Gerrish alongside him Rebecca, manacled hand and foot, already feared life in Gloster Gaol might well prove very different to that at Lawfords Gate!

After what seemed like an eternity she overheard the driver tell Constable Gerrish,

*"Bain't much further now Zur, we be almost in Gloster."*

She had been allowed out three times during the forty mile journey, once to relieve herself behind a hedge, still securely handcuffed to the Matron but mercifully minus the leg irons, again to eat some unsavoury bread, tasteless cheese and take a few sips of stale water whilst they changed the horses at some obscure livery yard and finally when they changed horses again at an isolated coaching inn..

Sounds of the massive bolts on the first Lodge Gate were heard opening as the cart very slowly trundled on. Hearing those lock behind them the next set, on the second gate, were unlocked and the creaking of what must be a very heavy door told Rebecca they had arrived and she waited, with trepidation, to be released from her prison on wheels.

With barely time to acclimatise her eyes to the evening sun Matron, whom she had long decided was a wicked old crone, pointed to the pathetic bundle by her feet and yelled,
*"Pick up thy things n get theeself out!"*……

….only then did Rebecca glimpse her new home. From deep within the bowels of the grim austere building came indescribable moans, groans, screams, hysterical laughter and shouts, accompanied by an overwhelming feeling of despair, whilst from the other side of the high stone wall came voices shouting out orders and singing as sailors worked on their ships in the Docks. Returning to face her welcoming party Rebecca struggled to conceal her fear, all the while determined not to betray how, from first impressions, she was sure she had arrived in hell! Hell was indeed an apt word to describe Gloster Gaol. Forty years earlier for every criminal executed here three died from goal fever, with no segregation women shared their cells with every hot blooded man in the building, including gaolers and were actively encouraged to 'get with child' in order to 'plead the belly' and have a death sentence commuted to transportation. Animals such as pigs, poultry and dogs were part of everyday life and if you were unable to pay for your keep or refused to pay 'in kind' then the gaolers could and did make a woman prisoner's life very uncomfortable. Thankfully, since the late 1700's there had been no outbreak of gaol fever, dogs were banned, there was now a separate female wing and by an act of parliament prisoners no longer paid for their keep, however it had only been six years ago that pigs and poultry finally disappeared.

Taken before an austere looking man sitting at a plain mahogany davenport, large calfskin book and quill pen in front of him, Rebecca quickly realised none of her tantrums, pleadings, swooning, allusions of grandeur or claims to be of a fine upstanding County family would work on the Governor of Gloster Gaol. Barely raising his eyes to as much as acknowledge her presence, he entered her particulars in the Admission Register. Putting her age at around thirty six he

guessed her to be about five foot four in height, of stout build with long arms, her hair was dark brown with no sign of grey, her eyes were hazel in colour, however when he asked if she had any employment she chose to reply,
*"I constantly laboured caring for my sick husband whilst expected to milk and make butter from my own cows and raise other animals in order not to starve. I also cared for my children and household without the help of a kitchen servant"....*

....so he simply wrote 'Labourer' in the appropriate column.

However when he began reading the Prison Rules from a printed book, as he was obliged to do to every new prisoner whatever their crime, she sarcastically interrupted,
*"Kindly hand me the book as I think you will find I am more than capable of reading it for myself !"* thinking to herself, *"unlike you,"* scowling towards the Matron from Lawfords Gate, Constable Gerrish and a Turnkey hovering in the background, *"and certain other illiterate persons in this room."* Returning her gaze to an astonished Governor she announced, *"thanks to my family I received an excellent education!"*

Mr Symmonds, Governor of Gloster Gaol, later completed his Register thus; 'Rebecca Worlock, labourer who can read and write'

Believing she had adequately dealt with 'that insignificant little man and his Register and Book of Rules', Rebecca waited impatiently to be 'escorted' to the privacy of her own cell, instead she was bundled into one of four Lazeretto Cells in the Gate Lodge. Thinking this dingy room, no more than seven foot square, was to be her home for the next four months conveniently brought about one of her apoplectic faints, however once she realised it was only a holding cell she quickly recovered....too quickly for Mr Symmond's liking! Further humiliation came at the hands of the Prison Surgeon, Doctor John Playdell Wilton and two swarthy female gaolers who were intent on removing her clothing and forcing her to take a bath. She could not remember the last time she had taken a bath, probably before she married, these days it was just a quick wash down with cold well water. Of course she objected ...about having to take a bath in the first place, the lack of privacy and finally because the water was cold. All this having failed she simply complained for the sake of it.

Doctor Wilton was having none of it; in the seventeen years he had been Surgeon to Gloster Gaol, he had seen and heard it all before,
*"Worlock!, you have but two choices; you can agree to take a bath or,"* pointing to the pair of determined women standing either side of a battered old hip bath, *"my assistants will be only too happy to persuade you to change your mind."*

Rebecca could not have known there was little chance of a hot bath, medical opinion decreed allowing prisoners such luxury had a strange effect on their behaviour and no one was prepared to take any risks with a woman who's reputation had already gone before her!

Declared 'clean and wholesome' Rebecca lay shivering, almost naked except for a thin shift, as she was intimately examined should she later claim to have been with child on admission. No one, not even her despised husband, had ever looked at or touched her in such a way! Her ordeal over, she was declared 'not with child and free from infection' and her old brown dress, beige shawl, stockings and rough wooden clogs were returned to her. As a final act of humiliation a badge, which she was to wear at all times, emblazoned with her Prison Number was tied to her bodice.

# CHAPTER TWELVE

Doors creaked loudly behind her, keys turned noisily in their locks until finally Prisoner No 13 reached the female wing of the Penitentiary. Without warning or time to focus on the scene before her Rebecca was forcibly pushed into a cell already occupied by two other women.

Her vitriolic tirade against the gaolers and the other prisoners showed no signs of abating, as she demanded to be moved to the promised single cell. Expecting her own way as usual she failed to notice how she was becoming the centre of attention for every convicted female thief, burglar, pickpocket and low life to walk the lanes of Gloucestershire. With her reputation having already gone before her she was certainly fulfilling everyone's expectations. It was not every day a murderess joined their midst, the last one had been thirty eight year old Ann Tye from Dowdeswell back in May 1818.....and they hanged her! Ignoring the bemused looks from the other prisoners Rebecca continued to insist she be given the single cell she had been led to believe, by Mr Cowley at Lawfords Gate, would be awaiting her and, pointing towards the pair of bedraggled women currently occupying two of the three beds, she exploded, *"Why should I be expected to share my days with those creatures!!"*

She fiercely resisted when two turnkeys dragged her, screaming, into what she considered to be an overcrowded cell, refusing to accept it was up to the Governor where prisoners were placed. Finally, after being roughly manhandled back onto the empty bed for the third time, she was ordered to 'untie thy bundle and bide thy tongue.' Leaping up from the bed she followed the hapless guards towards the doorway boasting to the bedraggled horde gathering, spellbound, at the spectacle before them,
*"You insignificant people have no idea the influence my family holds in this County but, mark my words, once the Governor realises he has made an error, a very grave error, of judgment he will waste no time in carrying out my orders and,"* grinning arrogantly towards her two would be cellmates she hissed, *"by tomorrow I shall have my own cell!"*

Her two new companions had seen and heard enough. Losing patience, the pair sauntered menacingly towards her until, standing on either side, one whispered slowly,
*"This bain't no place t'be choosey bout thy friends so theese better get used t'doin what theese bid else thees'll find thyself in trouble frum those who be less understandin than we two."*

Roughly grabbing Rebecca's chin between her grubby thumb and forefinger her friend warned,
*"Knows what we means dearie!!"*

It was well before dawn, in fact the tiny barred windows high on the wall of her cell told her it was still dark, yet her companions, Prudence an habitual Cheltenham pickpocket and Nancy a Gloster shopkeeper accused of having defective weights on her scales, were already up and about along with the rest of the female wing, so there was no point in remaining on her uncomfortable old wooden bedstead with its itchy straw and horse hair mattress. Last night had been intolerable apart from lack of sleep and no fireplace to warm the night cells the thin blanket, no thicker than a piece of sacking, did little to keep out the bone chilling cold. Reluctantly clambering out of bed she stubbornly refused to ask why everyone was frantically tidying their beds, emptying their slop buckets and sweeping out their cells. Urging her to do the same they received a sharp retort,
*"How dare you to tell me what to do!"*

So they just shrugged their shoulders and mused,
*"Suit thee self but just wait till th'Governor n Matron d'get yer."*

Realising the Governor was expected Rebecca remained on her unmade bed concentrating on a mental list of conditions he would need to address before she would co-operate any further. However, with his arrival she was not expecting to be told that far from making demands she was never to speak to him unless he spoke to her first, nor was she prepared to hear him bark,
*"Worlock, in future by the time I arrive for my morning rounds you will have your bedding neatly folded, floor swept, slop pail emptied and your hands and face washed ready for your day's work!"*

Breakfast, for which she was allowed half an hour, resembled her pigs feeding at the trough in the orchard as everyone fought to get their share. The gruel and vegetables, this morning it was tasteless over boiled leeks, was warm, salty and as thin as well water, the bread was stale and the water had a bitter taste to it so she refused to drink it. Noticing some of the other prisoners were drinking buttermilk and one or two even sipped dishes of tea she demanded to given the same only for the guards to take great delight in telling her,
*"They aves special privileges n friends n visters, theese don't so thees'll just ave t'drink dirty water like the rest of um."*

She was put to work in the prison wash house sorting disgusting foul bed clothes and prisoners uniforms. Bed linen and uniforms were changed once a month and washed in a large copper boiler. By mid morning she was fit to drop, little sleep along with meagre portions at breakfast left her weak and, spying a very tempting wooden bench, she sat down to rest, only to hear the loud threatening voice of the taskmaster reminding her,

*"You're here to work not spend your days idling but, of course, if you can't manage the task perhaps you would prefer to stand at a table picking oakum instead!"*

By early afternoon she was close to exhaustion which was just what the National Penitentiary Act had intended, *"Prison Labour,"* it decreed, *"is to be the hardest yet most servile kind in which drudgery is chiefly required,"* and, after only one day in this awful place, she doubted whether she would survive until August.

Back in her cell at the end of an excruciatingly long day, facing another night with two unwanted unsavoury companions, she was extremely relieved when a guard came to take her to the Prison Chapel. Someone wished to see her.

The portly man, dressed in black, standing with his back to her turned as she entered the dismal Chapel and walked towards her, both arms outstretched, tattered old bible in one hand, as he introduced himself,

*"I am the Chaplain,"* adding, *"and it is my divine duty to care for your soul whilst you are here."*

Thinking he might be of some use at a later date Rebecca decided there was nothing to lose by, *"humouring the old fool,"* and, joining him in the battered front pew, she allowed herself to be led in a quiet prayer for herself and the soul of her dearly departed husband although she failed to understand why she was expected to pray for such a brute considering she was falsely accused of his murder!! Glancing around this miserable excuse for a House of God she thought it a truly dreadful place and, not feeling in the least bit repentant, found herself comparing it with Bitton Church. Here the plain glass windows were so filthy no light shone through whereas St. Mary's beautiful stained glass windows always sparkled when the sun reached them. The rows of worn out old pews, segregated so that social classes could not mix, showed years of shameful neglect, back at St.Mary's her family had their own red deal wooden box pew. The dilapidated pulpit from whence her companion preached hellfire and eternal damnation every day was so askew it looked as though it might topple over at any minute, how different to the one her family had helped finance at Bitton.

The Chaplain's monotonous droning voice brought her back from her memories as he ended their first meeting with his usual offer,

*"Should there be anything I can do for you my child,"* explaining how he

sometimes arranged for poorer prisoners to receive extra food allowances in the absence of any family support. Rebecca thanked him for his kindness by demanding,

*"Be so kind as to go to the Governor and tell him I am to have a single cell by suppertime or, failing that, by bedtime for I fear the foolish man does not fully appreciate my situation nor how powerful my family is in this county."*

Supper of cheese and vegetables was far worse than breakfast but Rebecca was so hungry anything would do, fortunately she was able to buy a small dish of tea, thanks to the 1d she earned for her day's labour.

Obliged to return to her shared cell she fumed,

*"So the fool of a Chaplain has not carried out my orders either, well he is not the only one who can go back on their word, next time I see him he will find that I can be equally uncooperative if I choose."*

Meanwhile she had no choice but to sleep alongside two women, a pickpocket and a fraudster, with whom she felt she not only had absolutely nothing in common but who were of the lowest class. Had she taken time to listen to what was being said about her she would have realised her feelings were entirely mutual and, after only two days, she was already an extremely unpopular prisoner.

A month later the prisoners in Gloster Penitentiary had become accustomed to the backlash caused by Rebecca and her crime. Hardened criminals, turnkeys and common gaolers, even the experienced Governor and Matron, were regularly subjected to demands, tantrums and insults in an attempt to get her own way. By using the daily visits from Mr Pleydell Wilton or his son, who had been assisting his father as the second Prison Surgeon for nearly eight years, she learned it was sometimes possible to get extra food or be allowed a day off from the unbearable laundry. Within a week of her arrival she tried to claim her monthly ague in a failed attempt to be excused work, although she had been prescribed camomile tea at bedtime for a cold. However the one thing she craved but consistently failed to secure was her own cell, despite claiming rheumatic pain and breathing difficulties in the hope the younger, more gullible Doctor Wilton would recommend a warmer cell. It was now late May and he decreed there was no need. Having failed to persuade Doctor Wilton Jnr that her monthly sufferings deserved a note excusing her from the laundry it then became his father's turn to be on the receiving end of her acid tongue when he also refused to give in to her demands,

*"Unlike you, my family physician, Doctor Roger Edwards, was better qualified to understand and more sympathetic towards my problems"* claiming, *"he often ordered complete rest!"*

This latest outburst cost her not only a rare rebuke from Wilton Snr. who delighted in reminding her,

*"If Doctor Edwards thought so highly of you and your family why was it partly due to his testimony at the Inquest into your husband's death that you were committed here, accused of his murder"*....but also a night in solitary confinement.

Incensed at having again failed to get her own way Rebecca consoled herself that, far from it being a deterrent, solitary confinement offered her the one thing she craved the most…a cell to herself, however that was before she saw the black, almost windowless *"Solitary"* cell that awaited her.

The first thing to hit her was the overpowering stench then, as her eyes became acclimatised to the darkness, the discovery there was no bed.

*"There is a perfectly adequate bed in your cell. If you obeyed the rules and controlled your tongue you would not be facing the prospect of spending an uncomfortable night on a cold flagstone floor,"* was the unsympathetic answer Mr Symmonds gave to the question he knew she was about to ask. A small hard pillow and a filthy piece of sacking was thrown at her, what fresh air there was came through a tiny, heavily barred window set high up on the wall but, judging from the overwhelming smell permeating the room, it was clear none was getting through. Surely she was not expected to spend a night in such a place as this without any light; please God they would allow her a tallow candle,

*"Candles bain't lowed n solitary,"* came a gratifying, almost jubilant reply, from one of the female guards.

As the night drew on Rebecca began to see her old cell and two unwelcome companions differently; at least you were provided with your own slop bucket. Here you were obliged to call out for a communal pail and, from what she could hear and smell, the gaolers tonight were a particularly evil bunch choosing to deliberately take their time, forcing those in solitary to squat on the floor in the corner of their cells. With the heavy cell door bolted, every noise from within the building increased in volume and she imagined all her enemies were gathering outside waiting to pounce. Therefore, even if the cold hard floor had allowed it, she dared not sleep for fear of what they might do to her. Returning to the Day Cell, with the luxury and warmth of a blazing fire, in time for breakfast her body felt as if it had received another severe beating from Thomas instead of a night on an unforgiving floor. Barely able to stand let alone walk, her unkempt hair and dark rings under tired eyes told everyone she had not slept but, stubborn to the end, she was not about to satisfy their curiosity by admitting it.

The Chaplain, now there was a loquacious man if ever there was one, what you might call pure 'fire and brimstone'. A man who retained all the old compulsion of a long gone clerical life, choosing to thunder out the same endless sermons every Sunday, interspersed with the occasional fist waving, shouting and thumping on the less than sturdy pulpit. Prone to declare *"Alleluia Praise the Lord!"* without warning, he expected the instant reply, *"and Amen to that!"* from his less than enthusiastic flock. Woe betide those who failed to respond or dare interrupt his evangelical flow, especially during Assize week when he had the added pressure of comforting condemned prisoners as he cleansed their guilty souls in readiness for the next world. Rebecca attended Chapel under duress and only because she knew the alternative was another night in solitary. Under different circumstances she would have insisted on sitting with the more socially acceptable prisoners, debtors maybe, but in an attempt to avoid the Chaplain she willingly sat at the back where he could not see her and send for her. These days she thought only of herself and attending Chapel gave her the opportunity to concentrate on securing an easier life, not for a moment did she consider her desperately unhappy children, currently being passed between various reluctant relatives whilst they decided which one should give them a permanent home.

The obvious choice was Grandmamma Mary but, with her daughter in Gaol charged with murdering her husband, her controlling younger husband had conveniently remembered a long standing promise to visit relatives in Somerset and she was currently away from home…apparently indefinitely and, as if this were not enough, the already hostile relationship between Peter Gerrish and the Worlocks had not been helped by the appearance of newspaper accounts and a Bonners Broadsheet boasting to know the, *"true, full and particular account of a most horrid and cruel murder committed on April 20th by Rebecca Worlock,"* now in full circulation throughout Bristol, Bath and Gloucestershire. Those reading Bonner's cheap Broadsheet who managed to decipher the smudged lampblack oil based ink print would learn all about her crime and, to Peter's tyrannical rage, realise she was his stepdaughter and that could jeopardize his aspirations to be fully accepted by sophisticated Bath society. Even those who knew the Flowers, but cared little for 'Gerrish or his high handed ways', recalled the childhood tantrums and agreed Rebecca had certainly surpassed herself this time.

As her incarceration continued Rebecca noticed how all the other prisoners mixed well with each other until she walked into the exercise yard or one of the dayrooms when all conversation abruptly stopped as pairs of suspicious eyes fixed on her and extra gaolers appeared, as if from nowhere. Dutifully queuing for her meals she often refused to eat the food placed in front of her, consequently she lost so much weight Dr. Wilton Snr eventually noticed and instructed the Governor to give her extra mutton broth. Smug at successfully convincing the Prison Surgeon, whilst still hankering after her own cell, she misguidedly thought she might try the same with the Governor by complaining about Prudence and Nancy,

*"I constantly suffer from disturbed sleep for fear at what they might do to me during the night."*

When that failed she asked,
*"Why should I be expected to share my days with the likes of them,"* before suggesting as a compromise, *"If you will not allow me my own cell at least arrange for me to share with people of my own class, a debtor about to be discharged will do."*

Still smarting at being forced to give her extra food Mr Symmonds, naturally, would hear none of it.

May turned to June and Rebecca languished in Gloster Penitentiary, more or less tolerated by her fellow prisoners, as she waited for her day in court. Back in Bitton her three children were currently living with Robert and Sophia, even though they already had six mouths to feed and could ill afford three more. Martha was close to exhaustion caring for an almost totally crippled John and, thanks to a diet of mercury, fifteen years of constant childbearing (two dead babies, several miscarriages, three surviving, another on the way) and over work, there was no way Samuel and Zipporah could even consider taking them in. Finally, after a family meeting at which neither John nor Martha were invited, it was agreed the children would take turns to live with different aunts and uncles until their mother's fate was decided after which, if she hanged, something more permanent like the Poorhouse or an Orphanage must be found.

Peter Gerrish could not understand why anyone in their right mind would wish to visit Gloster Gaol but here were his stepsons insisting they not only make the long journey to see Rebecca but suggesting their mother accompany them. Now, whilst he was powerless to stop them, he knew he could certainly prevent his elderly wife from going anywhere near Gloster. The boys offered to travel in short stages, over several days, resting at night at Coaching Inns in the hope it might encourage their mother to stand up to her husband for once but, holding her tiny hand in his accustomed firm controlling grip, Peter argued,

*"Your dear Mamma is not to consider such a journey, she is far from well, can you not see how it would be most unwise for her to contemplate travelling so far,"* Desperately searching for any way in which to deny his wife the chance

to see her firebrand of a daughter he surmised, *"Why, I doubt if even old John Worlock will be well enough to travel to Gloster for the trial as I understand he too has been deeply affected by your sister's actions."*

With Peter having brought the Worlocks' name into the conversation, George Flower chose to remind his mother of the wretched lives her grandchildren were said to be leading and suggested she might take them in and give them a loving home, at least til they knew whether Rebecca would ever be coming back. Mary opened her mouth as if about to say something only for her husband to swiftly interject,

*"They carry their father's name, therefore is it not for his family to take responsibility for their welfare."*

Rebecca and the Chaplain continued their stormy meetings in the Prison Chapel where, as always, they clashed should he dare broach the subject of her husband's death and her part in it. Nevertheless he knew she must somehow accept her very dangerous situation and realise she could hang. Thus it was during his weekly discussions with Mr Symmonds and the elder Dr. Wilton, regarding a small band of disruptive prisoners amongst the 150 or so currently serving their time, that her behaviour and ignorance of her perilous situation was raised,

*"Well gentlemen,"* informed Mr Symmonds, *"I may have a possible solution for I have this very morning received this,"* waving a crumpled piece of parchment above his head, *"from her brothers asking if they might visit."*

Taking this as a sign of Divine Intervention, the Chaplain asked,

*"If I may be allowed a brief meeting before they are taken to her I will ask God to move to impress upon them the seriousness of their poor sister's plight."*

Far from raising her spirits her brother's visit simply plunged Rebecca further into the depths of despair. Denied any physical contact, forced to talk between a metal grating, she declared she would have preferred to have seen her children as well and showed she had not changed, demanding,

*"Why are they not with you!"* even though she knew Gloster Gaol was not the best of places to bring young children.

*"They are being well cared for by Robert and Sophia Worlock"* was all George could say.

*"Do not lie to me George, Sophia Worlock never liked my children because they are brighter and cleverer than her nincompoops, so why does she suddenly feel sorry for them and want to care for them whilst I languish in this place and"* stopping only to take a breath, *"where is Mamma and why are the children not with her?"*

*"She is far from well at the moment and not strong enough to travel,"* George lied, how could he tell his sister the real reason their mother never answered her letters, would not send a lawyer to see her and refused to take her grandchildren away from their miserable existence had nothing to do with her health? Although Mary had truthfully returned home with a chill from her latest visit to Publow it was Peter, with no wish for his wife to become embroiled in yet another damaging Court Case, who was preventing her from following her heart. They also had no answer to her accusation,

*"And another thing, you rarely visited me during the years I was married to him!"*

How could they ever confess to still being a little bit afraid of her, intimidated by her tantrums and false illusions of grandeur at being a Flower…they were millers and brewers not Lords of the Manor like Uncle George…she needed to look across the river at Saltford to possibly claim that. Nor could they dare tell her they felt sorry for Thomas, often going behind her back to ask after his health whenever they met his father or brothers but, once their scheming stepfather planted the idea of hatred in her gullible brain, there was certainly no point in revealing that, contrary to family beliefs, they had always respected the Worlocks.

Plucking up enough courage they asked what she did to pass her days and were immediately subjected to rantings about how she laboured in the laundry for a meagre 1d a day, about how she missed the fresh milk from her cows, the eggs from her chickens and, although she had never been very good at baking bread, how at least hers was better than that on offer here. As if suddenly prompted by her desperate plight George reached into his waistcoat pocket and took out a leather drawstring purse containing some coins, passing it through the metal grill to his sister he whispered.

*"Mamma sends this, she says you may be in need of a few comforts,"* hoping his sister would not see the lies in his eyes.

Did she mix with the other women, they asked. Her answer was sudden, abrupt and dismissive as she shook her head, turned up her nose in disgust, staring at her brothers, eyes wide open in disbelief,

*"What possible reason is there for me to wish to mix with the kind of people found in this place but,"* holding up her rough gnarled hands in case they planned offering some unwanted advice, *"spare me your pity I will not be here for much longer because the Assize Jury will find me innocent and I shall return home!"*

Mindful of his earlier conversation with the Chaplain and convinced his sister had lost none of her wilful stubborn ways during her incarceration in this dreadful place, George dared to ask,

*"Do you know what will happen if you are found guilty, the best you can hope for is transportation but,"* lowering his voice to little more than a whisper, *"do not forget you could hang!"*

Her frenzied screams were heard throughout the visiting area, two turnkeys, closely followed by the matron, arrived to see what all the commotion was about whilst someone had automatically gone for the Governor.

With Rebecca's hysterical protestations of her innocence and accusations that they were no better than her mother, Peter and all the Worlocks put together, still ringing in their ears the four brothers walked dejectedly back to their horses and the long journey home but not before George admitted to the Chaplain how he had failed to make his sister see reason over her situation. Listening as the locks turned in the massive prison doors behind them they reluctantly agreed that, on this occasion at least, Peter Gerrish was probably right and it had been a mistake coming here. By the time they reached Bitton, tired and exhausted, the following day they had decided not to visit their sister again but to wait until August when she appeared at the Summer Assize.

At the June Vestry Meeting it was unanimously agreed for William Clarke, Overseer of the Poor for Bitton and William Matthews, Acting Overseer, to start the long laborious task of preparing all the Parish Documents needed for the Summer Assize. The charges to be laid against Rebecca were *"Felony and Petit Treason"* and, by the middle of July, both men were meeting regularly to discuss their progress. Reverend Ellacombe was acquainted with the present situation and because he was not present at the Coroner's Inquest, preferring instead to comfort John, Martha and the children, he gave William Matthews a full account of his involvement on that dreadful Friday morning. Mr Ludlow, a well known Barrister on the Oxford and Gloucestershire Circuit, had been approached some time ago and he now confirmed he was free to prosecute. All that was required was for the evidence and a small retainer to be forwarded to his home in Shrewsbury, via his clerk. Dutifully, in mid July, a retainer along with copies of all the Coroner's Depositions were sent to Mr Ludlow's for his perusal. The next day the Overseers met to decide which of the witnesses not called by the Coroner should be questioned.

They began with Elizabeth Amey, who was employed by Mrs Stephens and could testify that Rebecca had bought poison from her employer. Two days later William Clarke told his wife he planned to be away from home all day, *"busy on the Worlock Matter."* fortunately she did not ask what would be keeping him out for most of the day. Had she known he was planning to visit Robert Worlock in an attempt to talk to Mary Ann, who was by all accounts living a wretched life there with her two siblings, Mrs Clark, being a local woman who knew all about the children, would have advised great caution.

Robert Worlock readily admitted he had only taken in his brothers' children out of loyalty. Unfortunately his wife viewed things differently and expected the three extra mouths to earn their meagre crust. On first meeting Mary Ann, the Overseer saw a thin, pale child, ragged clothes hanging from a skeletal body, large sad saucer eyes peering from a dirty tearstained face. Concerned over the treatment the two other children might be receiving he asked to see them as well, only to hear from Sophia,

*"The boy be elpin at th'Slaughterouse and t'other girl be with Martha elping with th'old man."*

Annoyed at hearing his old friend and colleague described in such a derisory way, William Clarke angrily retorted,

*"I assume you are referring to your father in law Mr John Worlock!"*

Robert lamely tried to make up for Sophia's shameful remarks by interrupting,

*"Now scuse I Zur, but tis only out the gudness of er art n pity fur our Thomas' un-appy situation she offered to give is little uns a lovin ome. Mother casn't look after three young uns an care fur father, our Lizbeth and er usband be caring for Garge and there bain't no more room, Sophia n Richard do feel they've dun thur bit what wiv bein mixed up wiv taking our Thomas over t' Keynsham and then bein spected to go all the way to Berkeley fur the Carner and as for our Samuel and is wife, well they be aving trouble feedin their own brats what wiv is illness an another babby on th'way."* The eldest of John and Martha's boys ended his pathetic attempt at defending the heartless treatment his wife was giving to his dead brother's three children with a cold calculated warning, *"but if she be found guilty and d'hang fur is murder then we be goin to the Parish to get um put into the Poor House."*

When the Overseer suggested they were the only family the children had, Sophia angrily interrupted,

*"Scuse I Zur but what bout them Flowers up Goldun Valley, or as thee fergot?"*

William Clarke struggled to control his anger. No! he had not forgotten there was another Grandmother but, on this occasion, his business was with the Worlocks and he still insisted on talking to Mary Ann ...alone! At Sophia's prompting Robert made it clear he wished to be present. Overseer Clarke on the other hand was equally determined he would do no such thing because it was obvious the child was terrified of them and as long as they remained in the room there would be no chance of getting to the truth. However as Mr Clarke had further questions for the pair they were told to go about their business but remain nearby.

Despite his important position within the community William was a kindly man, content to take his time to gain the confidence of a very frightened Mary Ann until she trusted him enough to gradually respond to his gentle questioning. She repeatedly asked after her mother,
*"Be it true what Aunt Sophia d'say an she killed father cus she ated im and that she be goin t'ang and then we'll be put in th'Poor Ouse cus no one d'want us, not even Grandmamma Mary!"*

William Clarke was appalled at what he was hearing and could not believe a woman, with youngsters of her own, could be so evil and gain such pleasure from making three innocent young children, who had not only watched their father die in agony but now faced the possibility of never seeing their mother again, suffer so much. By the time he finished talking to the child he knew she had fetched the beer from the Chequers and that her mother had taken it from her on the doorstep before sending her out to look for Honor and John but, realising she had forgotten to pass on the message from George Hook, she returned home to see Rebecca mixing white powder into the beer after which father had become ill.

William stood up to leave only for Mary Ann to pull gently on his hand to innocently ask,
*"Zur, twas it th'white stuff muther were mixin in father's beer what made im sick,"* adding *"ee always sid we was t'tell th'truth an tis wickud to tell lies. I only done what ee sid, I didn't tell no lies."*

Clarke thought how, at a future day in Court, such simple words from this innocent young child might well hang her mother.

Robert's, of course, was a much different story. His was full of bitter resentment at the way Rebecca treated his brother, blaming her for the way the Flowers and then the Gerrish's always looked down on them,
*"Least we bain't got no murderess in th'family n if she be found guilty an do ang what be thik family gonna do then?"*

Overseer Clarke was shocked to hear such talk and wondered whether the children might indeed be safer in the Poor House. At least there they would get regular meals and be free from the influence of a family who clearly despised their mother and would not be content until she was either executed or transported. Making his weary way home he was already planning a visit to Henry Ellacombe to discuss urgent arrangements for the children to be removed before further suffering could be inflicted upon them.

As soon as Anne Ellacombe opened the study door William Clarke could see from her husbands cluttered desk that he was very busy and, feeling he was intruding, immediately apologized,
*"I know it would have been more convenient to have made an appointment but I have something of a delicate and urgent nature to discuss that will only take ten minutes of your valuable time."*

Henry Ellacombe rose from his desk and walked towards his visitor, hand outstretched, as he gently guided him into one of two comfortable armchairs in a large sunlit bay window where, once settled with a glass of claret, he assured his visitor,
*"My dear fellow of course you are not interrupting, in fact,"* gesturing towards his untidy desk, *"you call at a very opportune moment as you find me struggling with Sunday's sermon but, at a loss of what to say, I have instead turned my mind to the restoration of the interior of our beautiful Church. What would you think at my suggestion we remove the old double pews in place of, how can I say, new life in their stead, then, once I have sorted out the pews I intend to concentrate on designing a piece of machinery to assist with the ringing of the bells."*

From the impassive, unresponsive look on the face of Overseer Clarke Henry realised there was obviously something much more important to discuss than changing the interior and helping the bell ringers of St Mary's.

The Curate was not surprised at hearing such a pitiful story; Anne had already raised the children's plight from both her own observations and those of the other Sunday School teachers who were witnessing their distress at first hand. Whilst most of the labourers' children attended regularly, the three Worlocks only came when household chores allowed and they were timid scrawny little things, always hungry, poorly clothed and often showing one or two bruises!! Thanks to their near starvation diet any food placed before them swiftly disappeared. During the next hour the two men discussed what they thought was best for the children should their mother be found guilty and how the final outcome would affect everyone. They agreed that, thanks to Bonner and his Broadsheet, both families and the inhabitants of Bitton and Oldland must prepare themselves for a certain amount of notoriety should there be the expected Guilty verdict. As Henry busied himself clearing his desk William sat in silence, shaking his head in disbelief as he read and then re-read the Curate's well thumbed copy of Bonners Broadsheet. Words such as, 'a horrid murder,' and, 'a true and particular account of a most horrid and cruel murder,' leapt out from the page but it was the final paragraph 'the eldest child, who fetched the offending beer, will be giving evidence against her own mother,' that said it all. Both men were in complete agreement about what would happen if Rebecca was to hang….another Bonner Broadsheet would appear along with inquisitive ghouls and hoards of the plain nosey, intent on viewing the 'scene of the horrid crime' for themselves. Harry Bonner claimed Rebecca and Thomas lived very unhappily together because he had only recently discovered she had 'formed an imprudent attachment to another man', but then as now no one knew if such a man existed or whether it was simply a case of a false rumour to increase circulation. Ellacombe promised to do his utmost to ensure the children enjoyed a more bearable life until their mother's fate was sealed after which, fully expecting the death sentence, something of a more permanent nature would have to be arranged.

With William Clarke on his way home Henry abandoned his sermon and his plans for St Mary's and took a slow contemplative walk from the Rectory towards John and Martha's cottage, all the while thinking how he was going to broach such a sensitive subject with an elderly couple who had suffered so much over the years and were only just coming to terms with the possibility their beloved son had been poisoned by his wife.

Late July was proving to be a real heat wave. There had already been tragic loss of life in the north of the County with people collapsing in hayfields or drowning in Mill Ponds and Rivers in desperate attempts to keep cool. John Worlock was not a well man, he had never fully recovered from his sons death and because he was no longer able to attend Church Henry visited him instead, spending many a sweltering roseate evening simply sitting, often in complete silence, drinking Hester's excellent cider or sharing a pinch of snuff as they gazed out across the tiny orchard with its abundance of argumentative hens, snuffling pig and grazing cows. On his last visit he imagined the number of animals seemed to have increased, only to be told that Hester had taken on Rebecca's two cows, numerous chickens and old sow. Choosing his words with great care Henry desperately looked for the best way to tell them the children of their murdered son were suffering, mentally and physically, at the hands of those entrusted to look after them. By the time he finished his unenviable task John was in tears at what he saw was his inability to be the proper head of the family whilst Martha was seething with anger at both her failure to notice what was happening and the callous behaviour of her eldest son and daughter in law because, although it was accepted Sophia was responsible for the care of the children, she believed Robert could and should have intervened,
*"She be is wife after all."*

Although it would not be easy and it would need the support of their daughters still living at home it was agreed for the three children to come and live with them whilst urgent enquiries were made regards a permanent home.

Finally, before returning home, Henry decided to make just one more house call.

Initially Mary Gerrish was very pleased to see the Curate, she did not receive many visitors these days and courteously invited him into the front parlour, a rare honour indeed, until she realised the reason for his visit when her welcome became decidedly cool,

*"Mr Ellacombe surely you cannot expect me, a lady of advancing years, to take on three children I hardly know. They were always made welcome in my home, it was their mother who chose to stop visiting and, as we were never blessed with any of our own, Mr Gerrish could never cope with a young family now, therefore it might be better for them to remain with their own kind or be placed in the Poor House."*

Had Henry not been a gentleman and a man of God he could have argued if only she had not believed every word her husband uttered against his stepdaughter and stood up to him from the very beginning and insisted Rebecca, Thomas and their children be made welcome, then maybe they would not be in the situation that now presented itself and she would not be suggesting her grandchildren might be better off facing life as orphans in the Poor House. Undaunted Henry persisted, if she was not able to offer her grandchildren a home, even on a temporary basis, would she consider contributing towards their care, thus keeping them from the Poor House Gates. At the suggestion she might part with some of her money she indignantly replied,

*"Reverend Ellacombe! since becoming financially embroiled with that dreadful business between Mr Cater and Mr Bevan over my late husband's weir and the death of my brother in law over at Saltford eleven years ago, after yet more legal expense, the Flowers are not so prosperous as they were and there is absolutely no way I will be able to help support those children!"*

Looking at the old woman sitting in front of him, thinning straggly grey hair hidden under an old muslin cap tied tighly under her chin, dressed in a faded pale cream cotton day dress fastened tightly under a sagging bosom, threadbare reticule dangling from an even older belt, an equally drab fichu draped around her hunched shoulders, Henry Ellacombe found it hard to believe that Mary was once regarded as a local beauty, known for wearing elegant pastel coloured clothes, her hair tastefully dressed with matching ribbons and a compassionate heart towards those less fortunate than herself. Henry naturally asked after Peter.

*"Unfortunately he has ridden into Bath on business and plans staying there overnight, otherwise he could have explained our problems himself, however,"* fearful Henry was planning to call and press him with the same questions, *"I cannot say for certain whether Mr Gerrish will be back tomorrow, so it would be better not to call unless absolutely necessary but, if you do, I must insist you do not mention my daughter or my grandchildren because, thanks to that Bonner person and his dreadful publication, my husband is beside himself with rage at the damage such scurrilous lies may have caused to his business plans. In fact that is the very reason he is staying overnight in Bath and although I am far from well and no longer strong enough to travel great distances he has left instructions that we are to leave for Somerset the moment he returns."*

Mary Gerrish' selfish cold-hearted attitude played on Henry's mind and as he strode home the words 'how are the mighty fallen' from the Old Testament in his beloved Bible came to mind when he remembered the story of David in the Second book of Samuel verses 1 to 27. In many ways the mighty Flowers appeared to have somehow fallen since the halcyon days of Lamorock. Now his widow was pleading poverty claiming to be so short of money she was unable to even manage a few pence a week to prevent her three grandchildren entering the Poor House…or was there another reason. Mary had unwittingly confirmed what people were already suggesting and Peter Gerrish, obviously troubled by the report in Bonner's, clearly preferred it was not known that Rebecca was his step daughter. However, as long as her three children remained in the district then so would the stigma and, ultimately, the scandal.

Back at the Rectory, Henry accepted it would be best for all concerned if the Worlock children were found a permanent home with a kind, God fearing family as far away from Bitton as possible and after supper he decided to begin the task of finding such a home, in the meantime however he knew exactly what to use as his text for Sundays sermon. With Peter and Mary Gerrish conveniently away from home he would take those words from Samuel together with some from a quotation first written back in 1672 and preach on how, 'Even though the mighty be fallen they should never forget blood is indeed thicker than water'.

Meanwhile William Clarke, having left another Worlock abode, was making his weary way home also convinced it was now imperative for the three children to be found new homes. Richard and Sophia Jenkins lived near Thomas and Rebecca and had savoured describing what their violent relationship was like, or at least how it appeared through their biased eyes. According to Sophia, *"She hated im an were always puttin im down, she never ad no time for er neighbours til he took ill then she knew she weren't goin t'manage wivout im."*

Apparently the children, who all took after their father in looks, led dreadful lives at the hands of their fiery mother and often escaped next door when *"she ad one on er"* Sophia delighted in adding. However, it was from Richard Jenkins that Mr Clarke learned,

*"She often stormed round to th'Chequers shoutin n ollerin about ow he were wastin er money, afore turning on the reglers sayin ow they oughta be ashamed of emselves."*

Sophia added, barely hiding the sarcasm in her voice,

*"Tis strange ow she were so high n mighty, accusing folk of wastin money buying ale but still spected er muther t'and over zum Flower money, money made from sellin their ale to th'Chequers."*

Returning to Thomas' final illness William Clarke was eager to hear Richard's account, only for Sophia to, once again, interrupt,

*"If she'd ave let im,"* jabbing a finger towards her husband, *"take Thomas to Doctur Watts down Bitton or Doctur Wingrove up Narth Common, stead of makin im go all th'way t'Keynsham he might ave bin saved!"*

Richard confirmed, once over at Keynsham it was Rebecca who did all the talking, apologising to Doctor Edwards for wasting his valuable time before he even had chance to either speak to or examine her poor husband, how he knew what Thomas was like and how he never 'thought of anyone but himself!' Richard also said that, during the days leading up to her husband's death, Rebecca repeatedly refused to send for John and Martha insisting there was no need because he would recover like he always did, but when she discovered Sophia had sent for them behind her back her initial response was to declare she couldn't cope with, 'a cripple and that fat old woman up here getting in her way,' only to change her mind and declare, 'well at least she'll be able to look after him.'

*"Mrs Jenkins, was Rebecca referring to your mother?"*

*"Course she were, she didn't wanna care fur our Thomas any more than she ad too, she never ad since the day they wuz married so why bovver now he were dyin?"*

Two days later William Clarke called on Doctor Watts who also agreed it would have made more sense to have brought Thomas to him rather than make him endure the journey to Keynsham but, in view what he already knew about the couple along with what he had since learned, he wondered whether it was just another way for Rebecca to add further pain to her long suffering husband. Yes, he knew the Worlocks and yes, he always found Mrs Worlock a very difficult woman to deal with but then so did everyone else and yes, he had examined all three of her children a few months earlier when she brought them to see him demanding a powder for the itch in their groin.

*"And did you prescribed a powder?"*

*"Yes, I gave her enough for three treatments."*

*"And would you consider the powder to be in any way dangerous if swallowed?"*

*"Certainly, as would any powder" but Mrs Worlock assured me she would be using it immediately, therefore I felt there was no danger of that happening."*

*"If she had mixed this powder into her husband's jug of ale could it have caused his death?"*

Doctor Watts thought for a while,
*"On its own probably not, just severe sickness but mixed with another substance and his already failing health then,"* raising his eyebrows, *"who knows?"*

Recalling the opening of the body prior to the Coroner's Inquest, William Clarke reminded Doctor Watts he had testified the cause of death was poison, was that still the case….

*"Oh yes, there is absolutely no doubt, Thomas Worlock was definitely poisoned!"* was the Doctors emphatic reply.

# CHAPTER THIRTEEN

Pushing the bowl of thin tepid fatty liquid away from her, Rebecca thought,
*"How on earth do they expect me to eat this?"*

It was all very well for the Chaplain to boast how he was there yesterday when each prisoner was served with 8oz of fine boiled beef and claim today's so called nourishing pea soup was made from the leftovers…he was not expected to eat it or go hungry. One spoonful was enough, it was just as unsavoury as all the food in this place and if the cleric had indeed spied some fine beef then it certainly was not offered to her nor had its gravy gone into the stock for this disgusting soup because the mouthful she misguidedly swallowed tasted like the remains of highly spiced peppered gristle. Whatever the ingredients the result was as inedible as the lump of hard stale bread that accompanied it.

Lying on her bed later, hunger brought on her bad dreams again and she was back home feasting on her own bread, cheese and milk from her cows and little eggs from her chickens, even the scraggy bits of meat Thomas brought home tasted better than the meat on offer here. At the thought of her dead husband and their life together her mind drifted back to when Mamma, always eager to please Papa, made it perfectly clear his business friends came first and she was constantly encouraged to *"go down to Martha's if you are that bored,"* which was how she first got to, *"know"* him. Resting against the cold stone wall, eyes closed, arms crossed tightly around her raised knees drawn up under her chin, she remembered the exciting weeks before and just after their marriage when he had been such a caring passionate man before the drink got to him and he became a violent, insatiable, demanding bully. He knew there were others before him although he never asked who they were and it was only when she said her illness was a miscarriage that he decided, because no one knew she was with child, there never was any baby and it was just another of her lies. All he had cared about was getting back into her bed, such was his eagerness to follow in his revered brothers' footsteps and produce another Worlock boy for the family business. She was sure his treatment was the reason it had taken so long for her to give him a live child, only to be blamed when it was a girl instead of the desired boy. Looking for a scapegoat Rebecca found one in Martha and began muttering to herself,
*"Of course she never dared speak to her precious son about his selfish behaviour towards me, but that was only to be expected considering she was continually brow beaten by John and all her other sons. Just like all the other*

*ill bred women in the village she was expected to compliantly fuss and fret over her men. "*

Thinking back, she convinced herself how her mother in law was not the only one to tell lies. Thomas had been less than honest about the success of the family butcher's business, in the vain hope he would be accepted into her mother's circle of friends. If only he knew how they ridiculed him and his vulgar ways behind his back. He was not and never would be what was expected as a suitable husband for her and it was obvious now why Mamma and Peter had been so against the misalliance. On the other hand it was abundantly clear the Worlocks greedily thought there was much to gain financially from her family, which was probably why they raised no objections.

Opening her tear stained eyes, she took in her dreadful surroundings. Hers was a lonely existence. She could see other women walking about the yard and day cells arm in arm, talking and laughing. No one came to her with a hand of friendship, even the gaolers treated her with indifference, choosing to approach her only to bark their orders. In the laundry the Task Master continued to threaten the oakum table should he catch her shirking. The Chaplain persisted in his futile attempts to get a confession, both Wiltons ignored her sufferings and were refusing to endorse any further comforts and she had long given up insisting the Governor move her to another cell. Taking a deep breath Rebecca sighed as she again muttered to herself,
*"Heaven forbid that I should ever agree with that milksop my mother married but he was right, I should have chosen one of my distant Somerset cousins. Who knows, I might have been mistress of my own house with servants instead of suffering a drunkard who treated me as little more than a common skivvy and expected me to live in a hovel. "*

How conveniently she forgot her present trials and tribulations were a direct result of her own selfish actions. No one forced her to pursue and marry Thomas and no one planned for her to end up in Gloster Gaol about to go on trial for his murder; so maybe it would have indeed been better if she had chosen someone more suitable and acceptable to her family.

Rebecca knew the real reason there had been no reply to the two short notes she had been permitted to send to her mother was probably Peter, whom she was convinced was making her suffer as punishment for thwarting his plans to marry her off to someone of his choosing instead of allowing herself to be seduced by an illiterate Worlock. In truth Peter, recognising Rebecca's untidy scrawling hand on the tell tale parchment, Mr Symmonds seal on the back, ensured they were never seen by Mary, quickly despatching them to the back of the fire where he felt they belonged.

Rubbing her neck and shoulders, as if erasing another imaginary beating, she was not even sure she ever loved Thomas in quite the same way he plainly loved her, especially after the early days, but no matter how hard she tried all she could remember was how swiftly she grew to hate him once she had snared him into the marriage she needed to escape her tyrannical young stepfather. Then, within weeks of their wedding, his refusal to employ the promised domestic servant and his callous treatment gave her the excuse to claim to have suffered a miscarriage after which what little love there was died. Even Mary Ann, Honor and John were conceived, not through mutual love but from drunken lust on his part and cold unfeeling duty on hers.

Thinking about the Coroner's Inquest, how could she ever forget being denied the chance to defend herself against the accusations of the people she once looked on as friends. She would be the first to admit she always expected her own way, hadn't Mamma warned her it would get her into real trouble one day, but what was so wrong in wanting her brute of a husband to remain so weak he would leave her alone. How was she to know that pennyroyal mixed with a small pinch of the powder Doctor Watts had given her for the children's itch, despite being told on no account must it be swallowed due to its harmful nature, stirred into his ale would fail to keep him away from her. In desperation there really had been no alternative but to increase the dosage knowing his health would deteriorate, when that also failed what else could she do but gradually add more and more of Mrs Stephen's rat poison, never believing she would kill him.

Four months incarceration in Gloster Gaol had given Rebecca time to reflect and consider what her defence would be when the time came. She would explain how she never planned for things to go so badly wrong, if only Mary Ann had not returned with that accursed message from George Hook she would have had ample time to fix the beer with just a tiny amount of rat poison leaving the remainder for another time. Instead she had no choice but to pour all the powder into the nearest thing to hand…the mug of beer. She planned to throw the poisoned ale away once Mary Ann had left to look for her brother and sister and, going against all her beliefs, walk to The Chequers herself for a fresh jug but, as she recalled, Thomas was in a foul mood that day and demanded she give him, *"thik beer now or thees'll feel the back o my and so God elp me!,"* so, not wishing to receive another beating but wanting to teach him a lesson he would never forget,
*"I did exactly as I was bid!"* she whispered to herself.

By the end of July the Overseers had spent many hours preparing all the desired documents for Rex v Rebecca Worlock for Murder at Gloucester Summer

Assize, between them they had drawn up the indictment, prepared fifteen copies as requested by Mr Ludlow. Next they retained a local Solicitor, Mr Osborne, to gain his views and to ask him to assist Mr Ludlow by opening the case in Court. Like his colleague, before making up his mind Osborne asked for copies of all the paperwork then, once he was familiar with the situation, William Clarke spent some time listening to his initial opinion. In early August, William Clarke joined Henry and Anne Ellacombe for luncheon in the Rectory garden before spending over two hours taking very long particulars of evidence during which their conversation once more turned to the future of the three children, currently living with John and Martha, should their mother hang.

Anne Ellacombe assured him,

*"Well Mr Clarke you will be pleased to learn that since their return to their grandparents there have been no more bruises and they appear to be eating better because we no longer see them ravenously clearing their plates but, whilst the younger girl and the boy are beginning to smile and appear to enjoy Sunday School, Mr Shipp has expressed concern over the eldest child. She rarely speaks unless spoken to and when she does it is in a quiet almost scared little voice. She rarely joins in any of the classes but chooses to sit quite alone in a corner gazing at the pictures in a Bible Story book to which, I understand, she has taken a great fancy."*

Three days later, with less than two weeks to go until The Summer Assize, the Overseers were frantically making sure all the witnesses were aware of their part in the proceedings. William Clarke returned to The Rectory to serve Henry with his Subpoena adding how he intended to call on John and Martha to serve Mary Ann with hers before going home via Richard Jenkins to serve him with his. The mention of John and Martha's granddaughter prompted Henry to advocate,

*"William, take great care with the child, thanks to a certain Aunt, who should have known better, she is absolutely terrified of being responsible for condemning her mother."*

Although their father's sister, their other Aunt Sophia, had taken care of the three children during the first terrible hours following their father's death and treated them kindly, Mary Ann was fully aware, from overheard conversations, of her father's dreadful final hours and her mother's apparent utter contempt for him. Sadly, by the time she had been allowed to see him he was past knowing who she was. Placing her rough chubby hand on William Clarke's steadying arm Martha Worlock tearfully whispered,

*"Tis no wonder she be suffrin so when she d'know er words cud send er mother to th'gallows?"*

The Overseers now concentrated on the medical evidence, particularly the differences of opinion between the three Doctors following the Post Mortem and as Doctor Watts had already given his version that just left Doctors Edwards and Wingrove. Hiring a horse, William Clark first made his way up to North Common to see Doctor Wingrove. During the two hours the men spent together William Wingrove stubbornly refused to change his story,

*"Thomas Worlock's vital organs gave all the signs of having been poisoned. I have seen many cadavers during my medical career and I know a poisoned corpse when I see one,"* was his resolute answer.

When the Overseer tactfully suggested Roger Edwards might disagree, it quickly brought about the response,

*"My opinion was and still is that the cause of death was poison,"* adding, a touch tetchily, *"but as I cannot speak for Roger Edwards maybe it would be best to ask him yourself!"*

The end of another weary day saw William Clarke arrive home late in the afternoon, but even then his work was far from done as he sat down to write to Doctor Edwards, requesting an appointment to discuss his evidence concerning the 'Worlock Matter'.

The following morning found William back in the saddle wearily travelling over to Keynsham where, after a further two hours, he left with another written statement. Roger Edwards was still not completely satisfied that the cause of death was poison, considering past medical history and the fact Thomas had been told on more than one occasion to stop drinking or it would be the death of him. Nor was he convinced the powder Thomas produced, claiming to have saved it from being thrown away by Rebecca, was poison because it was brown in colour and, *"Worlock claimed to have seen white stuff floating in his beer,"* whilst, *"the sample I examined was of vegetable extract, almost like hops, something you might expect to find in cheap ale."*

At the insistence of his wife, Overseer Clarke spent the next few days at home. He was no longer a young man and she could clearly see the stress and strain of so much travelling, along with the worry of ensuring nothing was overlooked, beginning to take its toll. After two good nights sleep and a few days rest the Overseers met again to decide how to interview the remaining few witnesses. Elizabeth Amey, who lived with Mrs Stephens in her Apothecary Shop in Kingswood Hill, and Doctor Watts, were served with their Subpoenas after which they concentrated on preparing more legal briefs, fifteen in all, before drawing up and dispatching a final fair copy to Messrs. Ludlow and Osborne. Everything was as ready as it would ever be and both men prepared to leave Bitton for Gloucester and The Summer Assize; they planned being away from home for some seven days, but before leaving they made one more brief visit to John and Martha to ensure Mary Ann was still willing, however reluctantly, to appear before the Court as planned. Satisfied, they took their leave knowing the child would return either with her mother a free woman or with the dreadful news she had been condemned. Sensibly, under the circumstances and after the briefest of discussions, both men agreed now would not be a good time to visit Mr and Mrs Gerrish!

Behind the grey, unforgiving walls of Gloster Gaol hidden away in her dank, dismal cell deep within the Penitentiary Rebecca waited, still not completely accepted by everyone thanks to her occasional airs of misguided grandeur, with no idea whatsoever about how she was going to defend herself, apart from pleading she had suffered at the hands of a violent husband whom she was sure would one day beat her to death. She had long accepted there would be no defence lawyer, even though her mother could have easily paid for one. The only person who probably understood was The Chaplain who, undaunted, resolutely continued meeting her in the Chapel, ever hopeful of a confession. With time running out he was persistent if nothing else, visiting her every other day before returning to his lonely room to complete his Journal and observe, *"Visited Worlock in the Chapel again, she is extremely stupid and incurable of her dangerous position."*

In the Penitentiary life was one of constant drudgery and hard labour with only short breaks for the most disgusting tasting food imaginable. Once a week, when the Chaplain was present, eight ounce portions of tough indigestible beef and vegetables miraculously appeared on their plates; he should be here on other days and see what was served then. Since her arrival more than thirty prisoners had fallen ill and several had been taken to the Infirmary in Southgate Street suffering from diarrhoea and bilious attacks. Rebecca still disliked the Chaplain intently and suffered his tedious sermons under duress, knowing the alternative was 'solitary'. By deliberately sitting at the back of the Chapel she always managed to leave before he saw her and sent one of the turnkeys to fetch her in order to persevere in his desire for her to make a full confession. Although it had backfired once or twice and she ended up on bread and water for being insolent, she knew if she could convince the elder Dr.Wilton she was starving there might be extra mutton broth again and, what's more, he was also known to prescribe the odd wine glass of cheap brandy, mixed with a mild sleeping draught, for those more *"excitable"* prisoners …Well, she thought, *"I can be as excitable as any other prisoner…if I choose."*

However, there were times when attending Chapel could be interesting. Those who refused to wash or shave on Sundays and regularly missed morning worship were denied their daily ration of bread, therefore petty thieving from those who complied was a frequent occurrence. Occasionally the Chaplains' regular banal sermons were enlivened by a few hard liners who chose to sit in the front pews intent on disrupting proceedings. Should they create too much mayhem the Governor would have them forcibly removed and punished, after which The Chaplain entered his thanks in his Journal for the 'efficient way' in which Mr Symmonds acted in removing those, 'determined to spoil Divine service.....Alleluia, praise be'!

Despite Prison Rules that decreed, *"Prisoners must wash every day and take a bath when ordered by the Surgeon,"* all the women, including Rebecca, were lousy and infested with fleas and lice. Not one of them was totally free from a foul itch, running sores, boils, eye infections, scrofulous tumours or stinking abscesses on their bodies. However, neither Wiltons were duped into excusing them from their labours, instead they were taken to the prison infirmary, consisting of two rooms, three cells and a dispensary, where the unfortunate women were applied with bread and water poultices and given disgusting medicines, often against their will, to clear the system. In extreme cases of diarrhoea their buttocks were blistered and a fomentation applied to their feet. Occasionally, however, there were those whom no one would ever be able to help. Anne Hawkins, for example, was already lousy when she arrived to join Rebecca and Prudence after Nancy was released and things did not improve even after one of Dr. Wilton's special welcoming baths. Naturally she was not allowed to keep her own clothes but was given a complete set of prison uniform including a spencer, though it was summertime and not really necessary. Still refusing to wash, even her hands or face, the old woman claimed she would never recover so long as she was sharing a cell with a murderess and a thief. Knowing she would never get her own way and poignantly reminded how history appeared to be repeating itself, Rebecca and Prudence listened intently as first the Governor, then the Surgeons dismissed her various complaints, ordering another bath and a further set of clean prison uniform instead. Returning to his room Wilton Snr. sat down to write his Surgeons Journal, *"Told her she was getting no better because of her refusal to wash and that her complaint would heal. Neither my directions nor her own suffering can induce her to correct,"* adding a few days later, *"very chesty and clamorous, hit out with fists, I am convinced she is sane, however, in a straight jacket for her own safety but told her I was not deceived by her apparent insanity."*

Within twenty four hours 'Crazy Annie', as she had been cruelly nicknamed by the others, was gone and Rebecca and Prudence prepared to welcome a new face amid rumours *"Annie"* had been confined to the Lunatic Asylum, 'for her own good.'

Back in her cell after another exhausting days labour and a most unpleasant meal of salt rice and gruel mixed with pepper and ginger, all Rebecca craved was sleep in the hope all her worries about next week would leave her head. She was therefore not expecting any visitors. Apart from her brothers' disastrous visit she could not remember the last time anyone had willingly wanted to enter this place to see her but, swiftly running her grubby hands through her dirty, lice ridden hair, splashing cold water on her tired face, she threw her old shawl around her shoulders and followed an increasingly impatient gaoler.

Two men waiting in the Committee Room, the part of the Gaol specially set aside for visiting Magistrates and Lawyers, decorously rose to their feet as Rebecca entered. This pleased her no end, as did the revelation from Mr Twiss, the younger of the two, that he was her defence council, *"and this gentleman,"* gesturing towards a short, shabbily dressed man standing behind him, *"is my clerk."*

Feeling an immediate lift to her spirits, thinking her mother had finally decided to help her, she mistook Twiss for a junior, employed by her family's Solicitor, and enquired,
*"But, where is Mr Parker?"* adding, with an air of superior disbelief, *"for I fear he has left it very late to prepare a strong defence."*

Both men appeared slightly indifferent and it was left to Mr Twiss to explain, *"I am afraid I am not familiar with a Mr Parker."*

Undaunted, believing he had probably been retained by her mother without Peter's knowledge, Rebecca inwardly questioned,
*"Is this the best Mamma could get for her money, a bungling fool and a dwarf?"* but, reluctantly grateful nonetheless, she urged, *"very well Mr Twiss you will have to do I suppose."* Indicating for them to sit down Rebecca ordered, *"Come, we have very little time to waste, there is much you need to know if we are to secure my freedom next wee...."*

Raising a hand to stop her mid sentence Mr Twiss said softly but very firmly.

*"I feel you do not fully appreciate the situation, I have been retained at such short notice and so inadequately briefed there cannot possibly be an effective defence but,"* with an air of resignation in his voice he glanced at his clerk before saying, *"we will do our utmost with the time and evidence we have to plead for transportation rather than execution."*

*"You are obviously expecting me to be found guilty just like the rest of them,"* was all Rebecca could bleakly manage to say, such was her despair at hearing his dismissive assumption, *"clearly my mother has only employed you at the last minute in an effort to look good amongst her friends back in Bitton, that*

*way they will at least believe she did her best by providing me with a barrister, however incompetent."*

*"Mrs Worlock, your mother has not retained us. We, I mean Mr Twiss, is here to offer you the simple defence your family has thought fit not to provide,"* was the clerk's cautious, slightly embarrassed reply, *"and you must understand from the evidence set before us it is highly unlikely any Jury will find you innocent."*

His pessimism was well founded. He knew her trial would be hurried over in one day and whilst Mr Twiss would be able to cross-examine all the witnesses currently gathering in Bitton he would not be allowed to directly address the Jury. He was also familiar with the behaviour of the wily prosecution counsel, Mr Ludlow, and knew he would present evidence of which they had been kept in ignorance.

Rebecca felt a familiar wave of anger surge through her. Well if the best she could expect was transportation then she would defend herself and turning to the fawning pair before her, in their old breeches and gaiters, threadbare coats and foul neck cloths about their be-whiskered chins, she stood to leave but not before defiantly announcing,

*"Pray do not concern yourselves on my account gentlemen, I shall inform the Judge of my dreadful sufferings endured at the hands of a brute of a husband myself. I will readily confess how I was convinced he would one day kill me and was forced to do something to save not only myself but also my innocent children from his constant rage. His Lordship will surely take pity on me and see I was a much aggrieved injured woman,"* as she rambled so her words were getting louder and louder and at times incoherent,

*"Mrs Worlock!!!"* Twiss shouted, forehead glistening with sweat his voice raised in mounting anger, *"let me make one thing absolutely clear, you will not, do you hear, not be permitted to say anything at your trial, that,"* added with more than a hint of self gratification, *"is why I have accepted your defence, do you understand!"* his voice now risen to its climatic crescendo.

What the lawyer and his clerk conveniently omitted to say was how they had been chosen, at random, by an unimportant court official earlier in the day who, knowing how much Assize Court Judges appreciated the niceties of a mediocre defence, decided it would look good for Prisoner Worlock, if not his own future career, to have some vestige of an answer, however hopeless the cause. The pair standing before Rebecca came from an itinerant band of inexperienced lawyers and their shabby clerks who pursued Circuit Court Judges competing for cheap briefs that might pay a guinea or so, considering themselves fortunate to get one that paid half that amount.

In early August Sir Edwin Bayntun Sandys, High Sheriff for Gloucestershire, travelled from Miserdon Park, his family home near Cirencester, to await the arrival of His Honour Sir John Richardson and his entourage. Sir John, who would be sitting in judgement over the Summer Assize, began his long legal career in 1793 at the age of twenty two. Twenty five years later he was appointed a Serjeant at Law and knighted by the Prince Regent himself at Carlton House the following year. Sir Edwin met His Honour's entourage on the outskirts of Gloucester and escorted the party to his lodgings where, in view of the long journey and his failing health, Sir John took a well earned rest. Later he was to be lavishly dined by all the dignitaries and splendour the Gloucestershire County elite could muster. Sir Edwin, resplendent in his blue velvet Court Dress, magnificent embroidered waistcoat and black satin breeches and Lady Sandys, equally radiant in an exquisite gown bedecked with jewels, entertained Sir John's party to an evening of dining, friendly harmony and mutual good company. Later, once the ladies had left, when he realised the calendar of prisoners stretched to nearly fifty, of which six were women, Sir John strongly hinted to those assembled gentlemen who were to make up his Juries how he expected them to keep within the allotted time because he had promised his wife, the Lady Harriet, they would take a holiday in Malta where he was working on drafting a code of laws for the island and suggested half an hour as an acceptable time to spend on each deliberation.

Next day, it being the start of the Summer Assize, everyone attended divine service at the magnificent Cathedral and pondered over His Grace The Bishop of Gloucester's usual blood curdling Assize Sermon before, after much coming and going, eighteen more notables, eager to fulfil their duty as jurymen, gathered in readiness.

Meanwhile, a few hundred yards away behind the grey walls of Gloster Gaol, the Chaplain was making his own arrangements and, much to the relief of most of the inmates, had already omitted morning prayers on account of The Assize.

Nine witnesses, including Mary Ann, had lumbered their way from Bitton crammed into Isaac Huntly's hired cart. With barely room for the driver on the box, Richard Jenkins had perched precariously on the rumble, such was the lack of space and, with the Parish footing the bill, a reluctance to pay for second one. After several stops and changes of horses the weary travellers eventually reached The Green Dragon, a less than salubrious hostelry in Southgate Street, their home for how ever long it took to decide Rebecca's fate. Doctors Edwards, Watts & Wingrove, Reverend Ellacombe and the two Overseers travelled separately whilst William Joyner Ellis joined them in time for supper, after which everyone prepared for the day they would stand in front of Sir John and testify how Rebecca had, in their opinion, murdered her husband.

At last the party was complete and, warned not to discuss their part in the trial with anyone, they eagerly took full advantage of the hospitality on offer. Mary Ann was given into the safe hands of Sarah Butler not, as expected, Aunt Sophia Jenkins. Henry Ellacombe believed it would be best for the child to be kept away from her family less she over hear unnecessary distressing comments about her parents. The child was to play an important part in the proceedings and no one knew how she would react when she saw her mother again after four months.

Under strict orders to attend Gloucester County Court on the first day of the Assize and to remain ready to be called at a moment's notice, Rebeccas' accusers dutifully presented themselves at the Courthouse every day during the first week. Now, as they entered the second, the small room set aside for them was slowly losing its attraction. Overflowing with every kind of inhumanity such a place could attract, it was little wonder skirmishes broke out. Drinking, smoking, gambling and all kinds of depravity regularly took place in quiet corners in an attempt at easing the boredom. In the case of *"Rex v Rebecca Worlock for Murder"* it was also unfortunate that, along with those eager to point their accusing finger in her direction, one or two men of straw arrived from Bitton eager to give their support in her favour.... ....provided the price was right.

Rebecca, meanwhile, waited in vain for a further visit from Mr Twiss, for another chance to plead to be allowed to speak at her trial, remembering how he had spent their first and only meeting telling her there was very little chance of an acquittal because the evidence against her was so strong, especially since it was rumoured her own daughter was the prosecution's main witness. Now, with only days to go and no return visit, she assumed their next meeting would probably be in Court.

With the dawn light of Monday August 14th two very different scenes unfolded within yards of each other. In her cell, far from yet so very close to those she had ever loved or cared for, a dishevelled, desperate Rebecca prepared for her day in Court. Deep in her thoughts she failed to see a surly gaoler standing in the doorway, sneering pleasure coming from her rasping voice as she barked, *"I gotta messuge fur thee, frum thy legul man!"* Rushing about the dark cell Rebecca frantically scrambled to make herself tidy, anxious to appear decent when Mr Twiss arrived, only for the guard to cruelly stop her in her tracks by snarling, *"Bain't no use changing thy clothes, cuz he bain't yer he just sid he wants thee to tek a bath afore thee leaves an th'Guvner says t'give ee these,"* tossing a set of prison issue uniform onto the bed.

When she first arrived in this hell hole Rebecca carried a small bundle containing, amongst other things, Aunt Partridge's precious green, red and gold damask gown which she intended wearing in Court. Miraculously it had remained safely hidden. Now she was being told the Governor was insisting she wore prison uniform.

Aware of how her day in Court would end and probably because she was speaking civilly to him for a change, Mr Symmonds listened sympathetically as Rebecca, freshly washed but woefully untidy in her ill-fitting uniform, pleaded to be allowed to wear her great aunt's gown,

*"It is the only thing I have to remind me of my family. My young daughter will be in Court today and we have not seen each other for such a long time, please allow me to wear something she has seen before so I will not be a complete stranger to her."*

Unwrapping her precious bundle, hidden for so long under her bed, Rebecca stared in dismay at the crumpled heap of brightly coloured damask. Things did not improve when she put it on, it hung loosely about her shoulders accentuating her dramatic weight loss. Unable to suppress the tears she fell back onto the edge of her bed, head in her hands and for the first time in four dreadful months sobbed uncontrollably. Feeling a gentle arm around her quivering shoulders she glanced up to see Prudence, her cellmate for all those months, sitting next to her. The bewildered look on her face brought about a simple answer to unasked questions,

*"Nun of us as sin thee cry real tears afore, you always made us think theese were a cold artless woman, wiv no feelins but, watchin thee now, you bain't no diffrunt frum the rest of us."*

Rebecca found herself whimpering, *"thank you, thank you so very much,"* as other prisoners crowded about her holding her shaking hands, placing arms around her trembling shoulders as they encouraged her, all the time hiding the nagging doubt in their voices as they assured her,

*"Th'Jurys bowned t'believe thy story and you'll be ome wiv thy children afore nightfall."*

Reality, however, was a very different matter. Rebecca was amongst habitual petty criminals who had seen many, charged with lesser crimes than hers, come but rarely leave unscathed through the secure wooden gates of Gloster Gaol. They knew there was little chance of freedom or transportation to another life on the other side of the world and by the end of today's shenanigans she would be in the Condemned Cell awaiting the hangman instead of celebrating an expected happy family reunion. May God have mercy on her poor unhappy soul because she would never see any of her family again!

Matron and The Governor came for her at seven, by which time Prudence and the others had found and adapted a piece of old ribbon into a makeshift belt giving Aunt Partridge's legacy some shape, the remaining excess material fell loosely over her hips and was partially hidden by the large shapeless coat. Mr Symmonds, whilst agreeing to her wearing the gown and coat, insisted she appeared tidy and presentable in every other way and so, in return, Rebecca said she was willing to wear a fresh muslin cap from amongst the discarded uniform, which hid most of her now greying hair, exchange her old worn out clogs for a decent pair of prison issue and put on a clean pair stockings to save her the indecency of exposing bare ankles. Sadly, the finished outfit was bereft of any bonnet. The one she had brought with her had not survived the long months of incarceration and it was the one thing her friends could not find for her.

She shuffled from the day room, feet in manacles, to a cacophony of shouts, whistles and cheers until, reaching the door leading to the exercise yard and ultimately the outside world, she turned to wave a last goodbye knowing she would never return here nor see any of its occupants again.

Around the corner and not for the first time during this Assize, the Courtroom was filling up at an alarming rate; such was the curiosity in sending poor unfortunate souls to the Gallows. Though there was no sign of Judge, Jury or Prisoner the crowd was already impatiently jostling for places. Outside in the foyer Rebeccas' brothers hastily made their way towards the seats specially reserved for the families of both defendant and victim. Like those at The Green Dragon they had also been in Gloucester desperately waiting for today to arrive. However they had sensibly chosen to avoid the others by taking a room at The Ram, a Coaching Inn in Northgate Street, instead. By arriving early they knew they would be spared the discomfort of sitting near Peter Gerrish or, worse still, the heartbreak and wrath of the Worlocks. Fortunately, although it was still very early and there were not many seats to be had, they found four immediately behind the dock facing directly towards the Judge's bench. Now, when their stepfather or their childhood friends arrived, they would be obliged to sit elsewhere. With a sigh of relief they saw Robert and George Worlock walk into the Courtroom without their ailing father or the unstable Samuel and thanked God they were spared having to meet or sit with them but that did not stop them sensing the Worlocks' eyes burning into the backs of their necks as they heard them take their places a couple of rows behind. To their right, as they faced the bench, they saw the Jury assembling and prayed they would listen fairly and justly to their sister's plight. Directly opposite the Jury elegant strangers, personal friends of Sir John and Sir Edwin, were taking their seats in the especially reserved section, scented handkerchiefs to their delicate noses, such was the stench. Behind these fashionable dandies any remaining seats were swiftly being taken by the cream of Gloucestershire Society and those who, from sheer curiosity, willingly paid for the privilege of watching the trial of possibly only the sixth woman to be sentenced to hang in Gloster since the Gaol opened almost thirty years ago.

Naturally Lady Sandys and her houseguests were there. As the wife of the High Sheriff she had been busily planning her Assize House Party for months. There had been concerts, plays and even a ball but today was the culmination of all her efforts... the last day of the Summer Assize and the rare chance to witness the trial of a murderess. In her excitement her Ladyship was overheard explaining to one of her guests,
*"I know not who is to be tried here today but she may hang and we ladies have been making great preparations for dressing,"* leading a bemused French visitor sitting close by to observe to his indifferent neighbour alongside him,
*"I fear you people look upon these meetings as a sort of family party, is that not so my friend?"*

Behind Robert and George, high up in the Public Gallery on uncomfortable wooden benches, people were pushing, jostling and fighting for seats. Women, some with babies at the breast, scrambled for the remaining seats, consumptive street sellers coughed and spluttered whilst the odour of unwashed illiterate labourers alongside their equally filthy wives contributed to an unhealthy atmosphere of stinking putrid air. In the foyer no amount of fighting, arguing or shouting could persuade the hard pressed Ushers to allow any more into the overcrowded Courtroom. It was already full to capacity, people were crammed in the stairwells, passageways and doorways such was their determination to get in because, as one regular was heard explaining.

*"T'aint evry day we gets t'see a murderess!"*

Out of sight, in the crowded claustrophobic room set aside for witnesses, young Mary Ann Worlock was suffering such agonies as she never thought possible. In fact Doctor Watts questioned whether the child was physically strong enough for the day's traumatic events. She was refusing to eat; last night and this morning she had only agreed to drink some warm milk because Henry Ellacombe warned her Granny Martha would be very angry to hear she was refusing to eat. The Overseers paced the floor like a pair of expectant fathers, convinced they had forgotten something. In another part of the building Mr

Ludlow and Mr Osbourne nonchalantly sat in two comfortable armchairs preparing to enter Court, already congratulating themselves on obtaining a conviction, such was their confidence of Rebecca's guilt and the inexperience of the unfortunate Mr Twiss.

Meanwhile back in the Penitentiary Rebecca, shadowed by two turnkeys, reached the exercise yard where a decrepit covered wagon was waiting. Glancing at the cart she was reminded how even the poorest farm labourer back home in Bitton had better than this. Waiting alone by the wooden steps at the rear she assumed the driver and gaoler standing alongside were gentlemen and looked for an arm to hand her up; when no such help was forthcoming she realised, as with the rest of her life, she was entirely on her own and clambered aboard all the while hampered by a large amount of unwanted damask.. Fear and the overpowering stench of the previous occupants met her as she took her place on the hard wooden plank reaching across the back of the cart and she instinctively held a trembling hand to her mouth in an attempt to stem the urge to be sick. Even the guard who took his place next to her, placing handcuffs to her wrists, was forced to reluctantly admit,
*"They baint s'brave when tis time t'pay fur their crimes!"*

Unlike earlier times, when she faked illness just to get her own way, this time her head swirled as everything before her began to spin until, unable to stop herself, Rebecca felt herself sliding towards her companion as her head fell sideways on to his shoulder. On a longer journey both the Gaoler, and his companion at the reigns, would have taken full advantage of the situation, Rebecca would not have been the first female prisoner the pair had raped in the back of a prison cart. However there was no way he intended to miss such an opportunity as this!

Feeling hands roughly exploring under her skirt, Rebecca assumed they belonged to Thomas and knew if she readily submitted it would soon be over. As they lumbered along Rebecca sensed there were no familiar sounds coming from the nearby docks, nor was there any fresh air seeping into the wagon, even the noise from the horses' hooves was different.

Within minutes of the cart shuddering to a halt sounds of locks opening, followed by men's voices, could be heard as the back opened up and she was ordered to get out. This time there were no shortage of rough grabbing hands as she was manhandled to the ground. Temporarily left on her own as the unwary occupants of another cart, from Northleach House of Correction, received the same welcome, Rebecca had time to cast her eyes around what appeared to be an enclosed stable yard, not dissimilar to the one at the back of The Chequers, with cobble stones under foot, bags of hay hanging on dirty lime washed walls and numerous stone buildings hidden behind locked doors. Turning her attention from the cart she spied a large dark archway and, looking closer, could just make out burning torches secured to the wall and wondered whether it might be stabling. With barely time to enjoy the fresh air she was dragged towards one of the locked doors and down a dark flight of stone steps. As she stumbled she tried to stop the searching hands of her two guards as they too found their way all over her body but, with her wrists securely manacled behind her, resistance was useless. She tried to scream out but as she opened her mouth it was immediately covered by a filthy hand along with the words she never thought to hear again.

*"Bide thy tongue ur else!"*

Their lust satisfied she was thrown into a windowless room before being forced into a cell, no bigger than her pantry at home, with hardly any room in which to move and only a small plank across the back wall on which to sit. Ordered to, *"sit thur and don't make no fuss, dos ear!,"* she was handed over to another pair of tormentors as the first two disappeared, no doubt eager to assault another poor unsuspecting soul. Outside her cell the large dark communal room, lit only by a small burning torch high up on a wall, was full of common prostitutes, pickpockets, horse thieves and all the vulgarity the County had thought to throw into the simmering cauldron known as the Summer Assize. Along one wall was a small blackened fire place which, as it was mid summer, mercifully was not lit because the heat in this underground cavern was already overbearing. From the depths of a dark corner came pitiful moans and groans of someone or something in a great deal of pain and anguish…afraid to leave her cell to investigate Rebecca sat in silence hoping the poor creature, for she was convinced the noise was not human, would soon be put out of its misery. Cruelly the noise did not come from the mouth of any animal but from one of six ragged vagabonds, drunks and lunatics, barely alive as they huddled together on a cold unforgiving flagstone floor in a pit about five foot deep, waiting their moment before a Magistrate.

Rebecca knew from the muffled sounds that the Courtroom was directly above her and suspected her brothers, brothers in law and step father were probably there. Deep in thought she was not expecting her cell door to be slammed, trapping her in complete darkness. Overcome with fear she screamed, kicked and clawed at the door till her hands, now free of it's shackles, were red raw, begging them to open it or else she would be dead before reaching the dock.

After what seemed like an eternity someone opened the tiny Judas hole and a man's voice gruffly yelled,
*"Shut thyself up or else!"*

Pounding frantically on the door she pleaded with whoever owned the voice to show some mercy and allow her to relieve herself. When the door was finally unlocked she collapsed exhausted at the feet of her faceless tormentor as a large wooden slop bucket was left outside her cell and it was made clear if she intended to use it then, just like solitary, she was expected to squat in front of the assembled rabble. Suitably relieved, they mercifully relented and allowed her a small rush light candle whilst agreeing for the Judas hole to be left open, reasoning she would not be in their company for long because word was ...

*"Judge be on is way."*

Staring at her bruised bloodstained hands Rebecca wondered how much longer she was to endure such inhumane treatment and what she had done to deserve such cruelty, conveniently forgetting that in the eyes of a Coroner's Jury and the Worlocks she was guilty of murder! However, she knew she would need to control her well documented temper, a temper already beginning to stir inside her, if she was to convince an Assize Jury of her innocence!!

Outside in the summer heat, gambling was intense amongst those unable to gain entry to the Courtroom, as bets were laid on whether she would hang or go home to her family. No longer in her claustrophobic cell but sitting, chained to the wall, on a bench in the equally oppressive communal room waiting to be called, Rebecca tried to block out all the turmoil around her. She was fretting over what they had done to Mary Ann to turn her against her when she should be telling them what a brute her father was and decided, with little or no confidence in Mr Twiss and his grubby little clerk, that her only option was to plead with the Judge to let her defend herself despite the objectionable man insisting she would not be allowed to say any such thing.

*"Worlock stand up!"* came a loud, unseen voice from the darkness. Standing up, as best she could, Rebecca found herself being roughly manhandled by more exploring hands as she was hauled across the room and through the battered door leading to a spiral staircase. Glancing up she saw daylight and heard voices, women crying, men shouting, court officers calling for order, pleading for people with no business with the Trial to leave, and knew that somewhere amongst it all would be those whom she once looked on as friends.

Gradually the Courtroom above fell silent as a door behind her opened, lending some welcome light into the dark abyss, and two female gaolers entered the communal waiting room provoking the discarded dregs of humanity within to suddenly rise up like some huge writhing mountain of unwashed bodies as they begged in vain for mercy. Gathering voluminous amounts of surplus damask under her arm, leg irons about her ankles, Rebecca shuffled and stumbled up the steep winding stairs. Tripping over the last step, fearful of what awaited her, she closed her eyes as she desperately fumbled for something, or someone, to guide her. Shuffling sideways, hands blindly outstretched before her, she came upon a cold metal rail whilst behind her she could feel the outline of a hard wooden bench. Opening her eyes she was met with row upon row of hostile faces, all looking at her with hatred and condemnation in their hearts and for a fleeting moment she found it very difficult to breath. Reaching out to the two women at her side, fearing she might faint, she found herself longing for the sanctuary and solitary seclusion of the dreadful cell beneath her feet.

The baying mob had waited long enough. Many had walked miles and queued since early morning to secure their seats, now she was standing before them and, unable to contain themselves, they started whispering then muttering until finally their voices joined in a loud crescendo of screams…

*"Murderess, Poisoner, Husband Killer….Hang Her !!!"*

Turning round towards the Public Gallery behind her Rebecca had never seen so much hatred on peoples' faces and desperately searched for someone, anyone, prepared to show her some compassion. Facing the bench again her gaze fixed on the twelve elegantly dressed members of the Jury sitting to her right, their grim faces telling her she would find no solace amongst them today. Next she spied a lone, less stylish, figure sitting at a desk in a small alcove, quill pen and paper in front of him, mistaking him for the Clerk of the Court. He would in fact be responsible for ensuring her crime and, ultimately, her fate appeared in all the local newspapers. Bonner did not hold a monopoly on newspaper reporting nor, sadly, was he the only one eager to condemn her in print. Her only hope lay with Mr Twiss, who was nowhere to be seen and had not even paid her the courtesy of a second visit. It was clear he had little or no understanding of her situation since he had taken great delight in suggesting hers was not only a lost cause but he had been retained far too late and given insufficient information to prepare any kind of defence in time for the Summer Assize.

Returning her gaze towards the Public Gallery her eyes searched through the reserved family seats. She found her stepfather first and expected some acknowledgement but his response was to drop his head and stare down at his feet. A few seats away she spied Robert and George Worlock. Neither had taken their eyes from her since she stepped into the dock and from the cold countenance in their eyes she knew she would find no understanding there either. Her spirits rose considerably when she found her brothers sitting a few rows from the Worlocks and expected some vestige of brotherly recognition but even they found it difficult to look at her for long.

As the screams, abuse and threats increased Rebecca finally accepted there was not one person on whom she could look for comfort and slumped back on her hard wooden bench knowing she was entirely on her own.

# CHAPTER FOURTEEN

Ludlow and Osborne appeared to welcoming shouts, cheers and screams unlike Twiss and his clerk who were greeted with boos, hisses and a great deal of verbal abuse. The Prosecution, resplendent in fine wigs, a relic from the Court of King Charles 11 following his exile in France, and elegant black gowns were in stark contrast to the Defence in their old moth eaten hand me down wigs and rough faded second hand bombazine gowns. From behind the large leather chair, standing empty but majestic above the Court, a loud voice called for order, and gradually the overcrowded room fell silent as the same hidden voice ordered,

*"All Stand,"*

Everyone turned as Sir John Richardson made his regal way from a door behind the bench. Reaching his chair, he deliberately moved the bouquet of fragrant herbs and flowers placed before him to prevent the filthy throng beneath him breathing jail fever and typhus in his direction, in order to get a better look at the creature standing in the dock before him. As he fixed a cold piercing glare over a pair of grubby spectacles perched precariously on the end of a large bulbous nose, in her direction Rebecca instinctively felt very scared and knew this man, like the rest, would show her no mercy.

The Charges of Petit Treason and Murder were met by a further deafening chorus of cheers, whistles and obscenities which not only completely obliterated Rebecca's defiant plea of *"Not Guilty"* but brought about another deafening outburst from the crowd, accompanied by the suggestion that Sir John should,

*"Hang th'bitch now, don't waste thy time wiv no trial!"*

Mr Osborne rose to briefly outline the case, making sure he faced the Jury not Rebecca, as he suggested,

*"The Worlocks enjoyed thirteen years of a less than harmonious marriage and it is fair to say they were totally mismatched from the day they stood before the altar of St. Mary's Bitton, since the accused was known to be an extremely selfish and bad tempered woman who cared for no-one but herself."*

Hearing this Rebecca was on her feet, shouting loudly,

*"You are a liar, I was not selfish, and I cared deeply for my husband!"*

This sudden outburst caused Sir John to call order and bellow,

*"Silence, I will not allow such outbursts in my Court!"*

Mr Ludlow slowly rose to his feet, acknowledged his inexperienced adversary Mr Twiss, then faced the Jury with a dramatic flourish as he explained, *"Gentlemen, the evidence you will hear today will leave you in no doubt as to the prisoner's guilt"* and, with a flamboyant wave of his hand, he called for the first witness.

For a very brief moment nothing happened until, following a second call, the small frightened figure of young girl appeared. At the sight of the daughter she had not seen for over four months, the daughter she had last seen being dragged screaming from her father's deathbed, Rebecca cried out, *"My dear, dear children, my dearest Mamma, Oh Papa why are you not here!"* before looking at her daughter and silently prayed, *"do not, for the love of God, believe all the lies they will have told you about me!"*

But of course the terrified child heard none of her mother's words, the noise coming from the crowd made sure of that. Sir John, ignoring the real culprits, called for order and again, threatened.

*"Worlock! I shall have you taken to the cells below and continue this trial in your absence if you persist in hindering these proceedings,"*....adding, with already a hint of prejudice in his voice, *"you may well be accustomed to getting your own way elsewhere but that is not how I conduct any Court of mine and the sooner you realise that then the better it will be for all concerned."*

Back on her uncomfortable bench she listened as Ludlow cleverly questioned Mary Ann about the events of April 17th when she had witnessed her mother mixing some white powder into the jug of beer she had bought for her father at The Chequers. Asked if her father had said anything the child whispered, *"He sid he wanted t'know what were in th'beer I fetched frum Mister Hook's but I told im there weren't nothing."*

Looking at Rebecca, whose eyes were firmly fixed on her eldest child, Ludlow, chose his words carefully, before continuing, *"Tell me my child, what did your father say, or do, when he realised his ale had made him ill?"*

With sad, dark, saucer eyes fixed on his face Mary Anne replied, *"Ee shouted at muther sayin she ad done fur im this time an told me t'go n fetch Mister Hook so's ee could look at th'beer"*

Pausing for a moment to gain the most impact Ludlow then asked in a quiet, almost compassionate, voice, *"And on your return what else did you see?"*

*"Muther were in th'outouse washing father's mug in a bucket of water."*

*"And did anyone else see your mother doing this?"*

*"Oh yes, Mary frum the Chequers an Missus Butler frum next door were there an father asked Missus Butler to look at what were floatin in is beer. Then father took ill an Uncle Richard n muther went with im to find a Doctur."*

Ludlow lowered his voice.

*"Mary Ann, you are a very brave grown up girl to stand here today and I know you miss your dear father very much but can you tell us about the day he died?"*

On hearing this Rebecca screamed out,
*"How could she have any idea what it was like living with a man like him, why are you expecting her to speak of such things?"*

*"Worlock!!"* bellowed Sir John, hammering his gavel on the bench in front of him, *"I will not allow such outbursts in my Court ...do you understand!"*... before composing himself and, turning to Mr Ludlow, to encourage *"pray continue."*

Mary Ann, with subtle prompting from Ludlow, told how she was not allowed to spend much time with her father during his final days but when she had been taken, together with her brother and sister, to say their goodbyes she didn't believe them when they told her he was dying because, in the past, he always got better.

Cross examined by Mr Twiss, who also emphasised she must be a good girl because father always told her to tell the truth, she was asked whether this was the first time Thomas had been taken ill with a stomach upset,
*"Oh no, he were always ill but mother always got im better."*

*"What happened to the 'stuff' you say was floating in the cup?"*

*"Don't know, mother throwed it away."*

Sarah Butler took the stand next to a further torrent of abuse from Rebecca,
*"You just couldn't wait to get your own back and turn my daughter against me could you!!"*

This brought about another rebuke from Sir John after which and to more rapturous cheers from the crowd, Ludlow rose once again to begin carefully extracting more damning evidence.

*"Mrs Butler, please tell us what you saw at the Worlock's house?"*

*"She"*, pointing at Rebecca, *"were in a right fright cus er usband were sayin he'd swallowed summut in his beer what made is mouth burn an there were*

*sum white stuff on a table but when he asked er what mess she'd put into is cup she said twere baking flour."*

*"And in your opinion Mrs Butler was it baking flour?"*

*"No Zur tweren't no baking flour."*

*"That's cus twere poison that's why!"* screamed the hysterical mob as Sir John again called for order, rapidly losing patience, threatening to clear the Court and send the ring leaders to the cells below.

With some semblance of order restored, Ludlow turned to the Jury.

*"Preferring to believe his next door neighbour rather than his wife, Thomas Worlock demanded to know if the white stuff was not baking powder, as she claimed, then what was it, only for that woman,"* pointing towards the dock, *"to accuse her own children of mixing some powder Doctor Watts had given her some months ago and which she had surreptitiously hidden in some paper between two books by the clock. She even suggested the girls had used the paper to curl their hair thereby accidentally mixing it into the beer."*

Returning his attention to the Witness box Ludlow continued,
*"Mrs Butler, did you hear the prisoner blame her children for their father's illness?"*

*"Yes Zur an,"* facing the Jury, *"when she blamed um fer mixing powder in their father's drink ee shouted at er fur leavin poisun near little uns and wanted t'know why andn't she locked it away."* As planned, this dramatic outburst had the desired effect as twelve men all nodded their heads in agreement. Ludlow continued,
*"Were the Worlocks a loving couple?"*

Shaking her head whilst suppressing a laugh Sarah Butler replied,
*"Lor no, they wuz always arguing Zur an......"*

*"....and Mrs Butler!"* Ludlow impatiently prompted,
*"an she were always threatnin to zun to put im out of the world."*

*"She was always threatening to soon put him out of this world, thank you Mrs Butler!!"* and with those words, delivered slowly and precisely, reverberating about the room, Mr Ludlow gave way to Mr Twiss.

Twiss rose to question Sarah only to repeat the same questions already put to Mary Ann, before turning to other matters.

*"Mrs Butler, was this the first time Thomas Worlock had been taken ill?"*

*"No he were always ill with stumuck pains."*

*"Had you ever seen any white powder on those occasions?"*

*"No Zur but ee were wus this time."*

*"That may be so but on this occasion did you see any white powder either in a bucket or on the table?"*

*"Yes, but th'stuff in th'buckut were whiter than th'stuff on the table."*

When Twiss suddenly stopped his questioning to stand motionless next to his table, everyone assumed he was about to bring his cross examination to an abrupt end. No one therefore expected any further interrogation,
*"Mrs Butler, when did the threats to put him out of the world and his illnesses begin?"*

*"Bout a yer ago."*

*"So up until then would you say the couple were happy together?"*

Sarah had little choice but to reply.

*"Most a th'time, unless ee ad th'drink in him."*

*"In your opinion why did things change?"* however before she could reply she was reminded, *"remember Mrs Butler, you are on Oath before God to tell the truth and I would therefore advise you to think very carefully before you answer."*

*"When he tuk t'drinking n spendin is time round Garge Hooks place,"* was the whispered reply.

Mr Twiss, keen for as many people as possible to hear what she had just said, suggested,
*"Mrs Butler not everyone, especially the Jury, will have heard your answer. Let me ask you again and this time, please, raise your voice slightly. What made things change in the Worlocks marriage?"*

*"He tuk t'drinking round Garge Hooks place,"* was all the hapless woman could say.

*"And please tell the Jury what happened should he return home drunk Mrs Butler?"*

*"He ould get vilunt,"* she whispered…

*"Louder Mrs Butler if you please!!"*

*"He ould get vilent !!!"* the unfortunate woman was forced to almost shout, such was the noise reverberating around the room.

*"He ... Would... Get ...Violent!!!"* ...Mr Twiss repeated slowly and deliberately, emphasising the word Violent, *"and what happened to her,"* pointing towards the dock, *"every time Thomas Worlock returned home worse for the drink, Mrs Butler?"*

Not wanting to be branded a liar Sarah had to admit, *"She zumtimes gotta beatin,"* adding, as if from personal experience, *"but so do other wives and they don't murder their usbands!"*

Ignoring this last comment, Mr Twiss dismissed the unfortunate woman with a brusque, *"That is all Mrs Butler."*

Returning to her seat, relieved her ordeal was over, Sarah was met with an icy glare from Rebecca who silently hoped her neighbour would rot in hell for the lies she believed she had told today, little realising Sarah had been cleverly led by Mr Twiss into testifying that Thomas' excessive drinking had resulted in not only his deteriorating health but had turned him into a vicious wife beater as well.

*"Call Mary Hook,"* was the next name the increasingly restless mob heard as they waited impatiently for the more credible witnesses to appear, witnesses who would spare nothing in describing all the gruesome gory details behind the agonising death of Thomas Worlock, Butcher of Oldland Common!

Mary Hook, daughter of the Landlord of the Chequers, stood before the Jury a proud young lady, proud that at last her opinion was considered important enough for her to be called to give evidence in a murder trial. Back home she was no more than the family skivvy, expected to help with the everyday running of her parents' Ale House, helping her mother with the food for the table and spending whatever time was left helping her father and her sixteen year old brother George look to their customers. At busy times she was usually found serving ale, from the barrel, at the back door. However the jobs she hated the most were cleaning out the brass spittoons and sweeping up the filthy sawdust left on the floor every morning. Today was different, today she was standing in a Court of Law before an important looking Judge and a Jury of twelve fine gentlemen. Dressed in her very best dress she was the centre of attention as she waited to be questioned by two equally important looking lawyers.

Sensing she was a simple country girl, raised in fear of her parents, Ludlow suggested Mary knew the difference between right and wrong and that it was a sin to tell lies. Fearful of her father, who was to follow her into witness box and was waiting in the adjacent room with all the others, she agreed she was a good girl. Even Mrs Ellacombe said so when she used to go to her Sunday School and she never told lies. Content in the knowledge he had scared her enough to tell the truth, Ludlow assured her he expected nothing else, and smiling fatherly towards her, he peered over his glasses and began his questions.

*"Miss Hook, tell us about the Worlock's house on the day Mr Worlock took ill?"*

Having rarely been addressed as Miss Hook, especially by such an important looking man, Mary felt very confident as she explained,

*"She,"* nodding towards Mary Ann now sitting with Sarah Butler on benches specially reserved for those witnesses who had already given evidence, *"comed fur some ale fur er father. She gave I th'jug an I drawed sum from th'barrel into a pewter pot afore pourin it into er jug, then she went ome an I went back t'me work."*

*"But it was not long before your friend came back, very upset, saying her father had taken ill after drinking some of that beer and Mrs Worlock over there,"* pointing back towards the dock but not even bothering to look at its occupant, *"was saying it was because the beer was bad and Mr Worlock wanted your father to come to his house straight away, is that not so Miss Hook?"*

*"Yes zur but fathur were busy an muther don't like Missus Worlock an Missus Worlock don't like er so I went,"* was Mary Hook's matter of fact reply.

Holding up his hands in mock horror Ludow demanded.

*"Now, why would Mrs Worlock blame your father's beer as the cause of such a serious illness?"*

*"Cus she said I gived Mary Ann bad beer an she wanted t'get me in truble cus she don't like me neither,"*

*"And what did Mrs Worlock say was wrong with the beer?"*

*"She sid there were white stuff in it."*

*"And was there Miss Hook?"*

*"No Zur, there weren't nothin in the beer nor the jug."*

*"There was nothing, no white powder, in the ale you sold to Mary Ann Worlock?"*

*"No Zur, there weren't",*

*"Did you see any of this so called white stuff floating in Mr Worlock's beer mug?"*

*"Only what were left aftur Missus Worlock throwed it away Zur, but I seed some white powder on a table."*

*"Did anyone else see this white powder?"*

*"Oh yes Zur, Mister Worlock said there'd bin bout a teacup of it in is mug but Missus Worlock ad rinsed it in a bucket but if I were t'go to th'outouse an look fur th'bucket there might still be some there an,"* nodding towards Sarah, still trying to compose herself after her ordeal at Ludlow's hands, *"Missus Butler were there as well."*

*"And did you see any white powder in this outhouse Miss Hook?"*

*"Oh yes Zur,"* came a confident reply, *"twas just like what I seed on the table... rough just like salt."*

*"But did Mr Worlock not wish to keep some of the powder...to maybe show your father...after all the so called bad beer was bought from his Ale House?"*

*"He sid he tried free times t'stop her,"* pointing at Rebecca in the dock, *"frum throwin the white powder away but he weren't strong nough."*

Mary Hook's ordeal at the hands of Mr Ludlow finally ended when she confirmed leaving the Worlocks once Thomas and Rebecca left, *"to look fur a Doctur."*

Twiss stood up and immediately tried to discredit Mary's ability to know whether the white powder, scattered liberally around the Worlock's house, was ordinary salt or the powder sent by Doctor Watts for the children's groin infection, asking instead that Rebecca be given the benefit of the doubt until someone better qualified to identify what it really was gave evidence. The hint that a Doctor, along with all his gruesome evidence, was about to be called caused the room to erupt again and to force Judge Richardson to once more threaten to clear the Court of the ringleaders unless they came to order.

As expected George Hook followed his daughter to a welcome of disappointed groans from an increasingly agitated, impatient crowd anxious for the speedy appearance of the three Doctors, fast becoming bored with what they considered were mundane witnesses. Well they would have to wait a while longer yet.

George readily admitted he only went the Worlock's house after his daughter returned home insisting he should, if only for the sake of his licence. Accusations were being made about bad beer and mysterious white powder because, unlike previous occasions, Thomas was showing no sign of recovery this time. Expecting to find the house empty and therefore reluctant to go alone, he asked his friend William Short to accompany him. However, when they got there they found Mary Ann, on her own but deeply distressed and worried about her sick father, quite happy to let them take a look around and it had not taken much searching to find the rough, glistening white powder his daughter had mentioned. In fact he testified how there had been little attempt to hide it as it was about an inch thick all over the bottom and sides of a bucket in the outhouse.

Twiss rose to his feet.

*"Mr Hook do you believe the prisoner poisoned her husband by adding some unknown white powder to his drink?"*

*"Yes Zur I be certun she did fur im!"*

*"But if that is so why did she not destroy all the evidence instead of leaving it for you and your friend to find?"*

George Hook shot a cold hard glance towards Rebecca, who was glaring at him as if wishing he would burn in hell, before admitting,
*" I bain't in no position t'answer fur th'actions of th'likes of she!"*

*"You are not overly fond of the prisoner are you Mr Hook. Would you care to tell us why."*

*"She'd bin alright if only she'd just let er man be, stead of ounding him so."*

*"Now, why would she be hounding him?"*

*"Cus she thinks she be better than im an didn't want im to be a mixing wiv the likes of...."*

*"...the likes of who Mr Hook, and why do you think Thomas Worlock should have wished to spend his time in your Ale House instead of at home with his wife?"*

*"Cus we made'n welcome, not like she"*, pointing in the direction of Rebecca, *"she never wanted im...., not like other wives did."*

*"And why do you think that was Mr Hook?"*

*"Well, she was always naggin im fur being full of the drink Zur."*

*"But he was always full of the drink, wasn't he Mr Hook, drunk and violent with your beer wasn't he Mr Hook?"* Turning to face the row of twelve elegant gentlemen, knowing he could not address them directly, Twiss continued, *"Mr Hook, pray tell the Jury whose money do you imagine Worlock was spending on that drink...not his...because he didn't have any til he believed he had found an heiress, so maybe it was hers don't you think?"*

Feeling aggrieved, as if he was the one on trial not the woman he and his customers loathed so much, George Hook stuttered,
*"Well if you ask me, every man's titled to is mug o ale Zur."*

*"But not when he is already a very sick man who turns violent towards his wife when he's drunk. Were you aware your ale made him violent towards his wife Mr Hook?"*

*"Zum said she deserved it Zur!!"*

*"Mr. Hook!!!"* shouted Mr Twiss with more than a touch of exasperation in his voice, *"were you aware that by encouraging Thomas Worlock to drink at your Ale House you were not only contributing to his failing health but also to the sufferings of his wife and three young children, who now have no father?"*

Desperately searching for way out of a corner George declared, *"Well he always got better didn't he?"*

*"Thanks to the care and devotion of his long suffering wife, who now stands accused of his murder. No more questions!!!"*

William Short was next to face Ludlow and was welcomed into the witness box by yet more impatient yells and catcalls from the assembled rabble. Yes, he had accompanied George Hook to the Worlocks cottage. Yes Mary Ann was there and let them both in to take a look around the cottage. No, the Worlocks were not there because Richard Jenkins had taken them to find a Doctor on account of Thomas being very sick. When asked why there was a need to visit the cottage in the first place William replied,
*"Cus she,"* pointing at the creature in green, red and gold damask sitting defiantly in the dock, *"claimed young Mary ther"* nodding at Mary Hook sitting next to her father, *"ad sold bad beer an she were sayin she ad sin white powder spread all round the place."*

Taking a deep breath Ludlow asked,
*"And was there white powder spread all around the place, as Mary Hook claimed?"*

*"Well Zur, tweren't zactly all round the place cus she,"* pointing again to Rebecca, *"ad made sure most on it bin washed away but we found zum in a buckut in th'outhouse."*

*"Mr Short, other Witnesses have suggested the powder resembled salt, is that what you thought?"*

*"Well Zur, it didn't taste like salt."*

*"Good God man! are you telling us you tasted the stuff?"* exclaimed Ludlow with a show of mock theatrical horror that would have earned him a place alongside the divine Sarah Siddons in Drury Lane or the Theatre Royal in Bath, *"Please describe its taste and how you escaped becoming the prisoners second victim!!"*

The flamboyant style of the Prosecuting Council was clearly lost on William who simply replied,
*"It burnt me mouth an made my tongue swell up but Garge gave I zum water from th'well in the yard and by alf a hour I wer better."*

Twiss suggested William knew the powder was probably harmless, why else would he have been foolish enough to taste it and hinted Thomas' illness was caused, yet again, from drinking too much beer. To his final question of whether Rebecca was capable of poisoning her husband William naively replied,
*"I ouldn't know, I bain't th'sort she d'care to mix wiv."*

Richard Jenkins was called. Yes, his brother in law and his wife were a very disagreeable couple at times, *"Especially she!"* pointing yet again to an increasingly dejected Rebecca. Yes, he often overheard her threats to put him out of this world. Yes, he had taken the couple to Keynsham to seek out Doctor Edwards and Yes, he recalled hearing Sarah Butler assure Thomas the white powder was definitely not baking flour.

*"Mr Jenkins"* asked Ludlow, *"pray tell the Jury how the prisoner explained the presence of white powder in her husband's beer?"*

*"She sid t'were her two little maids, she sid they must ave mixed it in be accident,"* came the accusing reply.

Ludlow turned to face the Jury, giving a wide sweeping gesture with an outstretched arm, before turning back in the direction of the assembled mob to reiterate, accusingly, slowly and precisely,
*"Gentlemen, she was even prepared to blame her innocent young daughters in a desperate attempt at hiding her crime. I therefore put it to you, what sort of mother would do that to her own children, if not a guilty one?"*

Hearing these damning words, the Courtroom descended into uncontrolled pandemonium with furious stamping, shouting and screams of,
*"Hang th'bitch now, she bain't worth waitin fer the Jury, just give er to us!"*

Sir John desperately tried to call order, officials were sent amongst the throng in an attempt to seek out and remove the troublemakers. Finally, with some semblance of order restored, a visibly shaken Richard Jenkins was asked to continue.

*"Mr Jenkins, whose suggestion was it to take Thomas all the way to Keynsham. Surely Doctor Watts in Bitton or Doctor Wingrove up at North Common would have been closer?"*

*"She,"* pointing to Rebecca, *"told I t'go to Doctur Hedwards cus he were th'family Doctur."*

*"But so was Doctor Watts, did she not turn to him for the so called white powder she was claiming had been accidentally mixed into the beer?"* suggested Ludlow but, before Richard had chance to answer, he hastily continued *"How did your brother in law endure the journey to Keynsham?"*

*"He were in agony Zur."*

*"So, a shorter journey would have saved him a great deal of further pain would it not Mr Jenkins?"*

*"Yes!"* came the short emphatic response.

Sensing the Judge was keen to call a recess, Ludlow ended by asking, *"Did the prisoner say why she wished to consult Doctor Edwards rather than Doctor Watts or Doctor Wingrove?"*

*"She sid Dactur Watts ouldn't know ow to treat er usband, she sid he were only good enough fur they in the Poor Ouse."*

*"So Doctor Watts cares for the poor souls in Bitton Poor House?"*

*"Aye Zur."*

*"And your sister in law considered Doctor Watts unfit to treat her sick husband yet she had no such concerns when it came to taking her children to see him. Why was that do you think?"*

*"Probably cus he knowed ow she treated our Thomas!"*

Twiss rose to his feet, with no idea how he was to counter such damning evidence, to an impatient muffled cough from the Judge as if to say, *"Be brief man, be brief!!!"*

*"Mr Jenkins, Doctor Watts had never treated your brother in law so how would he have known anything about his care?"*

*"Cus people d'talk and the way she made'n suffer were all round th'village Zur."*

*"Oh, so Doctor Watts, who was never called in to examine your late brother in law during any of his illnesses, would have been expected to make a diagnosis from village tittle tattle!"*

Richard did not reply to this and was about to leave the witness box when Mr Twiss asked him one last question.

*"Mr Jenkins, I appreciate it is only natural for your wife to be extremely upset but is she not just looking for someone on whom to place the blame?"*

*"Zur, tis true we be all grievin fur er brother but if you 'm trying t 'accuse I of lying then you 'm wrong cus I've told thee th'truth and she, " [pointing directly towards Rebecca,] "were party to is death. "*

There were no further questions but, as Richard took his place alongside the others, Rebecca was on her feet cursing and screaming,

*"I hope God makes you and that slut of wife rot in hell, along with the rest of her accursed family, for all the lies you have told. "*

For a brief moment the room fell silent, everyone's eyes turned to Sir John, even the Prosecution and Defence Councils remained in their seats. Finally the exhausted Judge called a recess, ordering the Court to be cleared and for all the doors to remain open to allow a change of air and to give everybody a chance to calm down.

Back in Court a half an hour later it was obvious no one had taken heed of Sir John's advice such was their reluctance to lose their hard fought for places. Instead the mob had simply reshuffled, leaving friends to guard their spots whilst they took it in turns to leave the room; however, everyone was now back concentrating on eating the food brought to sustain them through the day. Meanwhile, outside, for those who could afford it, cider, ale, meat pies and the like were freely on sale and were also being brought back, in vast quantities, to the Courtroom. As the temperature of the August sun increased so did the composure, behaviour and excitable state of a rapidly increasingly bacchanalian mob. By the time the Jury, Sir John's private party, Lady Sandy's guests, Rebecca's supporters and accusers returned to their seats the atmosphere in the Courtroom was already close to fever pitch as everyone eagerly awaited what they all knew would be the final act of the day's drama. The same, however, could not be said about the legal teams as, suitably refreshed and fortified by a good glass of claret and whatever sustenance had been placed in their rooms, they each prepared in their own way to resume the fight for Rebecca's life.

Sensibly Peter Gerrish had avoided the Worlocks and his stepsons. However he thought the trial was going well and there was nothing to indicate the Jury would find his stepdaughter anything but guilty, then he could return home to her elderly mother and that would be the end of the whole sordid affair because as long as there was just the slightest chance Lamorock Flower's daughter might be spared then Mary would remain ever hopeful of bringing her and her brats to live under his roof....and, considering his views plus all the things he had said about the Worlocks in the past, that must never happen!

Rebecca had enjoyed no such luxuries in her tiny cell beneath the Court. To distant screams and cries from other female prisoners, obviously suffering at the hands of the same pair of uncouth gaolers that had earlier thought it was their right to violate her, she toyed despairingly with a chunk of stale bread along with a lump of mouldy cheese balanced on a mound of almost raw uncooked cold potato, served on a battered tin plate and briefly remembered, not for the first time, how good her own bread with some freshly churned butter and large piece of tasty cheese from her own cows or a slice of her own pork, washed down with a mug of cider, had once tasted.

With everyone gathered, the Court awaited Sir John who, due to his declining health, had wisely chosen to take just a simple dish of tea and a piece of seed cake.

Mr Ludlow, fully refreshed by his liquid luncheon, rose from his seat and prepared to open the afternoon session. To cheers, shouts and ear piercing whistles, Roger Edwards entered the Witness Box. From the confident manner in which he gave his evidence and from the way he answered his questions it was clear this was not the first time he had appeared before a Judge, although if pressed he would have to admit he was more accustomed to appearing before a Coroner's Court, testifying to a cause of death, or sometimes in private before a Magistrate in his rooms, witnessing or swearing to the legitimacy of some deathbed last Will and Testament. Like those before him, he testified he knew the Worlocks as a most unloving couple and that it was always Thomas who was in need of his help because the poor man was constantly ill. He concluded by admitting he was not at all surprised, although a little annoyed, to find the couple at his door one evening in April. Anticipating Twiss would pick up on the suggestion he was not best pleased to find the Worlocks on his doorstep Ludlow asked,

*"So, why were you displeased to find the Worlocks on your doorstep, after all were they not patients of yours, did they not pay their bill on time?"*

*"Yes they, Mrs Worlock that is, always settled my bill. I suppose I was more annoyed because they interrupted my family's supper with what appeared to be just his usual problem, a problem for which I had only recently treated him."*

Inviting Roger Edwards to continue, the Jury heard things were slightly different on this occasion because, for the first time, Thomas claimed he had been poisoned, even producing some white powder saved from his mug of beer as if to prove the point,

*"Doctor Edwards,"* queried Mr Ludlow, holding his hands together before his face, as if at prayer, *"be so good as to tell us your opinion of the so called alleged poison?"*

*"Well I doubted it was poison, possibly vegetable powder, although not hops,*

226

*however twas clear something had upset him as he was complaining bitterly of being uncommonly sick."*

*"Doctor Edwards, I understand you have since had the opportunity to investigate the so called poison further, pray tell the Court of your findings?"*

To a room surprisingly silent, Roger Edwards continued.

*"Certainly, Worlock complained of sickness and pain in his stomach accompanied by a burning sensation in his throat which he blamed on the white powder he claimed to have saved from being destroyed by his wife. I placed a small amount, about an eighth part, of this powder in my mouth."*

With this revelation came loud gasps from the assembled mass that remembered an earlier witness confessing to doing the very same thing and looked to Ludlow, fully expecting a repeat of the theatricals, only to be disappointed as he urged, somewhat impatiently.

*"Yes yes!, we are already aware that someone else was careless enough to try something similar...pray continue!!"*

*"It was free from roughness with the appearance of jalap. An ounce of jalap might produce so much sickness as to occasion inflammation of the stomach and it is possible death might be occasioned by taking an ounce of jalap but..."*

*"But!, Doctor Edwards, but,"* pressed an impatient Ludlow.

*"But, I have never seen or heard of such a case and jalap does not produce a burning heat nor is it a white glossy substance."*

*"Can I take you on two days, to when you saw the deceased again? How would you describe him then?"*

*"Extremely ill,"* a subdued Roger Edwards replied, shaking his head, *"so ill in fact, I feared he was in great danger and told him so. He still complained of sickness and pains in his stomach but was also in a high state of fever and unable to retain any food. I prescribed another, stronger, powder in the hope things might improve but was obliged to warn the family the future did not look promising."*

*"You felt he might not survive?"*

*"I was sure he would not survive!"*

*"Doctor Edwards, just one more thing if you please. Mr Twiss has suggested Doctor Watts would not have been in a position to treat Thomas Worlock because, although he knew all about his constant illnesses from 'village tittle tattle', he never actually examined him. Can you add anything to that?"*

*"But of course,"* taking a deep breath Roger Edwards explained, *"Samuel Watts and William Wingrove are old friends and we use this friendship to discus any patient with whom we may have a problem in the hope one of us can offer support in ways of treatment. Therefore, with the Worlocks' already the talk of the district it was only a matter of time before they became part of our conversations."*

*"So what ever it was that ailed him would have been well known to Doctor Watts, is that not so Doctor Edwards?"*

*"Indeed Mr Ludlow, that is exactly so."*

Mr Twiss rose to cross examine and began by asking Roger Edwards to re-affirm the couple were well known to him, that he had been treating Thomas for inflammation of the stomach for some time and he could therefore see no reason for him not making a full recovery as he had done in the past, before taking his questions further.

*"So, Doctor Edwards,"* mused Mr Twiss, *"when the prisoner and her husband arrived on your doorstep that fateful night you did not consider things to be any different than before?"*

*"No, Worlock appeared as he had always done, a poor sickly fellow but I do confess to having never seen him quite so ill before and it was the first time he mentioned anything about poison."*

*"You have already told the Court how you assured the couple he had not been poisoned, I presume you still hold that belief and have not altered your opinion?"*

Roger Edwards always knew this question would surface sooner or later so he took time to consider his answer, especially as it was known he had initially disagreed with the findings of his colleagues over the cause of death, before finally saying,
*"In the beginning yes I did say that but...."*

Taking a leaf from Ludlow's book Twiss impatiently insisted,

*"No buts Doctor Edwards if you please, either Thomas Worlock was poisoned or he was not!!"*

However, for some inexplicable reason, before Roger could give his answer Twiss abruptly told him he had no further questions and sent him to his seat.

At this the crowd, convinced they were being cheated by the Defence, descended into uproar and began chanting for Doctor Edwards to return to the witness box and describe, in full, the state of the body and the true findings of the Post Mortem. Ludlow, sensing this final session could easily surpass this morning's shambles, was astute enough to know how to use the crowd to his advantage. Rising to his feet, he turned round in a circular movement pressing the palms of both hands down as if to quell the noise, before announcing, *"Rest assured, the prosecution intends recalling Doctor Edwards."*

Satisfied, order was restored and the next witness called.

Reverend Henry Thomas Ellacombe said he had been Curate of Bitton for just over three years and knew the Worlocks and Flowers as members of his congregation. At the mention of her family name Rebecca glanced across at the Judge hoping to see some sign of recognition. Instead the unemotional look on his granite like face never altered, in fact he was more interested in writing his notes than looking in her direction at all.

Like the rest of the village Henry was acutely aware of the tempestuous relationship enjoyed by the couple, but because he chose not to get involved, unless asked, he had been unfamiliar with the true situation until he was called to see a very sick Thomas, after which everything soon became clear.

*"Everything soon became clear?"* queried Mr Ludlow with a certain amount of surprise, *"Pray tell us in what way did everything become clear Reverend Ellacombe?"*

*"Well, far from visiting a sick parishioner as I expected, I found a dying man and all I could do was prepare the poor wretch to meet his maker. I was led to believe he had been given some bad beer which, in turn, brought about one of his attacks."*

*"One moment if you please,"* interrupted Mr Ludlow, hand in the air as if stopping an imaginary horse and carriage from crossing the square outside the Court House, *"who told you his illness was due to him drinking bad beer?"*

*"Why, Mrs Worlock of course, she always cared for her husband at times like this and was the natural person to know the cause of his present condition."*

The Curate continued to testify how he had spoken at length to Thomas, who was fully aware he was dying and complained of having something like a fire burning within him,
*"Knowing there was not much time, I urged him to allow me to hear his last confession. However Mr Henderson, one of my Churchwardens, arrived to take down his last Will and Testament after which we were left on our own and he was able to make his peace with the Lord."*

It had been Doctor Edward's suggestion that Henry, as his spiritual guide towards the next life, should ask Thomas what had taken place over the last few days and the rapidly intoxicated mob could barely control their frustrations when they heard the Curate had learned nothing from the dying man.

Ludlow next turned to Thomas' last Will and Testament, and waving a piece of paper about his head, he announced,
*"Reverend Ellacombe was present when the dying man indicated his wishes and,"* pointing excitedly to a signature on the bottom of the piece of paper, *"his name is clearly here as a witness!"* However there were one or two things Ludlow did not quite understand and he expected Henry to know all the answers. Why, for instance, did a dying Thomas expressly wish his meagre estate, worth no more than £50 by all accounts, to go to the one woman who had done so much to make his short life such a misery? Henry, who had long decided Ludlow was nothing more than an exhibitionist and a posturing bully when performing in front of a Judge and Jury, replied softly,
*"Why not, she was his wife and always nursed him back to health during all his other illnesses."*

Not content with that answer Ludlow pressed,
*"But why was she only to inherit if she remained a widow and did not remarry?"*

*"Do not most husbands make that stipulation?"* asked Henry.

*"Reverend Ellacombe, tis rumoured the prisoner had taken a lover, something her husband had only recently discovered, is that so?"*

Henry, who was now more than a little annoyed at such intimate questions, countered,
*"Unfortunately I am the wrong person to ask."*

*"Oh and why is that?"* pressed an over confident, sarcastic Ludlow.

*"How many people do you know who would wish their Curate to know they had taken a lover?"* was Henry's flat reply, unimpressed by Ludlow's impertinence.

Henry Thomas Ellacombe M.A. was proving a very shrewd, clever and, at times, unco-operative witness, more than a match for the normally unflappable Ludlow, who was suddenly very eager to dismiss him from the Witness box.

*"Reverend Ellacombe, I understand you did not testify at the Coroner's Inquest?"*

*"That is correct. I chose to spend the hours after their son's tragic death with his elderly parents, his father is a very sick man. However I gave a full deposition to the Overseer a few days later. Did I do something wrong Mr Ludlow?"*

*"No, no, of course not,"* flustered Ludlow for once slightly lost for words, *"however I believe you spoke to the prisoner following the Coroner's Inquest, could you tell us what transpired during the conversation?"*

*"When I explained the findings of the Inquest to Mrs Worlock and how there was strong evidence she had bought poison some weeks before, she immediately denied any involvement, declaring she loved her husband too much to have done such a cruel thing. She asked to speak to the Coroner but this was refused and by the time she left for Lawfords Gate House of Correction I had returned my attention to the care of her three young children."*

*"Have you spoken to the prisoner since that day?"*

*"No, I understand from the Prison Chaplain that she is not keen on any spiritual guidance at present."*

*"One final question, you were present when Thomas Worlock died, would you describe it as peaceful?"*

*"Not in the beginning for he was in considerable pain, unable to keep even sips of water in his stomach. However, once Doctor Edwards gave him a large dose of laudanum which, thank God, he was able to retain, I think it is fair to say his passing was as peaceful as could be expected. He did not die alone, he was surrounded by his family and his passing was with God."*

*"Was his wife part of this family gathering around his death bed?"*

*"Yes, he died in her arms."*

This revelation suddenly reignited a somewhat subdued mob who, thanks to the soaring August heat and increased alcohol consumption, had grown ominously quiet, and pandemonium erupted as they screamed, chanted and hurled more abuse towards Rebecca sitting impassively in the dock,
*"Th'only time she willingly eld im in er arms was when he were dyin an wouldn't be a problem to her n'more!"*

Doctor Samuel Watts followed the Curate into the witness box. He confirmed he was a Surgeon, lived in Bitton and, like his colleague William Wingrove, was present when Roger Edwards carried out the Post Mortem; however in the absence of the Coroner the examination had taken place without him. Doctor Watts stood in silence, as if waiting for some kind of guidance, before Mr Ludlow asked impatiently,
*"Well and what did Doctor Edwards's knife tell you?"*

*"The stomach contained four to six ounces of brown fluid which was placed in a bottle to be analysed. There were several livid spots on the lining which had*

*a corrosive appearance as though lunar caustic had been applied and, whilst the liver looked fairly healthy, the lungs were in a putrid state."*

*"Was there anything else that might point to the body being poisoned?"*

*"No, not really,"* was the nonchalant reply.

Realising this was not what the Jury was supposed to be hearing, Ludlow turned on Samuel and bellowed,

*"Not Really! Not Really! Come Sir, you assisted at the dissection of a body, supposedly poisoned and now expect us to believe there was little evidence of that being the case!! ?"*

Doctor Watts was of the same ilk as Henry Ellacombe and recognised a posturing bully when he saw one, so speaking softly, slowly and very clearly just to annoy Ludlow, he confirmed.

*"Although the liver was tolerably healthy, the brown fluid from the stomach was not flaky and the intestines did not have the same appearance as the stomach. It did not necessarily prove the body had not been poisoned."*

Growing more irritated, and wanting him out of the Witness box for the same reason he had wanted to be rid of Henry Ellacombe, before he also planted seeds of doubt into the minds of the Jury, Ludlow asked one final question,

*"Doctor Watts, despite what you have told the Jury today do you believe Thomas Worlock died of poison?"*

*"Yes!"* came the immediate and confident reply.

As Twiss rose to cross examine, the mob suddenly turned on him and began stamping their feet and chanting,

*"Twer Poison! Poison! Poison!"*

This was the final straw for Sir John and his patience finally reached the end of its very short tether. Pointing to a particularly vociferous group of intoxicated men creeping menacingly close to Mr Twiss, he motioned to the ushers to clear them from the Court and remove them to the cells below. Matters deteriorated further when their equally drunken cohorts, determined they should remain, resisted any attempt to remove them from the room. Egged on by those sitting in the Gallery and even one or two of Sir John's party, who were spoiling for a quarrel, things were rapidly getting out of hand when, from somewhere deep within the building, six hefty gaolers appeared armed with cudgels, sticks and fetters. From where she sat Rebecca recognised two of them and could only watch helplessly as order was brutally restored. Sir John also watched but more approvingly, as the ringleaders were removed with blood curdling ferocity leaving a reticent, bruised and battered crowd behind. In his high

backed leather chair, His Honour, slightly agitated, mopped his brow and straightened his wig as he tried to regain as much composure and decorum as possible, before glancing at the two distressed barristers sitting in stunned silence beneath he gruffly advised,
*"Mr Twiss...pray continue if you please,"* as if the last few dreadful moments had never happened.

Already rendered temporarily speechless, Twiss had not been sure what to ask Doctor Watts before the dreadful outburst, but now it was all over his mind was a complete blank. Desperately playing for time he grabbed a glass of water in his trembling hands and took several large swigs. His reluctance to continue was lost on no-one, especially his adversary and the best the traumatised man could do was encourage the witness to explain why there was a difference of opinion over the cause of death, however even in this Twiss was unable to persuade Samuel Watts to change his belief that Thomas had died from poison. In answer to his final question,
*"Do you think the prisoner mixed poison in her husband's beer?"*

Doctor Watts replied,
*"That is not for me to say....but someone did."*

As everyone waited for the next witness so sounds, from those who had earlier dared to vent their anger on Mr Twiss, were heard coming from the room beneath the dock and Rebecca realised her two old gaoler friends and their colleagues did not just mete out their personal kind of rough justice on defenceless women.

Doctor William Wingrove stood in the witness box and readily admitted that, whilst he knew the Worlocks, he had never treated the deceased but agreed, under the circumstances, it would have been closer and more convenient to have brought Thomas to him or Samuel Watts rather than travel all the way to Keynsham.

*"Why was that so Doctor Wingrove?"* asked Mr Ludlow.

*"Because, apart from it being a shorter journey, one of us could have given him the same powder and his sufferings might have been eased all the sooner"* came the confident reply.

*"But, and I am sure Mr Twiss will be anxious to know this, you were not his Doctor. You say you were never called to see him, therefore how could you have possibly known about his past illnesses and how to treat him?"*

*"Mr Worlock would not have been the first case of inflammation of the stomach I had seen and I would not have treated him any differently from Doctor Edwards. Secondly the couple were well known throughout the neighbourhood, such was*

*their fiery reputation, and it was common knowledge that each time he was known to have been drinking heavily he suffered from a stomach upset."*

Mr Ludlow then turned to the findings of the Post Mortem and, after once again confirming William was the third of the trio of Doctors who carried out the gruesome task, asked him to tell the Court what he thought was the cause of death,
*"Poison."*

Now, this was what Ludlow had been waiting for!

*"You are quite sure Doctor Wingrove?"*

*"Quite sure."*

*"Despite your colleague, Doctor Edwards, having expressed some doubt?"*

*"That is for him to say, not me,"* was the instant, slightly tetchy reply.

Mr Twiss, now more composed, rose in a hopeless attempt at persuading Doctor Wingrove that maybe excessive drinking could well have been the cause of death, pointing out how, although he may not have been the Worlocks' Doctor and had never examined Thomas in life, surely he had learned from his colleagues how the man spent a great deal of his time at The Chequers drinking heavily after which he was always violently ill. William Wingrove, whilst accepting that might be so, was not induced to change his mind and reiterated,
*"Thomas Worlock was poisoned."*

As promised, Ludlow recalled Roger Edwards and wasted little time getting straight to the point,
*"Doctor Edwards, do you agree with your colleagues that Thomas Worlock was poisoned?"*

Suddenly the Court fell unexpectedly silent as all eyes fixed on the figure in the witness box,
*"I agree with my colleagues over the condition of the deceased stomach, which had livid spots possibly caused by corrosive sublimate, but I am still not fully convinced it was consistent with that of a body having been poisoned and whilst I initially believed the contents might be animal matter, sadly that was not the case."*

With doubts beginning to creep into the proceedings, Ludlow next concentrated on proving Rebecca had purchased poison and he knew with his next witness would come that proof and, hopefully, any scepticism about the cause of death would finally disappear.

# CHAPTER FIFTEEN

The appearance of Sarah Jenkins was met with a loud anguished cry from Rebecca as she recognised the one person who could prove she had bought rat poison. Ludlow stood smug and satisfied, confident from the expression of disbelief on her face that he had played his trump card and this particular witness would secure the guilty verdict.

Although she lived in Bitton with her mother Sarah claimed, *"I never sid er,"* nodding in Rebecca's direction, *"afore thik day outzide Moses Flooks ouse in Kingsood Hill end a March."*

*"Can you describe how she behaved when you first met?"*

*"She wer like a crazed madwuman, lookin fur zummon t'sell er summut t'put zumebody t'sleep and, cus I were sorry fur er, what wiv er aving a sick usband at ome, I told er bout Missus Stephens an ow she d'sell Godfreys Cordial an they reckons that be good fur teethin babbies."*

*"Tell me Miss Jenkins; was the prisoner happy with that information?"* Mr Ludlow wanted to know.

*"No!, she sid she wanted summut else, summut t'kill a rat an she didn't like old Mother Stephens neither cus th'old witch ouldn't sell her no rat poison less she were wiv someone,"* sniffed Sarah, still slightly vexed at the way Rebecca had initially rejected her hand of friendship.

*"And did you accompany her back to Mrs Stephens?"*

*"Yes Zur."*

*"But why, when she had already turned down your earlier suggestion of Godfreys Cordial?"*

*"Cus she promised to give I fruppence for me trouble that's why!"*

Such an honest admission, rather than please the increasingly restless crowd, served only to cast further doubt in the minds of those who believed Rebecca was innocent and before long their whispered accusations,

*"But, would she ave done it if there weren't no money."*

*"She were bribed just like she bin bribed now."*

*"Dussent ferget, Judas sold is soul fer three pieces of silver as swell!"* were clearly heard.

This unexpected reaction caused Ludlow to go onto the defensive,

*"Quite, but you did not ask for payment in return for help did you Miss Jenkins, you did it from the goodness of your heart did you not,"* before swiftly going on to ask, *"Tell us what happened once inside the shop."*

Feeling relieved at not having to explain her mercenary actions Sarah continued,

*"She,"* nodding towards Rebecca, *"told Missus Stephens ow she wanted summut to kill a rat which were in er ouse but afore she anded it over th'old lady sid to kip it out th'way a children."*

*"One moment if you please,"* interrupted Mr Ludlow, holding his authoritative right hand aloft again, *"please tell the Jury what the prisoner said on hearing this very sensible piece of advice?"*

*"She sid she ad none."*

*"Miss Jenkins,"* said Ludlow, waving the same right hand in yet another of his theatrical flourishes, his voice full of incredulity, *"I'm sorry, but are you saying the prisoner claimed she had no children, when in fact she had three?"*

*"Yes Zur."*

Facing the Jury Ludlow challenged.

*"I wonder what else she chose to lie about,"* before turning back to Sarah, *"pray continue Miss Jenkins?"*

*"After she got er poison we left th'shop but wunce we was outzide she sid there weren't no rat, just a ell of a man she were wantin to put t'sleep and if she got th'chance she ould do it that very night, if not she ould wait fur another time but she were gonna do it. Then she give I fruppence like she promused an sid I wun't to tell no one."*

*"But you did tell someone, didn't you Miss Jenkins?"*

*"Yes Zur,"* Sarah's voice was now no more than an embarrassed whisper, *"muther made I tell er."*

*"And what else did your mother do?"*

*"Nuffin till we eard bout thik poor man what died a poison up at Oldland and then she sid I were to tell someone what I seed, so I went an told Constable Gerrush an he sid I ad t'go th'Chequers n tell the portant gentleman who were staying there."*

*"You mean Mr Joyner Ellis, the Coroner?"*

*"Don't know his name Zur but he were there the day they found out how thik poor man died."*

Twiss rose to cross examine Sarah with absolutely no idea what he was going to ask her, such was the overwhelming strength of her evidence. In desperation he vainly tried to throw doubt on her claim not to have known Rebecca.

*"You come from Bitton, surely you must have known Mrs Worlock, especially in view of her family connections."*

*"Muther n me bain't bin in Bitton long an though I d'know who she be now she sid she didn't come t'Bitton to visut er family no more, so I never seed her afore we met by Mister Flook's ouse".*

Twiss next turned to the matter of payment in return for helping Rebecca and asked what she did with the money.

*"I went to th'ale house wiv me friends,"* came the honest reply.

*"Do you drink a lot of beer Miss Jenkins?"*

*"No more than most Zur."*

*"Had you been drinking on the day you met Mrs Worlock in Kingswood Hill?"*

*"No Zur, I didn't have no money, that be why I went wiv her cus twas worf fruppence and theese can buy a lotta ale wiv fruppence."*

Accepting he would never be able to prove whether or not Sarah was drunk and therefore not a reliable witness, Twiss reluctantly told her there were no further questions and she could sit down.

Ludlow then called Elizabeth Amey to the witness box,
*"Miss Amey, be so good as to tell us how you are employed?"*

*"I works fur Missus Stephens in her pothcree shop in Kingsood Hill, Zur."*

*"I believe you do more than that, you also live with her as her companion and house keeper, is that not so?"*

*"Yes Zur."*

*"Can we therefore assume from your long service in the Apothecary Shop, that you are familiar with certain powders and potions?"*

*"Yes Zur."*

*"I understand you saw the prisoner,"* nonchalantly waving in the direction of the dock but again not bothering to look at its occupant, *"and Miss Jenkins*

*over there,"* pointing to Sarah now sitting between Mary Ann Worlock and Mary Hook, *"buy some rat poison from your employer back in March of this year. Perhaps you could tell us what it was that was purchased?"*

*"That be easy Zur, t'was arsnic, just plain white arsnic."*

With the word *"Arsenic"* so a low whisper began rumbling around the room, increasing to an almighty crescendo til those nearest the dock, unable to contain themselves, turned on the few misguided souls who dared to think Rebecca might be innocent and screamed.

*"See! ... we knew t'were arsenic all along!"*

Rebecca knew she was done for. Up in the gallery her brothers realised she would not be coming home with them whilst her stepfather, had he known their thoughts, would have agreed with them for once. Robert and George Worlock, on the other hand, wanted the day to end so that they could at last have the satisfaction of knowing their brother had been avenged.

Feeling very satisfied at the way things were progressing Ludlow turned back towards the witness box,
*"Thank you Miss Amey, you have been most helpful,"* he fawned.

After a very long hot day the tired, sweaty, smelly crowd gathered in that claustrophobic Court Room were not the only ones affected by the overbearing heat. Sir John, who felt the proceedings had gone on far too long, was anxious to send the Jury out for their deliberation. He was therefore not pleased when Mr Twiss asked to call certain villagers wishing to give character references in Rebecca's favour.

At last all the witnesses had been given their day in Court and Sir John began his summing up by telling the Jury they had a very simple choice to make. Was Thomas really an incurable drunkard who, despite pleas from his family and Doctor, ignored their advice and drank himself to an early grave or did his wife hate him enough to buy arsenic, on the pretence of killing a rat, mix it into his mug of ale and cold bloodedly murder him. He stressed the evidence regarding the purchase of the arsenic should be taken seriously and Rebecca may well have been telling the truth about wanting to kill that rat, however as a country girl why had she not put her husband's young dog to find it or set a trap? Doctor Edwards testified how Thomas' constant drinking always brought on inflammation of the stomach, although he had been most reluctant to name poison as cause of death. They had all listened to the last witnesses, friends of the prisoner, say how she always nursed her husband back to health whilst others had earlier claimed to have overheard her threaten to kill him on more than one occasion. Then of course they must consider young Mary Ann

Worlock, a child of her age would not lie in Court. Sir John also thought it most unacceptable that three learned Doctors, colleagues for some time, were unable to agree over the findings of the post mortem. However, he felt there was ample evidence and the Jury quite capable of making their own decision. And with that impartial and fair summing up Sir John sent the Jury away for their deliberation, his earlier words about spending no longer than half an hour fresh in their minds.

As the Guilty verdict was announced the Court once more erupted into chaos. Rebecca slumped back onto the wooden bench; her eyes went curiously blank as though all sight had left them. She made a choking sound, trying to protest her innocence, as the mob demanded her immediate execution, chanting *"Hang her! Hang her!"* at the top of their voices. She desperately tried to pretend this was not happening and it was a story from one of her books until she saw her brothers, head in hands, shoulders shaking as though they were sobbing. Nearby the Worlocks, no emotion on their cold hard faces, waited patiently for the Judge to pass sentence. Peter Gerrish stared impassively up at the ornate ceiling as Roger Edwards and Sarah Butler carried an hysterical Mary Ann from the room calling for her mother. From the day he became involved with the wretched Worlocks Doctor Edwards had felt nothing but pity for the child. Not only she was the same age as his own dear daughter, Martha, but at thirty nine, he was near enough the same age as the unfortunate Thomas.

Leaving Mary Ann in the care of Sarah Butler and the Court Matron, Roger Edwards returned in time to hear the Judge address the Court and pass sentence.

*"Prisoner Stand!!!"* boomed an order from the unseen Court Usher. With the help of her guards Rebecca was roughly dragged to her feet, praying for mercy from the man sitting in the high leather bound chair facing her, but already suspecting leniency would not be found in the heart of a Judge who had already passed the death sentence on seven lesser criminals than her at these Assizes. Repeating the guilty sentence, Sir John recommended she spend what little time there was left to her in the mortal world in seeking the forgiveness of her maker then, as if from nowhere, the usher appeared carrying the ominous black square cap which he placed on Judge Richardson's head.

*"Worlock, the sentence of this Court is that you be taken to the lawful Prison from whence you came and thence to a place of execution and that you there suffer death by hanging, your body to be handed to the Surgeons for dissection afterwards. Your body will then be buried within the walls of the Prison in which you shall have been confined before your execution. May God have mercy on your unfortunate Soul!!!"*

Then, as the Courtroom erupted into the expected furore, the same Usher handed the Judge a piece of paper to sign and, calling order, Sir John continued,

*"The execution will take place within the gates of Gloster Gaol three days hence ....take the prisoner away!!"*

Rebecca remained slumped on her uncomfortable bench and unless she was revived they would have to carry her back to her cell at the bottom of the steep spiral steps. The mob, content with the verdict, were quickly dispersing whilst already planning to regroup at nearby taverns to reminisce and drink themselves senseless...but not before they all sauntered past the prostrate figure, lying in Matrons arms surrounded by guards and who was now causing so much concern Dr Wilton had been sent for, to hurl their final abuses at her.

Back in his room, Sir John, suitably refreshed and minus his official regalia, was deep in conversation with Henry Ellacombe who was preparing to visit the Condemned Cell because, notwithstanding a fair trial and death sentence, his Honour was convinced, once revived, Rebecca would vehemently proclaim her innocence and there would be *"tiresome talk"* of an appeal. Cosseted together in a secluded corner, speaking in an almost inaudible whisper, Sir John suggested,

*"I would prefer her to confess her guilt before they hang her but, as I understand things, there is no way the Chaplain will ever persuade her. Therefore might I ask you to use the next few days and your understanding of the situation to convince her otherwise."*

Governor Symmonds was already in the prison yard with Doctor Wilton Snr, The Chaplain and Sir Edwin when Rebecca emerged from the same wagon that had earlier taken her to Court. Making to return to her old familiar cell in the Penitentiary she was brusquely restrained by one of the three female gaolers with whom, it was explained, she would be spending her remaining days on this earth. She listened as Mr Symmonds read out the rules and regulations for those who were condemned, this time she did not suggest she read them herself,

*"From now on you will never be on your own; someone will be with you at all times, where ever you go. There will be no mixing with other prisoners, meals will be taken in your cell with your guard, you will take your daily exercise alone, the other prisoners will have already returned to their cells."*

Rebecca made to speak but was abruptly stopped by a different Governor than of old,

*"In future you will speak to me only when asked or through one of your guards,"* and with that the heavy wooden door letting in what remained of the early evening sun was slammed, the key turned in the lock and life returned to

its dark sunless seclusion. Anxious for none of the other prisoners to see her, Mr Symmonds and his party swiftly escorted her to her Cell.

So, this was the Condemned Cell, all 9 foot by 6 foot of it! Glancing about her, from the uncomfortable looking wooden bed with its straw mattress, small roughly hewn wooden table on which was placed a battered old pewter plate, mug and bowl, she felt nothing but despair. Further searching uncovered an old worm eaten chair whilst in a tiny recess, hidden behind a grubby torn sack curtain, a battered washbasin and jug balanced precariously on a sloping shelf. Spying a wooden slop bucket on the stone slab floor brought back dreadful memories of this morning's experience in the black hole beneath the Courtroom. What light there was came from a heavily barred window and a tallow candle fixed to the wall. Her eyes then fell on her gaoler to whom, like the Chaplain, she took an instant dislike.

Within the hour, slightly more settled and composed, she was back to her old self and had already decided the uncouth uneducated old hag they insisted shared what was left of her unhappy existence lacked even the basic intelligence needed to carry out a normal conversation. Well, that was fine because she could think of nothing they might have in common. Besides there was much to be done since the incompetent Twiss had clearly not thought of an appeal against her sentence. Tonight, after supper, she would insist Symmonds provide some means with which to write to the numerous influential friends she was sure would remember her father and want to help his daughter, the innocent victim of a serious miscarriage of justice. In the meantime there were many other things she was going to have to get used to, especially as a condemned prisoner she would now be expected to wear the prison uniform she had so despised when working in the laundry!

Despite a supper of disgusting spicy pea and beef broth Rebecca ate ravenously, such was her hunger and she had barely finished when she heard the sound of keys turning in the lock and a turnkey appeared to escort her to the Chapel. The Chaplain had asked to see her. Despite being securely locked behind thick wooden doors within high sombre walls, her companion insisted she accompany her and gained immense perverse satisfaction from watching as her male colleague set about roughly fixing chains and fetters to Rebecca's wrists and ankles. For the first time since their initial meeting back in April, the Chaplain sensed Rebecca was pleased to see him. Maybe she finally accepted the seriousness of her situation and was ready to confess her sins. Arriving breathless, but in very good spirits, she believed this man was just the person she needed and took his request to see her as a sign someone 'on a higher plain' was listening to her prayers and had guided his heart. Knowing how important it was to keep him on her side, fully aware of just how useful he could be, Rebecca smiled beguilingly as she tried to impress him with,

*"I must apologize for keeping you waiting. Supper was served very late this evening, normally I would not eat such a meal, in fact back in the Penitentiary I particularly disliked spicy broth but when you have not eaten all day any food comes as a blessing."*

Showing genuine concern the Chaplain asked,
*"Were you not offered anything during your trial?"*

*"Oh yes I was well cared for,"* she lied, *"but who would wish to eat in that place. However it is of no consequence, I am here now and so very glad to see you because I have something of a serious nature to discuss with you."*

The Chaplain stood for a moment, facing the altar in silent thanks at what he believed was to come, forgetting he had been in this position many times before. Inviting Rebecca to join him in the front pew, he gave a dismissive nod towards her guard,
*"You will be sent for when we are finished."*

*"It be agin the rules Revrunt!"*

*"When it comes to the Lord and a repenting sinner there are no such things as rules, you will leave us!!"*

Returning to Rebecca, who was smugly satisfied at the way he had dismissed the old slut, he joined her in the front pew smiling, hands clasped together as if at worship, already thanking God for what he believed was the answer to his prayers…instead he heard her harsh voice demanding,
*"I am expecting your support in an appeal against my sentence."*

She then began ranting about her brute of husband who beat her on a slightest whim until he became ill, which was quite often and usually after a heavy bout of drinking, when she was expected to wander the lanes searching the hedgerows for natural remedies with which to cure him because they could never afford to pay Doctors' fees. She explained away the poison found in his stomach as hemlock, gathered by mistake along with pennyroyal, such was her haste to find something with which to ease his pain.

The Chaplain sat in dejected silence watching Rebecca shuffle backwards and forwards, waving her manacled hands erratically in the air in a frenzied attempt at claiming her innocence. She readily admitted,
*"I truly needed arsenic to kill a big rat I had seen about the yard. Of course had it been in my father's house he would have set his hunting dog on it or called one of the men to lay down a trap. Twiss failed to mention that or how*

*my husband's dog was only a whelp and not big enough to take on an adult rat, nor did he once relate to my true sufferings at the hands of the cruel man I married and the number of times I nursed him back to health before his tragic death."*

Sadly the Chaplain had heard it all before, from those guilty of lesser crimes than hers. He had been in Court for part of the trial and verdict this afternoon and knew it was the correct one, all that remained now was to convince her any appeal would be fruitless.

Back in the Condemned Cell, Rebecca was sure the Chaplain would help her. Had he not promised to go straight to the Governor and arrange for writing material to be brought to her so that she could begin her fight. Top of the list of those she planned writing to was the Home Secretary Lord Sidmouth, unfortunately she was not to know he took full responsibility for dealing with social unrest in Britain even if it meant executing all prisoners, man or woman, found guilty of Murder. Nor was she aware of the latest Bonner Handbill, now freely on sale at a halfpenny a time, relating to *"The Trial, Sentence and Sorrowful Lamentation of Rebecca Worlock who now lies under Sentence of Death and is to be executed on Wednesday next for the Wilful Murder of Thomas Worlock, her husband,"* or that he had no scruples about calling her *"a wicked murderess"* whilst happy to accuse her of committing matricide.

The Governor and Chaplain sat in silence til the latter finally suggested Rebecca would never be content unless she had the means with which to write to her supporters. Both men agreed there was no point in appealing to Lord Sidmouth, who was out of the country at the moment. Even Mr Twiss had indicated it would be useless, and before leaving for London and his delayed holiday to Malta, Sir John had also confirmed the evidence was so overwhelming that even asking for the King's Prerogative of Mercy to change the sentence to transportation for life, would be a waste of time. Instead it was agreed to allow her whatever she wanted and agree to her writing to whoever she wished in the hopes it would keep her occupied til she kept her appointment with the hangman on Wednesday morning. The arrival of quills, ink and paper later that evening received a very mixed reception in the Condemned Cell; sheer delight from Rebecca, utter contempt from her companion. Throughout a restless night spent on an itchy straw pallet, Rebecca's head spun with long lost names and vague faces of those to whom she was going to write in the morning, so that by the time they brought her thin warm, salty gruel for breakfast, there were already some letters waiting to be sent on their way.

Rebecca decided her unwelcome companion, Sarah, was no different to any other illiterate servant, probably an ex convict or the child of an ex convict, she plainly knew no other life save for one inside a gaol. For someone from the lower classes, her devotion to duty was commendable. However, yesterday evening's confrontation with the Chaplain, when it was clear he wished to talk in private, showed nothing but disrespect for her betters and Rebecca decided it was pointless involving her in any conversation concerning the remaining influential people to whom she would be writing. Although it was very early, barely light, Tuesday was promising to be a hot, sultry day and Sarah, angry and exhausted after a disturbed night, stood impatiently in the doorway of the condemned cell, jug of cold water in her hand. Banging it down noisily on the uneven unsteady table in the recess she barked,

*"Wash an,"* throwing a set of prison uniform onto the bed, *"dress thyself in these cus theese got vizters!"*

It had taken less than one disturbed night to recognise Rebecca's defiant streak and, making as if to talk to her, Sarah managed to catch her unawares and swiftly gathered up Aunt Partridge' precious damask gown discarded on the floor, then before she had chance to stop her, to grab the matching coat draped over the back of one of the chairs. Standing helpless in a dirty shift Rebecca pleaded for the return of her precious clothes but Sarah, anticipating everything, was already in the passage outside the Condemned Cell before she turned on her charge, gestured towards the jug and basin and reminded her,

*"Make shure theese wash proper cus t'wouldn't do t'look dirty!"*

Realising it was futile to answer back, Rebecca glanced at the gloating woman, shoddy clogs on ugly feet, grubby gown, black teeth, foul breath, filthy face that had not seen soap or water for some time and a mass of greasy limp hair tucked under a disgusting cap, enjoying some kind of personal pleasure by taking the only remaining thing she could still call her own and thought,

*"Even my father's poorest labourers were cleaner than her and she has the nerve to tell me to wash properly!"*

Alone at last Rebecca prepared for her visitors. The cold water on her tear swollen face brought immediate relief but as she began to wash the rest of her body so her mind returned to life at the Mill with her sisters before Thomas tricked her into one of drudgery, fear and eventually hatred! Back then a young servant girl brought jugs of hot water to their room every morning and on very special occasions, like Mamma's tea parties or if there were guests for dinner, they were allowed to use some of the sweet scented soap Papa sometimes brought back from his business trips. Rummaging through the bundle of clean prison clothes Rebecca realised she had been wearing the same shift for the past four months and wistfully imagined its replacement was made from the same soft linen as those of her childhood. She desperately wanted to wash her flea and lice infested hair. Although they had provided soap and towels in the Penitentiary and she was made to take a bath only yesterday she still didn't feel clean, her head itched, her hair was beginning to fall out at such an alarming rate all she could do was keep what was left covered with an old cap.

Fully expecting to see Mr Twiss, or his clerk, with news of her appeal she began humming quietly to herself. Pushing back the threadbare curtain separating the washstand in the alcove from the main cell she was met with the spectacle of a scowling Sarah, head to one side, face like thunder, black squinty eyes glaring at her from an equally black coarse grained face, arms crossed over a large drooping bosom, in the company of two elegant strangers. Momentarily forgetting where and who she was Rebecca angrily demanded,
*"How dare you come in here without knocking, go away til I send for you!"*

A furious Sarah replied,

*"Well, th'Condemned Cell do offer most fings but bein privute bain't one on um,"* then, grovelling before the visitors, perfumed handkerchiefs firmly over their faces, she gestured towards Rebecca, *"this un, Zurs, be partial to givin er orders,"* pausing only very briefly before turning on her to angrily demand, *"an who be you t'issue yer orders Miss?"*

For a few seconds, although it felt much longer, Rebecca stood transfixed before Sarah disappeared with her elegant companions in search of some much needed early morning fresh air, such was the terrible stench permeating this part of the Gaol but not before she saw both men surreptitiously place some coins in Sarah's grabbing hands as a reward for allowing them to visit the creature they had seen condemned in Court the day before.

Back and eager to continue her merciless torment, Sarah stepped forward and indicated with a swift nod of her head that Rebecca was to remove her filthy shift. Meekly she pulled the shift up towards her shoulders and over her head until she was standing, naked and slightly afraid, in front of the open cell door in full view of not only Sarah but any male gaoler or turnkey who happened to be passing. Deliberately dressing slowly she pulled the rough shift over her head and down over her bare shoulders followed by the dreadful coarse prison uniform, all the while remembering how, as a young girl back in those halcyon days at Bitton, there had been beautiful gowns and dresses made by the best dressmaker Papa's money could buy, dainty shoes for Church on Sundays, warm cloaks for winter and gaily decorated straw bonnets for summer picnics.

Sarah made to leave, her shift over but still threatened,
*"I be goin now but when I comes back t'night theese better be-ave thyself, writin they things,"* pointing to the half written letters strewn about the old

table, *"be a waste a time cus people bout t'ang b'aint never saved, specially usband killers like thee.!!!!"*

With the new day came a new companion. When Frances, a tall austere woman, strode confidently into the cells Rebecca inwardly groaned as she removed her cloak to reveal a crucifix in one hand and a bible in the other; placing both on the table she suggested they fall to their knees and thank God for guiding them safely through the night, for the delights he had provided for her breakfast and for moving the Governor's heart into giving her the means with which to write to her supporters who, God willing, might secure her release. Never having been religious since she was forced to sit through Reverend Elwes endless sermons at St Mary's as a child and then being told it was God's will that had taken her beloved father and brother from her leaving her mother with seven children, to be tempted by a young fortune hunter, the last thing she needed was a religious zealot for a companion.

Dinner over, some more 'vizters', not the expected Mr Twiss 'and his dwarf' but Henry Ellacombe and the Chaplain, arrived. However, when Henry explained they were not there to offer a reprieve or with news of an appeal but in search of a confession, Rebecca made it abundantly clear if the Chaplain and Frances remained there would never be a confession, even if it cost a Christian burial and her soul remained forever in purgatory. Sensing a stalemate Henry tactfully suggested to his companion,

*"I fear we are keeping you from your daily prayers and there are other prisoners who would be better served if you carried them out. I am quite content to remain here, so perhaps we might meet in your Chapel at, say 4 of the clock, to discuss things."*

The Chaplain needed little persuading. Pious, God fearing Frances, however, was appalled and refused to leave, being most anxious to join Henry in his prayers for Rebecca's soul. Claiming the same *"rules be rules"* excuse as her predecessor it needed the intervention of the Governor before she agreed to leave. Undeterred, such was Frances' determination to be privy to any confessions made within the Condemned Cell, when the Chaplain eventually opened the door to leave she was discovered on her knees eavesdropping at the key hole. One look from both clerics and a piercing scream from Rebecca told her she may have overstepped the mark on this occasion and, gathering up her skirt, she scurried way into the darkness.

On their own at last Rebecca begged,
*"Please, Mr Ellacombe, can you not use your influence and let me spend what may be my last night on this earth alone. Can you not see the creatures with which I am forced to share my last hours?"*

Of course it was an impossible request. The Condemned were never left on their own because the risk of suicide would cheat the massive hordes, currently making their way from all over the County to gather under the gallows outside the main gates of the Gaol as they spoke, out of witnessing the gruesome end to her wretched life but, from what he learned about the previous night and from what he had just witnessed, Henry conceded,

*"I fully understand, but you really do not help your own situation. However I will ask the Governor if a more understanding companion cannot be found for the coming night."*

Not content unless things always went her way and never grateful, nor stopping to think about the consequences of her acid tongue, Rebecca dismissed Henry as if he were a family servant,

*"Kindly do so and another thing, have you met with Twiss because he should be here with news of my appeal by now?"*

Taking a deep sigh, more to maintain his composure than anything else because she plainly misunderstood the seriousness of her position and would never be content unless she heard the answer she wanted to hear, Henry explained,

*"I am afraid Mr Twiss, Mr Ludlow and Sir John have long since left Gloucestershire."*

So her pathetic ineffectual defence council had abandoned her just like a rat on a sinking ship. Well she was a Flower and perfectly able to stand on her own two feet without the help of him or anyone else for that matter. Just wait until Lord Sidmouth received all the letters from her supporters, he would agree to a reprieve and recognise how influential her family still were in the County. As Henry listened to a further tirade against *"all those inadequate small minded unimportant people in Oldland"* he found himself comparing her to her mother, another proud arrogant woman, who also doggedly clung on to the belief her family still held considerable power and he wondered how much of her daughter's suffering could be laid at the dainty little feet of Mary Gerrish.

To obtain Sir John Richardson's desired confession Henry skilfully brought Mary Ann, Honor and John into the conversation,

*"Your children deserve a place to visit, to grieve and to lay their flowers, well that will only be possible if you return to Bitton and I cannot arrange that unless you confess to murdering Thomas for I fear the Judge has determined you are to be buried here within the Prison walls. However if you confess I will allow your mortal remains to come home to Bitton for a Christian burial, which I will personally conduct....now,"* leaning towards her and taking hold of her trembling hands, *"please take heed of my words because there is very little time left to you."*

Rebecca asked after her children,

*"What have they done with them, will they be coming to see me? Do they know of what I am accused, where I am and what will happen if I there is no reprieve. Are you aware the two younger ones have never been christened, Thomas would not allow it?"*

Henry assured her,

*"They were at their father's side when he died and know you are charged with his murder as a consequence so, yes, they are aware of your situation. However, after tomorrow, they will need to be very brave when they learn you will not be coming home again and sadly Mary Ann is already back in Bitton."*

*"So,"* she whimpered, *"I shall never see them again,"* before burying her head in her hands and sobbing uncontrollably. Composing herself she asked, *"Who will tell them that I am never coming back to them in this world because the Worlocks will take great delight in giving them different versions of the truth?"*

Henry promised,

*"I will ask John and Martha to join me and tell them myself."*

*"Are they both well, my father in law was very much crippled and dependent on Martha the last time I saw him"* she haughtily replied, as if casually passing the time of day with a guest at one of her mother's afternoon tea parties, conveniently forgetting that by murdering his son she was probably the main reason for John's rapid decline in health.

*"Losing his son to your poison did not help!"* was Henry's curt reply.

Suitably chastised, Rebecca sensibly chose not to ask after the Flowers for which Henry was mightily relieved because, thanks to Peter Gerrish, he had been unable to talk to her mother. Therefore unless there was a reprieve Rebecca would leave her mortal world totally unaware her innocent children had been disowned by Grandmamma Mary, possibly on the advice of her young husband, to be farmed out amongst reluctant Worlocks until her dependable old mother in law, who was already caring for her crippled and very sick husband, had taken them in, but only on the understanding they went into an orphanage should she not return.

Rebecca was taking a late afternoon stroll round the lonely exercise yard when she was met by a small crowd of well dressed men, women and young children all clutching bibles. Like the two dandies who invaded her cell this morning they too had paid to gawk at the sinful murderess that was to hang tomorrow. They gasped, some genuflected and crossed themselves, as she emerged from the black hole of the prison, fettered hand and foot, they all shook their heads in disbelief as she shuffled past them, head bowed, unseen tears in her eyes. They all pressed silk perfumed handkerchiefs to their faces, thus preventing the stench from reaching their delicate nostrils, until finally, having seen enough, they walked away hands clenched in prayer leaving her to wonder how much more degradation there would be before it all ended..

Back in her cell, desperately trying to ignore what the heartless Frances had done, she demanded to know,
*"If you are such a God fearing woman why did you make me suffer in front of all those people?"*

Unrepentant, the fanatical Frances replied.

*"They cumd t'see watta awful sinner you be, an you cud ave showd a more grateful art seein as they've bin prayin fur thy soul in the ope theese'll see there be but one God, n'fact why bain't thee on thy knees askin im fur is fergivnuss right now!"*

Ignoring these furious outpourings, Rebecca went back to the uneven table, picked up her quill pen and declared,
*"You are wasting your time because I have done no wrong and there are more important things with which to occupy my mind other than asking your God for forgiveness,"* and with that she defiantly returned to her remaining letters.

Frances, fearful her pious friends would chastise her for failing to convert a disbelieving sinner to the ways of the Lord, suddenly lunged at Rebecca. Angrily snatching the quill from her hand, Frances brandished her dilapidated old Bible in her face and screamed,
*"Dussent thee know thy stupid evul wuman, there'll be undreds of people watchin thee ang tommorra, all on um wantin t'see thee dead an it bain't no good writin these!"* snatching up the completed letters Frances hysterically threw them on the floor, stamping them under her dirty clogs, *"cuz they all wants t see thee dead, even thy preshus famly aven't bothered with thee an,"* pausing to take breath she folded her hands as if at prayer, *"th'only person who can save thee now be the Lord Jesus imself!"*

Of course Frances was right, Rebecca had upset too many people in Bitton and Oldland to expect their pity and by late afternoon she expected to hang come the morning, so what did it matter whether she confessed or not so long as Ellacombe kept his word and, after she finished her supper of highly spiced almost inedible tough gristly beef along with the usual tasteless vegetables and stale bread, she sent word she wished to see him.

*"Tell him I have something of the greatest importance to discuss with him"* was all she would say.

Rebecca was taking her evening exercise leaving Frances on her own in the Condemned cell scarcely able to disguise her excitement. Anticipating Reverend Ellacombe might bring the Governor with him, she settled herself on one of the rickety old chairs, bible open at a suitable passage, in readiness for the moment she would, at last, witness the answer to all her prayers and be present when this sinful woman finally made her peace with the Lord. Walking into the yard Rebecca was met by another large, more aggressive, crowd but as far as she could see no one was carrying a bible. Acclimatising her eyes to the sunlight she fiercely searched for Frances only for the spectre of Mr Symmonds to appear before her, whereupon grabbing her firmly by one arm he turned to address the menacing throng gathering dangerously close.

*"This is the unfortunate creature who stands convicted of murdering her husband and hangs in the morning. Not only that but she resolutely refuses to confess to the crime and I therefore beg you all to ask almighty God to show His mercy upon her come the morrow!"*

After four months of incarceration Rebecca's mind was in turmoil. She now accepted she had never loved Thomas but had only used him as a means of escape, blaming him for frittering away what little of Papa's money they had given her. Her mother had denied her a proper inheritance or a dowry when she married. How could she know the stupid, misguided woman would marry a boy and allow him to influence her decision to withhold her rightful inheritance? Over the years no one had stood by her as the Worlocks forced her into the life of misery as the wife of an illiterate penniless and lowly carcass butcher, beholden unto his father for employment, in return for a pittance of an income. If only she cared to stop and think, just for one minute, about the reality of her situation and realised how, before she chose to tamper with his beer, Thomas was not only strong enough to work alongside his brothers but also earned a good living as part of a successful family business.

The noise of keys turning in the lock woke her from her dreams as Reverend Ellacombe, accompanied by the Governor and a woman she had never seen before, entered her cell. Mr Symmonds dismissed Frances with an abrupt wave of his hand and introduced Hannah who would be spending the rest of the night with her.

*"Frances will be assigned other tasks this evening and Sarah's special roles are needed elsewhere,"* was all he would say but Rebecca knew this was all Henry's doing and, grabbing hold of his hands, she thanked him for caring. She then turned, cold faced, towards the Governor and this person called Hannah.

Before taking their leave Symmonds whispered further instructions to the young woman,

*"She must be encouraged to sleep, Doctor Hagdell Wilton has left a strong sleeping draught to bring about that effect, however should it not work then there is further medication here,"* waving a battered old pewter jug, *"and do not forget there will be a gaoler outside in the passage at all times."* Turning to Rebecca he was obliged to ask,

*"Worlock is there anything else you require?"*

About to spend her last night in this world, aware she was to hang in the morning, there was nothing to lose so she replied,

*"Yes Mr Symmonds I fear there is!"*

For a painful few seconds an awkward silence descended over the Condemned Cell and Henry Ellacombe, fully aware of the exhibitions that had taken place in the exercise yard during the day and equally disgusted at such a spectacle, prayed she would not cause another scene whilst the Governor, prayed he was not about to be interrogated over his involvement, or lack of it, in there being no reprieve. Standing as tall as her five foot and four inches would allow, a defiant Rebecca began,

*"This morning I was obliged to change my own clothes for ...these,"* sensually gliding her hands over her still ample breasts, thin waist and bony hips, before gathering the skirt of her prison uniform with both hands and swaying from side to side, *"the woman guard, whom you have since dismissed, took a valuable damask gown I had been wearing, together with a matching coat, which was hanging there,"* pointing to the old wooden chair where, not more than half an hour ago, the zealous Frances had been sitting full of anticipation, *"yet despite my pleas for its return it still has not arrived. Can I therefore assume she has stolen it?"*

Symmonds truthfully said he was unaware of this and promised to make immediate enquiries, although deep down he suspected it was long gone. People like Sarah looked on the property of the condemned as theirs to dispose of as they wished and an outfit made from such quality material as damask, however old and filthy, would fetch a decent price in the Gloucester underworld. Seeing the uncomfortable look on his face Rebecca grasped at what she knew was her last chance to gain revenge on the man she blamed for her living hell over the past four months and continued.

*"That gown, Mr Symmonds, was a personal gift from my late aunt and the only thing I had to leave my children, I had planned to instruct Reverend Ellacombe to sell it for their benefit, however it now appears one of your servants entrusted with my care has cheated them out of it."* Hands on hips, eyes blazing like

large fiery saucers, she turned to face her adversary one last time, *"How many more times am I to be hawked out on public view and what news is there of my appeal?"*

Relieved her tirade appeared to have ended, all the Governor could say was, *"You will not be disturbed again and there is no news of your appeal but, rest assured, I will bring any decision to you myself,"* and with that he was gone, shaking his head slightly as he did.

It was a very pensive Henry Ellacombe who joined the Chaplain, Governor Symmonds and both Hagdell Wiltons for supper later that evening. Sitting in the dark, oppressive dining room of the Governor's Quarters with just the loud tick of the large clock on the wall for company no one found much to discuss. Glancing around the cheerless room Henry spotted a large ceiling lamp above his head which, had it been lit, might have given the place a better hue instead of which the few flickering candles only cast further shadows over a place that was already dismal enough. It was as if the room itself was in mourning, portraits of nameless grim faced men hung on dark recessed walls but it was much too gloomy to make out any family likeness to Symmonds or whether they were of his predecessors and Henry was not about to ask. Next his eyes rested on the large fireplace where, as it was August and in the midst of a sweltering heatwave, thankfully no fire blazed in the hearth although the wood and coals were laid should the weather change. The battered old poker and tongs were neatly crossed as if making some ritualistic offering for the wretch languishing in the Condemned Cell. Henry noticed a pair of threadbare arm chairs standing untidily either side of the grate and thinking of his own furniture in his study back at Bitton Rectory he imagined how even his beloved Anne, who always stood alongside him and supported him in everything he was called to do in the Lord's name, would have difficulty making a loving home for him and the children in a dreadful place such as this.

Apart from Henry, all the others had witnessed many prison hangings during their careers and although tomorrow would not be his first, there had been many during his short but interesting and varied life especially whilst with the Navy in Portsmouth, Rebecca would be the first woman to dance the hangman's jig and he was therefore extremely apprehensive about the whole thing especially when he recalled the chaotic scenes following an earlier hanging which, by sheer coincidence, had taken place almost three years to the day. He knew he was taking something of a risk by agreeing to allow another convicted criminal to rest in St. Mary's Churchyard but Rebecca was no Benjamin Caines and, apart from her behaviour as a child and the dreadful way she had treated her poor husband, she had never caused any trouble in the village so it was the least he could offer in return for a confession. If anyone, Peter Gerrish for example, objected he would point out that surely now was a time for forgiveness.

Unable to stand the intolerable silence any longer Henry finally spoke, to no one in particular but to anyone who cared to listen,
*"There is absolutely no hope for the wretched woman; she will hang in the morning?"*

*"Oh yes, there is no way she will be reprieved,"* whispered the more experienced Governor, *"Lord Sidmouth and his Government will see to that."*

*"Will they not reconsider...there are three young children who will be orphaned tomorrow,"* pleaded Henry.

*"No man is so sinful that he deserves to be murdered, especially by his wife,"* interrupted the Chaplain.

Doctor Wilton Snr. nodded in silent agreement, although his son remained silent, staring impassively at the wall as if in his own thoughts. Remembering how Rebecca constantly refused to ask God for forgiveness, the Chaplain continued,
*"There is little evidence she has been touched by God. Indeed both you and I,"* looking straight at Henry, *"have pleaded with her over several hours and the only signs of repentance came when I took the extreme step of threatening to withhold absolution and even then she only confessed once you agreed to take her home for burial!"*

Listening to words of agreement echoing between his fellow diners Henry dearly wanted to ask,
*"How would you know of life in a small village like Bitton, of the endless hardships and struggles Anne and I strive to ease amongst our congregation because, if you did, you might understand the actions of the poor wretch waiting in the Condemned Cell and,"* not asking for her to be adjudged entirely innocent, *"offer some measure of compassion other than the death sentence."*

# CHAPTER SIXTEEN

Rebecca reluctantly swallowed the sleeping draught and allowed herself to be guided to the scratchy uncomfortable bed. Despite her earlier misgivings, Hannah was not a bit like Sarah but kind and considerate, nor was she as virtuous as Frances with her ceaseless religious outpourings. There were no orders to wash and change, no thieving fingers taking what meagre possessions she still had, no fancy dandies arriving to gloat at her misfortune and there were no prayers thanking God for his infinite mercies from one of his crazed disciples. Instead there were soothing words of comfort, re-assuring arms about her shoulders and, above all, understanding.

Rebecca heard the sound of shuffling coming from the darkness of her cell and was about to accuse Hannah of waking her from her slumbers when she saw her brother George standing in the doorway, eager to tell her she was going home, possibly as early as tomorrow afternoon. She knew he would come for her but was nevertheless disappointed not to see her older brother Lamorock with him but, of course, he was with Papa at the Mill and far too busy. George said Lamorock would be waiting for her tomorrow. She asked after Mamma and was comforted to learn she was also waiting for her; she even had her old room ready. George did not stay long, there was much to do before tomorrow and it would mean an early start for them all. He promised to be waiting outside the Prison gates just before eight o' clock although she probably would not see him. Outside it was still dark and a light breeze was blowing through the docks, gently stirring the ropes and riggings of the heavily laden ships that, just like her, were waiting for the morning light to begin their long journey home.

Lying on Grandmamma's day bed, with its red and white dimity covering, she listened as Papa read the letters sent by his friends and business colleagues. Everyone supported her and he promised things would be fine once they were placed before the Home Secretary and she was not to distress herself, he had spoken to John and Martha who not only understood but agreed that Thomas deserved to suffer for being such a drunken brute and they eagerly awaited her return.

Clambering from her bed she stumbled frantically about the dark cell, lit only by a tallow candle, before collapsing back onto her uncomfortable heap of straw where she continued her conversation, this time with her elder brother Lamorock who was now sitting in Papa's chair explaining how he was on his way back to Bitton to ensure everything was ready for her return. Glancing over Lamorock's shoulder she could just make out a dark shape of someone standing in the recess and, thinking it was Martha, she complained bitterly about how impossible it was to care for the children what with Thomas being ill again. Hannah walked towards her and, placing two arms around her shoulder, gently lay her back onto her bed as Rebecca continued rambling incoherently to her invisible visitors.

Awake again she fumbled around in the darkness bumping into the table and knocking over one of the chairs in her frantic search for her family before tripping over a slumbering Hannah. Mistaking her for their young kitchen maid Rebecca began an angry onslaught,
*"Wake up, wake up, you lazy good-for-nothing girl and tell me where the Master is, did he not leave any message for me!"*

Although patient and more understanding than the dreadful Sarah and the pious Frances, Hannah was nearing the end of her tether and, with an exhausted tone to her voice, she pleaded,
*"There bain't no one, theese must get zum sleep!"*

Meanwhile, thanks to Hagdell Wilton's sedative and the Governor's *"further medication"* in the battered old grey jug outside her cell, an increasingly incoherent Rebecca continued to insist her family were indeed present,
*"How could you possibly know who has been here, you have slept most of the time!"*

Unable to convince neither Hannah nor the guard outside her cell, Rebecca sat on the edge of her bed, head in her hands, whimpering as she tried to clear her mind until, spying the now empty mug on the table, she realised the ale and sleeping draught had done their work and, no longer able to offer any resistance, she allowed herself to be put back to bed. Lying there in the dark, lucid for the very briefest of moments, she knew unless there was a miracle she would die in the morning and, surrounded by silence, she gradually picked out the sound of a sleeping Hannah and wished she had the means with which to end it all and cheat those who had remained behind after the trial just to see her dance on the end of a rope.

Rousing from her slumbers she was surprised to see Reverend Ellacombe in the darkness. She had long made her peace with him and did not expect him until the morning, surely it was not that time already. Maybe he was here to tell her he had changed his mind about taking her home ...but everything was arranged why else would her family have travelled all this way. Sitting together on the edge of her bed Henry read out a letter from Mamma. Powerless to leave

Gloucester he had written Mary a short note begging her daughter's forgiveness for causing so much trouble and amazingly she had received it because Peter Gerrish, the only person capable of preventing it from reaching its destination, was currently away from home, coincidentally in Gloucester on business. In her letter Mamma assured the Curate her dearest daughter must not concern herself about what people were saying, they had always been like that where the Flowers were concerned and of course she was forgiven, in fact as soon as she was back in Bitton she would waste no time in telling her so personally.

Rebecca sat bolt upright in her bed, the scratchy straw mattress refused to give her any rest. Apart from the tallow candle and the dim light straining through the Judas hole, the Cell was still in complete darkness and would be for some time. From within the cell she could clearly pick out the loud snores of Prudence and Nancy and knew it would not be long before they would be up busying themselves before the Governor arrived. Remembering the overbearing heat of yesterday the thought of spending another day working in the Wash House filled her with dread. The taskmaster could be a very unforgiving man at times and she often reached the point when she felt she was about to collapse from exhaustion. It sounded like Prudence was already up and about because she could hear that old familiar voice saying,
*"Didn't I tell thee you ouldn't be yer much longer, didn't I tell thee you ould be goin home t'thy family, well t'morra theese'll be going ome f'good so I've come to bid thee goodbye."*

Rebecca desperately wanted to take hold of her, to thank her for understanding and befriending her when none of the others would. She called out her name but with each cry there came no answer until she found herself shouting out,
*"Prudence, Prudence, PRUDENCE! Where in heaven's name are you, in God's name why don't you answer me!"*

You lost privileges for not having your bed made or your corner of the cell cleaned ready for the Governor, so with her companions already up and about, Rebecca sought to join them only to fall helplessly back onto the bed which creaked alarmingly as it scraped noisily along the stone floor, waking her desperately weary minder who was taking another illicit nap.

Hannah was becoming more and more concerned about Rebecca's lack of sleep and how it was going to affect her behaviour in the morning. Hagdell Wilton's sedative plus copious amounts of ale normally guaranteed a restful night but this particular prisoner was proving a rare exception. She had been awake and deep in conversation with her entire family most of the night prompting Hannah to consider calling for the guard more than once, so convinced was she that there really were people in the cell with them. There could problems and. thinking about all the hangings in which she had played her part, Hannah defiantly reminded herself that none of her other unfortunate charges had ever been carried to their execution through exhaustion or lack of sleep and determined,

*"This un bain't bout t'ruin me reputation cuz of who she thinks she be, cuz who'll git th'blame if she bain't able t'climb th'steps to th'gallows?"*

Sleep continued to elude Rebecca as her nocturnal ramblings increased and tested Hannah's patience to the limit until it finally snapped and, delving into a little bundle under her chair, she brought out a hidden flask of gin. Unfortunately, Hannah was not to know how gin only served to remind Rebecca of life with her despised husband. Nevertheless with hours still to go before dawn Hannah doggedly increased her efforts to convince Rebecca the only way either of them could hope for any sleep was with a few sips of her gin to enhance the effect of the Governor's ale and the Doctor's sleeping draught.

Outside, Wednesday August 16th already promised to be hot and sultry. Meanwhile inside the claustrophobic Condemned Cell its occupant continued entertaining her invisible visitors,

*"Did you not see my husband leave just then Hannah, he came to ask my forgiveness for the way he treated me when he had the drink in him. He said if only my family had not denied him my inheritance our marriage would have been very happy and there would have been no need for him to work for his father, forever killing animals. He said he could have helped run our Mill whilst I became Mamma's travelling companion."*

Tired, drugged and drunk, thanks to a second mug of ale into which Hannah had skilfully slipped a fair amount of her gin, Rebecca now staggered dangerously unsteadily about her cell waiting for the mercy of dawn which was at least two hours away.

With daylight creeping eerily through the small dirty window high on the wall, Rebecca anxiously searched for all the people with whom she had spent most of the darkness. Unable to find them she convinced herself they were in another part of the building waiting to take her home. Hannah tried to reason with her,

*"There bain't been no one yer but we two n im,"* cocking her head towards the door, *"outside all night. You just dreamed it."*

*"I did not dream it, my family were here my father even read my letters of support!"* Rebecca screamed, stamping an already unsteady foot angrily on the uneven flagstone floor. Losing her balance she collapsed into an intoxicated heap alongside her bed from where she raised a heavy insensible head towards Hannah, her brain swirling, desperately trying to focus her eyes to her

surroundings, before demanding, *"but how would you know, you have been asleep for most* of *the night?"*

Eager for no accusations of sleeping on duty to reach the Governors' ears, Hannah called the guard from outside the cell to confirm no one had passed through the door that night. Feeling safe, she joined Rebecca on the floor, placed a comforting arm around her shoulders and whispered softly,
*"No wun bin t'see thee, you dreamed it all cus you was crazy wiv th'Doctors medsune and th'Guvners ale."*

With all the 'medsun' gone Rebecca slowly regained her composure and, as the soporific effect of the previous night wore off, grim reality hit her. There was now little hope of any reprieve and she accepted she would be meeting her Maker all alone. With her brain slowly clearing she accepted neither Papa nor Lamorock had been to see her. What on earth made her think that when they had both been dead for over twenty years! She could not even be sure if anyone would be waiting to take her home later today because Mamma was now controlled by Peter Gerrish and he would never allow her nor her three orphaned children to return home to Golden Valley, so the suggestion that her own room was ready for her was also in her drunken dreams. Images of the Worlocks remained fresh in her mind but again she knew that neither Thomas, John nor Martha had been to see her, that too had been a figment of her drug and alcohol induced imagination, as were their assurances of forgiveness.

Hannah and the other gaoler could never remember sharing the condemned cell with anyone so lonely as Rebecca Worlock, even her supposedly close family appeared to have abandoned her.

With dawn everyone, from the most desperate prisoner to the Governor himself, woke early in readiness for what was to take place in a few hours time. Mercifully Rebecca had no idea what was happening in the chamber above the New Drop where preparations were well in hand for her appointment with 'The Finisher of the Law' as some people chose to call the hangman. Gone were the days when the Condemned at Gloster Gaol were publicly hanged from dilapidated wooden gallows on the roof, their pain, suffering and humiliation for all to see. Everything now took place in private away from prying eyes. The first indication the baying mob would have today was when her body hurtled through the newly installed trap door above the Gate Lodge, neck broken, eyes bulging and body twitching on the end of a strong rope. Naturally her tormentor, the hangman, felt decidedly aggrieved by these changes claiming he always gained immense pleasure from all the shouts and cheers from well wishers below. In fact he often ended his show by raising his hat and making a long sweeping bow to his appreciative audience beneath him.

Despite their best endeavour's not many people, except maybe the Governor, knew much about the dark elusive figure seen furtively wandering around the Gaol over the past days. Some habitual criminals, content to spend their time incarcerated behind bars, boasted of catching him creeping around the gatehouse, his face hidden by a large floppy hat whilst others claimed to have seen him deep in conversation in a cheerless corner of the Prison Chapel with the Chaplain. Whichever rumour was to be believed, it was safe to assume the hangman had been secreted in Gloster Gaol a lot longer than people realised and with Rebecca amongst eight prisoners sentenced to death that week, although she was the only one to end her pathetic days on the Gloster Gallows, it was quite possible he had been lurking about other Gaols in the County for some time before that. Much as he despised the man, Symmonds was expected to entertain the hangman during his stay but at least he was spared having to know his real name and simply referred to him as Jack Ketch, the nickname earned by all executioners following the ineptness of the real Jack Ketch when he dispatched the Duke of Monmouth on Tower Hill following the doomed Monmouth Rebellion. He was officially employed by the Government who decreed the County should pay him around £1 plus expenses, board and lodging for this week's work. It was a long cry from the days when his namesake depended on whatever the condemned could give him on the scaffold which, on a good day, might be a sovereign or even more should his client be wealthy, but little or nothing if they were poor. As the latter was usually the norm extra money came from various perks. Like the objectionable Sarah, the hangman got to keep or sell any unwanted clothes and he would have looked on the green, red and gold damask gown as his, had she not got there first. The more disreputable amongst them sold lengths of rope, fraudulently claiming they came from the gallows upon which celebrated criminals had died and there was a booming trade in gruesome relics, none more so than with Madame Marie Tussaud who was systematically collecting everything from clothes, locks of hair, pinion ropes, personal keepsakes to hanging hoods for her famous wax museum. Those suffering from cancer or an incurable illness but were desperate for a cure, bribed old Jack to place the limp cold hand of his latest customer on their tumour, cancer or wart, such was their belief it was a remedy that might bring about a miraculous improvement to their lingering death. It was not unknown to see wealthy cultured women readily bare their breasts in public to have the cold clammy hand of an executed murderer placed upon them. Eventually this macabre trade came to the notice of the authorities who had little choice but to pay for an official hangman if only because condemned wretches, about to be publicly executed, had enough on their minds and had no control over their pinioned hands with which to hold any coins, however meagre.

Up from her uncomfortable bed but, thanks to last night's alcohol, still slightly unsteady and unsure of her surroundings, Rebecca sat at the dilapidated old table with a confused dazed look on her face. Dressed only in an old shift, she toyed with the food before her, the fresh bread and real butter she had requested for her last meal no longer seemed so appealing. She knew there was to be no reprieve; Symmonds had just left after coolly telling her,

*"As there have been no instructions from my Lord Sidmouth or his deputy the law will take its course, they will come for you later this morning."*

So she was to die, despite all her protestations of innocence, all her letters to her fathers' old friends and claims to have been the victim of a cruel drunkard of a husband whom she never intended killing but whom she only wished to stop from hurting, not only herself but their three young children. Assuming she was alone for the first time since she entered the Condemned Cell, unable to see the gaoler outside keeping a distant but discreet watch because it was reasoned she might still try to cheat the hangman, Rebecca took the thin blanket from her bed and, wrapping it around her shoulders, gazed at her untouched breakfast and sipped the tea they had thoughtfully provided, unaware it contained yet more of Dr Hagdell Wilton's 'medsun'. As she waited for Reverend Ellacombe her befuddled mind returned to the day her world fell apart, when all he could do was pray for Thomas who was past help. Later when she was asked what happened how could she ever confess to only wanting to keep him from her bed...not kill him!!

Suppressing a tear she remembered Robert Henderson arriving to draw up Thomas' Will, Doctor Edward's warning that he could not last much longer and Robert frantically having to scribble down the remainder of his wishes before he became too weak to sign it. She had been so proud when Thomas had signed the Register after their marriage, unlike her stepfather who could only make his mark when he married her mother, but when he died he only had the strength to make his feeble mark on his hastily drawn up Will.

With her husband dead she soon convinced herself how thoroughly the Worlocks and his drinking cronies at the Chequers had done their work persuading him that, whilst she was determined to keep him from her bed, she had been more than willing for his place to be taken by another. Mindful of her flighty ways before they married, Thomas believed their lies and, whilst he had left her his pitiful estate, he denied her any future happiness by insisting she remain a widow and it was only hers til the children came of age....Well, whilst she was minded to confess to his murder she would take the identity of any secret lover, and whether he ever existed at all, with her to the grave.

A set of clean clothes and a small tumbler of diluted gin arrived along with the Chaplain who made another futile attempt at getting her down on her knees in prayer. Perplexed he pleaded,

*"You made your peace and confessed to Reverend Ellacombe. Therefore I beg you, in the name of God, to join me on you knees to ask him for the strength you are going to need today."*

Desperate for Henry Ellacombe to arrive, she was even more convinced she was right not to trust this man especially when, on more than one occasion, he had accused her of being extremely stupid for refusing to accept her dangerous situation and confess to murdering her violent husband. But accepting there was no point in continuing with the charade, she relented.

*"Very well, yes I killed my husband, what other choice was there, he was a brute and deserved to die!"*

Recalling his conversation with Henry the previous evening the Chaplain responded,

*"But, when you confessed to Reverend Ellacombe, only yesterday, you claimed his death was an accident. Now you are saying you planned it all along."*

The nonchalant shrug of her shoulders and the indifferent look on her face told him she was guilty and, silently handing her a copy of the Holy Bible, he suggested,

*"I hope this will give you the strength, comfort and solace for what is about to befall you,"* quietly adding, *"May your unhappy soul soon find everlasting peace."*

Rebecca truly believed Henry Ellacombe was different from the others. Although she had only known him since his arrival in Bitton as a young Curate, in her present unstable mental state she believed he was the only person who could save her from the gallows. She therefore clung desperately onto his every word, however insignificant, in the vain hope it could be interpreted as proof of her innocence. Naively believing he understood her unhappy situation at home, she mistakenly fantasised he was acting as mediator between both families over the care of her children but, although distraught during those first dreadful days in the Penitentiary, when the weeks passed with no visit from them, she accepted she would never see them again…at least not in this world and suddenly it became all Ellacombe's fault because now she was going to die and they would never hear her side of the story!

Henry arrived just as Rebecca prepared for her traumatic day and, embarrassed at finding her only in a thin shift, suggested now might be a more convenient time for the Chaplain to join him to search out Mr Symmonds. For the second time in nearly as many days she was given hot water with which to wash. Back in the Penitentiary it was cold or tepid depending on how long it had been away from the fire and where you were in the queue. They even gave her some soap. However these gifts came at a price…in the relative seclusion of the recess the once benevolent Hannah, now in complete but exhausted control after her long disturbed night, ordered her,

*"Wash thyself proper an give us thy dirty clothes,"* pointing at the shivering form before her, *"specially thik shift."*

Thinking they were quite alone, Rebecca allowed Hannah to help her undress and wash, completely unaware the surly guard outside was using his perfect vantage point on the other side of the metal grill to enjoy the rare sight of the naked body of a condemned female prisoner!

In a more secluded part of the Gaol, far away from the desolate scene in the Condemned Cell, Governor Symmonds, Henry Ellacombe and both Hagdell Wiltons awaited the arrival of Sir Edwin Bayntum who, as High Sheriff of Gloucestershire, was obliged to attend all executions carried out in the County. Sir Edwin had met with Symmonds only yesterday when, not surprisingly, the main topic of conversation was the recent Summer Assize. The Governor's admission that he was, *"mightily relieved,"* there was just one poor wretch left to send to her Maker brought about an equally frank response from the High Sheriff,

*"You are a dashed lucky man Symmonds. Thanks to Sir John I have witnessed no less than seven this week, in lesser Gaols in the County and I thank God tomorrows will be the last!"*

Back in the Condemned Cell Rebecca absentmindedly opened the bundle Hannah had left on her unmade bed. There was no point observing prison rules this morning, after all who or how would they punish her and she was overjoyed to discover the Governor, or maybe it was Hannah, had somehow managed to rescue Aunt Partridge's precious damask gown from the obnoxious Sarah. It was crumpled and extremely grubby but it was hers and now she could face the gallows suitably dressed instead of wearing the unacceptable alternative, a white burial shroud. By the time the Governor's party reached the Condemned Cell she was washed and ready but far from composed because with their arrival she knew death was not far away.

Beyond the Gaol an expectant exited mob was gathering, the whole of the city of Gloster and most of the surrounding countryside were currently spilling onto the streets. Those willing and able to pay up to 2/- had already found their places in nearby windows and on rented rooftops, whilst the side streets were

*262*

filled with the wagons and carts of those unfortunate to have only secured somewhere to stand and glimpse a distant view. Back in front of the Gaol the scene directly before the Lodge Gates was swiftly gaining a carnival atmosphere. Many had trudged miles on foot through the late evening or the early hours to ensure they had the best view in town only, having found their spot, to find there was nothing to do except join the party and descend into a long night of drinking and debauchery of every kind. By first light the city, especially the roads leading to Gloster Gaol, was jammed with drunk and disorderly crowds of men, women and children, all in celebratory mood, as if they were about to begin a holiday rather than witness an act of humiliation against a fellow human being. Taverns had been open since first light, pie men were doing a roaring trade, hawkers yelled out their wares and the increasingly wild crowd was becoming more and more mercurial as the hours dragged slowly by. In Barrack Square, with less than an hour to go, the space outside the massive wooden doors was crammed with the highest and lowest life Gloucestershire could muster. Pickpockets and thieves walked alongside street urchins, young dandies mingled with family parties, simple honest tradesmen and their wives passed the time of day with gentlemen whilst prostitutes and whores plied their special trade on street corners and behind every available high wall. Heated arguments prevailed between those still sober enough to believe Rebecca might be innocent and those too full of the drink to care so long as they had their sport, until word of her confession began circulating, then drunken scuffles became fierce fist fights as those, *"who always knowed th'bitch were guilty,"* demanded apologies from the doubters.

A confession, of course, meant brisk business for all the migrant street sellers and pamphleteers from Bristol who had descended on Gloster armed with the latest copy of Bonner's Lamentation for the soul of Rebecca Worlock, bought directly from his printing works late yesterday evening for tuppence a dozen, they were now selling at a ha'penny a sheet!

With the gallows hidden away above the Gate Lodge the knowledgeable mob no longer enjoyed the spectacle of a public hanging and there were those who felt deceived at the arrival of the New Drop. When public executions took place on the roof you saw how bravely or cowardly the condemned met their death. You also got to see the poor condemned creature walking, sometimes carried, into the prison exercise yard to have their leg irons removed and the noose placed around their neck. Often, to add to the atmosphere, the Governor and his official party were there and the prison bell would toll out it's dreadful sound. Now that was all gone, replaced by a long wait until the hangman, thought so competent by the Authorities they considered themselves fortunate to have secured his services, carried out these tasks in private.

With morning service suspended and all prisoners back in their cells the Chaplain swiftly made his way towards the Condemned Cell to join his colleagues where it was agreed that it would best if Henry Ellacombe were to enter first. On seeing him Rebecca grabbed hold of her mug, took another large swig of gin and let out a piercing pathetic scream,

*"No! No! Surely it is not time! I am not ready, please, please let me have longer, I must have more time to prepare!"* desperately glancing past her visitors towards the open door and beyond as if hoping to see someone with a last minute reprieve. Swaying uncontrollably against a decidedly unsteady chair she continued pleading for more time, *"Please, let me stay for a few more moments, my brothers have not arrived!"*

Henry Ellacombe, who was standing close by her right side whilst the Chaplain took up his place on her left, stressed quietly,
*"I am sorry but it is time, we can wait no longer. Do you wish to pray with us before we go?"*

Rebecca, desperate to gain more time, however short, readily agreed it would indeed be a very good idea for them all to fall down on their knees and ask forgiveness of all those she had wronged. Her prayers ended, Rebecca rose shakily and unsteady to her feet until, with a drug and alcohol induced tongue, she pleaded,
*"Sirs, please believe me when I say I never meant to harm him but he would have surely killed me if I had not done something. You cannot have known how I was abused over the years following our marriage and I could not bear one more beating ...and then of course there were my dear children."*

Not one word passed between the four men in the cell until Henry Ellacombe, desperate to break the dreadful silence, volunteered,
*"I am so very sorry, we did all we could but you must now resign yourself to your fate and come with us."*

The Chaplain, taking up the hint, placed himself in front of her,
*"My child you have already confessed your sins before God and I therefore offer you Communion if you should wish to receive it."*

It had been a good many years since Rebecca last received Holy Communion but as she closed her eyes to receive absolution she knew this really was the end, there could be no more distractions, no more excuses, no more putting off the inevitable and for the first time in months she felt at peace and ready to meet her Maker.

*"Am I to die a sinner or am I forgiven?"* she asked the Chaplain.

Looking at Henry for support he said the first thing to come to him.

*"God always welcomes a repenting sinner; therefore you are already forgiven in his eyes."*

*"In that case I am ready,"* then turning towards her Curate she continued, *"Reverend Ellacombe I have written some personal letters to my family, to my husband's family and to my poor children, will you,"* pulling several pieces of crumpled paper from the pocket of her equally crumpled damask gown and handing them to Henry, *"please make sure they are delivered to the right people on our return to Bitton."*

Henry nodded, despite knowing full well that any letters Rebecca sent to Bitton would remain unopened and probably find their way onto the back of the fire but what harm would this last act of kindness do at this late stage?

The door creaked open and, feeling more composed, Rebecca turned to Henry and said,
*"I am so very frightened, will you pray for me?"*

Leaving the Condemned Cell behind them they made their slow way towards the gallows. Reaching the passage beneath the Execution Chamber the Prison Chaplain began intoning the words of St John's Gospel.

*"I am the Resurrection and the Life, he that believeth in me though he was dead, shall live. And whoever liveth and believeth in me shall never die."*

With these words all confidence suddenly left her and Rebecca collapsed in a dead faint on the floor. Hannah rushed forward, handy bottle of gin at the ready, to assist the elder Doctor Wilton. Together they struggled to get her to her feet after which, with the Chaplain leading the way still chanting St. John's words, Reverend Ellacombe supporting her on one side, the younger stronger Wilton on the other and Hannah flitting in between, the prison bell began its doleful beat.

Back in the Penitentiary, all the other women sat in silence until Prudence broke the spell and whispered,
*"B'aint bin no reprieve then."*

*"Didn't spect none d'ist?"* someone asked.

*"Least she be goin ome like what she always wanted and er little uns'll know she n their father be at peace,"* was the best Prudence could think of in way of a reply.

Reaching the bottom of the steep spiral stone steps leading to the execution chamber it was clear Rebecca would never climb these unaided. A restless night despite copious amounts of alcohol coupled with a constant stream of imaginary visitors thanks to Doctor Hagdell Wilton's initial sedative and more gin for breakfast, meant she was having great difficulty standing let alone clamber up such a narrow flight of stairs. Aunt Partridge's voluminous damask gown flapped perilously close to her ankles causing her to stumble at every step. Once Henry Ellacombe and Dr Wilton felt it safe to release their guiding grip on her arms it took the combined efforts of Hannah and two gaolers, brought in especially from the Penitentiary, to steer an increasingly unco-operative Rebecca into the chamber of death.

Downstairs the official party was waiting, silent and bewildered, until Mr Symmonds whispered,
*"I always anticipated there might be trouble but I never expected her to be so agitated ... considering what she has consumed through the night."*

The mob gathered outside, especially those closest to the locked wooden front doors, listened and heard everything,
*"We can ear her screamin, she be fightin um all th'way, they be going to ave to make er stand on the spot cus she bain't goin quiet."*

Loud roars reverberated throughout the crowd as detailed accounts of Rebecca's fight for life passed from person to person changing, like Chinese whispers, until they reached a crescendo and she also heard them ....and fell away into another dead faint!

Sir Edwin, Governor Symmonds and the hangman waited patiently in the chamber of the New Drop; 'Jack' was in no hurry, the eventual outcome was not in doubt. Therefore what did it matter how long it took to send her off? 'Jack' had dealt with many a reluctant victim throughout his career but even he was beginning to think this one might be more of a challenge than most and maybe he should have listened to the Governor and agreed to an assistant hangman.

The door slammed loudly behind her and Rebecca saw the grim cross beam with its coil of rope for the first time. However it was only when she spied the lever and trap doors that she finally accepted the inevitable and whimpered softly,
*"So this must be the end. Soon I shall be with Papa and Lamorock who are already waiting for me in heaven."*

*"Notice how her poor unfortunate husband is nowhere in her thoughts,"* Sir Edwin was overheard whispering sarcastically to Mr Symmonds.

As the hangman moved towards her, pinion straps and hood at the ready, Rebecca recoiled and made to step back only to find her way blocked by

Hannah and one of the unfortunate gaolers who had struggled so furiously to get her up the stone staircase. Momentarily transfixed at the sight of the trap door directly beneath the noose, swaying menacingly from the beam above them, it gave them the chance to grab her arms and securely tie them behind her back. Another desperate struggle ensued as they tried to move her into position until flaying legs, hindered by voluminous red, green and gold damask, were eventually strapped together. After that all resistance was useless.

With everyone ready inside the Execution Chamber the front doors of the Lodge Gate sprang open to a roar from the restless crowd that surpassed anything already heard that morning or even during her trial. By now loyalty was divided, with as much noise coming from those who still thought Rebecca was innocent as there was from those who gained immense pleasure from just watching a hanging, irrespective of whether they were guilty or not. Hannah stood at the back of the room with genuine tears in her eyes. Despite the enormity of Rebecca's crime and her often haughty high handed ways she truly felt for this poor wretched woman and her situation but it did not excuse the fact she had murdered her husband and must pay the dreadful price.

Henry Ellacombe remained at Rebecca's side assuring her,
*"I am praying you will not weaken; remember in a few moments you will be in paradise."*

Listening for any sounds from which she could gain solace, Rebecca realised she could no longer hear any noise coming from the mob outside,
*"Are they waiting for me?"* she asked in a slow, slurred voice.

With the hood in place and the noose securely about her neck it was pitiful to see her inert body supported by Henry and the Chaplain whilst Sir Edwin and Mr Symmonds looked on. By now her head had fallen forward and she was completely oblivious to what was happening. Turning to the hangman, Sir Edwin, who had been spared the traumatic journey from the Condemned Cell, urged,
*"For God's sake get on with it man!"*

Without any further delay 'Jack' dutifully obliged….springing to the lever he launched Rebecca into eternity.

The thud as the trapdoor opened was met with screams, shrieks and cheers whilst, in the eerie silence of the execution chamber, no one spoke until Henry Ellacombe stepped forward to look down at the swaying figure gently twitching on the end of the rope,
*"May God bless your troubled soul Rebecca Worlock and,"* making a sign of the cross over her body, *"may you now rest in ever lasting peace"*…..

….it was just after eight in the morning and, although it seemd like an eternity, the whole tragic performance had taken less than fifteen minutes from the time they left the Condemned Cell! The hangman had used the long drop thus ensuring Rebecca was dead as soon as the noose took the weight of her body, her neck cleanly broken before she appeared thrashing violently on the end of the rope. The earlier method of using the short drop often left the victim to slowly strangle to death, sometimes taking 30 minutes or more and it was not uncommon for family and friends to pull on their legs to hasten the process.

Amongst the howling throng who had travelled many miles, not only see her trial but remained to witness her execution, were four brothers. Spying the red, green and gold gown swaying gently between the Lodge Gates of Gloster Gaol they felt nothing but despair at seeing their sister end her days in such a way. They had desperately held on to the vain hope there might be a reprieve, now all that was left was to wait until they could claim her broken body and take her home one last time. Meanwhile they had no choice but to allow the swell of the crowd to carry them and they felt themselves unwillingly drawing nearer and nearer to the lonely figure hanging limply from the gallows.

Within the hour Sir Edwin and the Governor were standing before a Magistrate seeking an order saying Rebecca had been legally executed, absolving 'Jack' of any crime. However when the official death notice was eventually fixed to one of the large wooden doors the crowd were still wandering aimlessly around the cold limp body hanging from the creaking length of rope and it took a determined prison turnkey to tell them to,
*"Get theeselves away back ome, there bain't n'more to be sin yer."*

Finally orders were given to close the heavy doors thus affording Rebecca some decency, however temporary.

Sir Edwin, relieved there would be no repeat of this morning's exhibition till the next Assize, gathered his party together,
*"Gentlemen this calls for some refreshment,"* and, waving his arm in the direction of the City *"shall we go, I have arranged something at my club."*

Those with little reason to know otherwise could have mistaken the carter for a common tradesman but to people around here he was not only a regular visitor, especially during the Assize, but they knew only too well what he was carrying. Therefore no one paid any attention as two sullen men furtively appeared at the rear of Gloucester Infirmary in Lower Southgate Street to unceremoniously remove a roughly hewn coffin and take it into a large dissecting room. The room was empty and bare but within the hour it would be full to bursting because, thanks to the Anatomy Act of 1752, it was perfectly legal to hand over the bodies of executed criminals to Medical Schools. It also proved to be a form of a deterrent to crime because people believed they would not be resurrected to the afterlife if they were not buried intact. However the Act did not stop the illegal trade in fresh corpses and a decent one could always be obtained, although it could cost up to £8.

In life Rebecca always desired to be the centre of attention at all times, but in death she would receive adulation beyond her wildest dreams. The woman who, four months ago, had turned the lives of a small South Gloucestershire village upside down and caused irreparable damage to two families; the woman who, three days ago, caused near riots when she appeared in Court charged with murdering her husband; the woman who, early this morning, had paid the price for her actions was still capable of causing a commotion even in death. As she waited so young educated men arrived and began jostling to get a good view of her. Taking their places on steep tiered rows, the first two reserved for the dressers the rest for medical students, their eyes strayed towards the naked body of an emaciated woman lying on a rough wooden dissecting table. News quickly spread about this morning's specimen; some students had even chosen to witness the execution just to get in the right mood which was probably why the frenzied scramble was more intense than usual. Complete strangers, with absolutely no medical interest at all but who had been invited by the Surgeon himself, appeared and selfishly placed themselves directly behind the dressers, effectively blocking the views of those wishing to learn something from the proceedings. Before long shouts of, *"Heads! Heads!"* were heard coming from the more seriously minded students, unable to get a clear view and witness one of the three compulsory dissections necessary during their medical training. The reputation of the Surgeon, combined with Rebecca's notoriety, was known throughout the County, something abundantly clear from the number of medical students, doctors and those wishing to witness this final act and it was taking all the efforts of the great physician's servants to control the violent determination of those intent on gaining entrance. Just like her trial, fights and mild altercations were breaking out between those waiting outside unable to get in.

The great sugeon made his entrance to a room packed like sardines. With no ventilation, save a small window to let in some light, body odour and the August heat was already overpowering. With not so much as a glance at Rebecca he turned to acknowledge his adoring audience before walking over to a small wooden table on which his faithful dresser had laid out the necessary plates, basins and dishes.

Those seated close to the dissecting table and who could almost reach out and touch her body, rose to welcome the great man with outstretched hands.

Had he been operating and Rebecca in need of life saving surgery, he would have probably stood before them in his second best frock coat. However, especially for today's event, he appeared resplendent in his best working clothes as befitted his bedazzled admirers. Standing with arms outstretched like a crucifix, he allowed his faithful assistant to wrap his favourite apron, stiff and stinking with pus not to mention dried blood from a previous encounter with a fetid corpse, around his waist and tie it in place. Everything was ready and the Surgeon turned and reached for his instruments.

To some it was over all too quickly and those students who had managed to stay without fainting or needing to be carried out by their friends, left holding their precious certificates signed by the Surgeon himself confirming they had witnessed yet another dissection. The great man himself had swiftly disappeared for a fine lunch with his elegant friends, leaving his dressers and servants to clear away the butchered remains of what was once Rebecca Worlock. The wooden table was washed down with cold water, the blood soaked sawdust covering the floor was swiftly replaced in readiness for the next unfortunate candidate and any limbs or organs, needed for future study, were placed in receptacles. With little or no dignity she was irreverently thrown back into her coarse rough wooden coffin, any unwanted remains were then roughly tossed alongside her mutilated body. There was no sign of the precious damask gown, that had mysteriously disappeared and was probably already on its way back to the lucrative Gloucester under world from whence it was rescued. Once the lid was firmly secured it was placed in a tiny lonely room, no bigger than a large cupboard, to await her brothers who would be taking her home tomorrow. For all Reverend Ellacombe and The Chaplain's promises of forgiveness she was not even afforded a night before the Altar in the Hospital Chapel.

Later that afternoon Henry met with George Flower to discuss his sister's journey home and her burial. He also took time to assure them that death was instant, the surgeons knife showd her neck to be broken. It was agreed it must be a very low key affair, especially since Henry knew Peter Gerrish, as a former Churchwarden, was objecting to his plans to bring 'another convicted murderer back to lie in Bitton Churchyard!'

Angry that anyone should want to cruelly deny them the right to bring her mortal remains home, whatever her sins, Henry quietly reassured George,
*"I promised your sister a Christian burial in Bitton in return for her confession and we both asked the good Lord and Thomas for their forgiveness. Now, whilst I can speak for God I cannot of course speak for Thomas, or the Worlocks, but I sincerely pray they will not object. Therefore,"* with a slight determined edge to his voice, *"be so kind as to send word to your stepfather that your sister*

*will be returning to Bitton at the earliest opportunity, possibly as early as this evening or tomorrow. Shall we say we will lay your sister to rest on Friday?"*

Despite strenuous efforts the plenipotentiary of Mary Gerrish and her surviving children received little support for his objections to his errant stepdaughter resting in Bitton Churchyard and, as promised, on Friday August 18th, with the golden sun of a hot summer's day now the red glow of an early evening, Henry Ellacombe led one or two members of her family along with one or two other brave souls to a hastily dug grave, devoid of any regular shape or appearance, on the very edge of St Mary's Churchyard, as far from her poor suffering husband's final resting place as was possible, where Rebecca was finally laid to rest. Henry encouraged the sparse gathering to accept all suffering was now at an end. It was time for forgiveness and, as if to emphasize the point, he had already decided to say so from his pulpit on Sunday whether the Gerrish's, Flowers or Worlocks chose to attend or not. The past traumatic days spent in Gloucester had given him ample time to contemplate and he already had his Sermon prepared....it was going to be.

*"How the Power of God's love can heal and forgive."*

John Worlock, buoyed by the relief the warm summer sun brought to his aching joints and the satisfaction of knowing his son's tormentor had finally paid the ultimate price, determined to visit the family plot and, ignoring pleas from Martha who knew how much physical and mental pain such an exertion would cause, made his slow shuffling way from their cottage to St Mary's. Reaching the grave he read his son's name, freshly engraved on the headstone beneath those of his baby son and daughter and his mind went back to when they lost, first John twenty six years ago, then Ruth seven years later and Thomas, his once strong son, four months ago. Taking a deep breath he let out a pitiful sigh then, shaking his head, he wiped tears from his cheek, crying aloud,
*"Well young uns tain't gonna b'long afore I be wiv thee."*

Making to turn away and struggle back to Martha his eyes were somehow drawn to the fresh grave amidst the dense overgrowth in the far corner and he found himself muttering,
*"Well she cassent urt I now so what arm be there in takin a look."*

Later that evening Henry Ellacombe walked to a grave alongside St. Mary's where, four months earlier, he had laid Thomas to rest,
*"In life you and Rebecca were unable to live in harmony, it is therefore time for you both to rest in peace,"* and, making the sign of the cross, he turned to slowly make his weary way over to Rebecca's grave where, standing out bright and gay, was a small bunch of hand picked flowers, the sort found in abundance along the banks of Boyd Brook.

*"So, someone cares for you after all Rebecca Worlock,"* he mused as, once again making a sign of the cross, he prayed, *"may you, like you poor husband, rest in everlasting peace."*

*"Well, who do you think it was who placed those flowers on her grave?"* Anne Ellacombe asked her exhausted husband over supper later that night.

*"What does it matter who it was my dear so long as someone, other than God, has forgiven her,"* was the only thing Henry could think of in way of a reply.

# TRUTH OR MYTH

I never planned to find a family murder; in fact I never planned to trace my family history either. I blame it all on Nanny Worlock ….aided and abetted by my father and husband.

Nanny Worlock died in April 1980 leaving me her tumble down cottage nestling on the banks of Boyd Brook in what was once the tiny Hamlet of Coneyore, now School Road, Oldland Bottom. My mother was born there and I spent most of my childhood there, knowing the cottage would one day be mine and, as the years passed, how it was her wish should I not want to live there myself it was to be sold and the proceeds put into a trust fund for my two young daughters. Everything was fine until a dispute arose with her neighbour over ownership and the ensuing years took me close to a nervous breakdown as I waited for a Judge to decide.

During one family Sunday lunch when, as usual, the conversation was *"the cottage,"* talk gradually turned to my other slightly more eccentric grandmother. Dad believed she had been a Muller's Orphan and, how he wished he had known more about her. My husband, knowing there were still many months to go before we were due in Court, took the hint and suggested it might be something we could look into. Realising we had no idea where to start I began by joining the Bristol and Avon Family History Society and, with their help, discovered she was never taken into their care.

Realising just how compelling and rewarding tracing your family could be, I decided to include the Worlocks, naively thinking I might uncover some hitherto unknown evidence crucial to the forthcoming Court Case. Bristol Record Office was then in the Council House on College Green and, trawling through the Church Records for St. Mary the Virgin Bitton, I found a burial entry for Thomas Worlock under which the Curate had thoughtfully added 'Died of Poison'; two pages on the same Curate had again thoughtfully added 'Hanged at Gloster' under the name of Rebecca Worlock. With this discovery so began years of searching into what lay behind the death, by poison, of my distant Uncle and that of his wife, on the gallows, four months later.

Having found such a brace of ancestors it was with some trepidation that I wrote *"Until She Be Dead,"* little realising that, twenty five years on, I would attempt a fictional sequel based on all the information uncovered during that time and that Thomas and Rebecca, who had led such stormy lives and suffered truly grim deaths, would have completely taken over my life.

Thanks to a fellow member of the Family History Society, I learned a fair bit about the Flowers. However little was known about the Worlocks or the Priggs, therefore most of their early years remain a mystery. According to the Marriage Register, Martha came from Swineford; her father's name was not given and I have been unable to find a Baptism for her anywhere; John was given as a Bachelor of the Parish but again there was no mention of his father. The only Bitton reference to John Worlock Snr. is on a £40 Bastardy Bond when his name appears in support of John Hulburd after the latter was named by Sarah Kaines as the father of her unborn child. John Hulbard came to Bitton from Marshfield with his brother William and was, by coincidence, a butcher. Did John Worlock Snr. follow his friends from Marshfield looking for work only for John Hulburd to take on his young son as an apprentice after which he naturally succeded him as the village butcher?

Parish Records point to the Flower's affluence and their link with Bitton from around 1558. They had their Mill, homes and land in Kelston and Saltford along with a family ancestry spanning throughout Somerset, whilst the best the Worlocks could ever claim was an unidentified slaughter house that does not show up on any tithe map, account book or rate book.

In such a small village, with their fathers meeting as business friends, Thomas and Rebecca probably grew up together and maybe became closer as their respected family businesses expanded. Her comfortable childhood was no doubt made all the more enjoyable thanks to a household of compliant domestic servants rescued from the Poorhouse. Consequently she was already accustomed to issuing orders and expecting her own way long before her father died. It is also clear from the various surviving legal documents that his early death left his widow wealthy, yet vulnerable and the arrival of the much younger Peter Gerrish played an important part in the story. With Peter for a stepfather and, ultimately, legal guardian, did Rebecca and her siblings feature in some grandiose plan to marry them off to especially chosen families, leaving her with no choice but to defy him. Was Thomas tempted at the thought of unlimited Flower money and freedom from labouring alongside his semi-illiterate father and brothers in their family slaughterhouse or did he simply covet her dowry and, expecting to be suitably rewarded, willingly become a scapegoat in Rebecca's desperate bid to escape a home life she believed had been made unbearable thanks to a stepfather only a few years older than herself. But of course it's quite possible the couple truly loved each other and it was their feuding families, who were to blame for its ultimate failure and the ensuing tragedy.

From the Coroner's Depositions, the Summer Assize Accounts, Bonners Broadsheets, Overseers Accounts and local newspaper reports, it is clear there was little love lost between Rebecca and her neighbours, her in laws, her husband and most of the inhabitants of Oldland. With no likeness we only have the brief and somewhat biased opinion of her written by the Governor of Gloster Gaol, an opinion which may hint at her family having already distanced themselves from her when we read his description of her in the Prisoners Admission Book. *"A labourer who could read and write,"* is hardly that of someone with a father who left an estate valued at around £1.500.00 (£48.000 today) a Grandfather and Great Aunt from whom she inherited £50 (£1.600.00 today) along with valuable pieces of family jewellery, clothes and furniture. She was even denied her £50 inheritance from her murdered husband when her brother in law, George Worlock, successfully applied for and was given the money instead

Did Thomas and Rebecca have a normal courtship, were they married with their families blessing, if so what made the educated daughter of a wealthy landowner choose the uneducated son of the local butcher when, with her pedigree and inheritance, she could have had the pick of the best Bitton or Bath Society could offer? With a sister already married with her own household, why did Rebecca not follow Honor's example because there is no indication of her ever having such a home or even where she lived. We know from the Coroners Depositions how the most vociferous of her accusers were her neighbours, common labourers, who not only lived in fear of her volatile temper but overheard her constant threats to soon put Thomas *"out of this world."*

Reverend Henry Thomas Ellacombe played a pivotal role; he not only witnessed Thomas' last traumatic hours but became embroiled in the drawing up of his Last Will and Testament, hearing the dying man's final confession and played a decisive part in the future of his orphaned children. With their son dead, Henry focused on the grieving family, choosing to take Martha and her grandchildren back to Bitton rather than remain to point an accusing finger towards Rebecca during the Coroners Inquest. Four months later he was at her side when she paid the ultimate price and stood firm against local opposition when he kept his promise to bring her body home to Bitton for burial. To further add to the myth that still surrounds her there remains a question mark over whether she actually returned to St. Mary's Churchyard or remained within the walls of Gloster Gaol, as was normal following executions and was what the Judge decreed at her trial. Nevertheless, it is due to Reverend Ellacombe that her name, along with her fate, appears in the Burial Register for all to see.

Life for Rebecca changed with the early death of her father, only to worsen with the arrival of Peter Gerrish and deteriorate further when he married her mother, the widowed Mary Flower who, at forty four, was twenty one years older than him.

The Overseers of The Poor Account Book gives an indication of just how much the ratepayers of Bitton and Gloucestershire paid for Rebecca's crime. Between June and August there were regular payments, from 6d for postage to a staggering £27 (£1.131 today) for the stay at The Green Dragon. Court Expenses and Disbursements totalled around £136 (£5,712 today) of which £118. 16s 0d (£4,980 today) was settled by the County Treasurer, leaving £18 (£732 today) for the Parish to pay.

Our first visit to Gloucester Record Office went well until they closed for lunch and we had an unplanned hour to 'kill'. Undeterred I asked the archivist for directions to Gloucester Prison. Once there I realised I hadn't the foggiest idea how I was going to get inside…so I sent my husband to knock on the door and ask…which was how we came to meet their unofficial historian and, two weeks later, found ourselves being escorted through locked gates and across the exercise yard, probably once so familiar to Rebecca, Prudence and Nancy. We were guided to a small portacabin where, on being invited to step inside (and over the remains of a man trap which, we were told, was often used to recapture escaped prisioners!!) we were met by a serving Senior Prison Officer with a wicked sense of humour. To *"make me feel at home"* he had even thought to lay out a replica hangman's noose on his desk! He explained he was currently researching the lives of all the executed criminals buried within the prison walls because the Cemetery was earmarked for an extension to the current prison and it was planned to exhume and re-inter their remains elsewhere. Having already searched through the archives on my behalf he confirmed Rebecca's remains were not amongst them, leading us both to believe she indeed rests in Bitton.

The agreed one hour meeting became two and half. On finally taking our leave he insisted on walking us back through that familiar exercise yard. Standing in the prison gate lodge, two thick wooden doors in front and behind us, he described in colourful detail what would have happened on execution day and, pointing towards the white painted plasterboard ceiling above our heads, suggested we were not only directly beneath the trap door but that I was standing just about where Rebecca would have been left hanging!!!

Boyd Mill still stands alongside the river so important to its history, about a mile up Golden Valley Lane on the Upton side of the Bitton and it is to those who once lived there and to those who live there today that I give my heartfelt thanks. These very kind people gave generously of their time and access to their memories as well as their privacy, thus allowing me to learn far more than I could ever have hoped. Unfortunately I still do not know for sure where the Worlocks had their slaughterhouse although Robert and George Worlock were both paying rates for a House and Land and Samuel Worlock was paying rates for a House and Garden on the Bitton side of the village in 1836, so maybe the clue is there somewhere. Similarly I do not know for certain where the doomed Thomas and Rebecca lived, except that it was close to The Chequers in Barry Road. Nor do I have any idea why such an ill matched pair married at all and, can only guess at what made her want to 'put him out of this world.'

Most of the characters in this book are real, their part in the tragedy created by me from the surviving records as I understand them. The murder and its aftermath is well documented in Parish Records, Local Newspapers and Bonner Handbills, whilst the Coroners Inquest Depositions give further insight into an unhappy marriage and the possibility that Rebecca may have been using natural remedies to incapacitate Thomas for some months before his death.

I often visit St. Mary's and stand by two family graves. The names of babies John and Ruth and their big brother Thomas are there; old John, true to his prediction made to his dead son, lived on for only two years before he joined them in November 1822 aged 71, followed by Phoebe, his sickly twenty-five year old daughter, in April 1824. Martha, dependable and strong to the very end, outlived them all and died, aged 87, in February 1841. Her one time friend but latterly old adversary, Mary Gerrish, fared little better and died, aged 66, in 1822 and lies, not at Kelston or Saltford with the Flowers but in Bitton Churchyard, as does her young second husband Peter who survived her by twenty years, remarried and died in April 1842.

Henry Ellacombe only partially fulfilled his promise to find the three children new homes. On two different dates in October 1820, Mary Ann and Honor were sent to start a new life in separate Orphanages in London. However, for some unknown reason John remained in Bitton, reliant on the Parish for annual handouts of 2/-, steadily falling under the disreputable influence of Uncle George Worlock until, inevitably, they found themselves in trouble with the Constable and on remand in Gloster Gaol. The pair were soon up before the Quarter Sessions in the same Courtroom once occupied by Rebecca, charged with stealing 'a fat ewe sheep, the property of James Britton'. They were both acquitted, unlike Uncle William Wilcox Flower who was, by an amazing coincidence, up before the very same Magistrate on the very same day charged with 'stealing two ewe sheep, the property of Abraham Brain', a crime which alone carried a sentence of seven years transportation. However, this was not William Wilcox' first offence, as he had not long returned from seven years transportation to Australia for stealing 'two fat pigs, the property of Robert Fisher'; this time he was transported for life.

Despite the serious nature of my research, the intervening years have not been without their lighter side. Very early on, as news filtered through the family, my father received two bizarre 'phone calls from two Worlock uncles. One suggested I should stop delving into things over which I had no control, whilst the other insisted that not only had there never been any murder otherwise he would have known about it but if I continued to *"forage about"* then I could end up *"discovering things best left alone!"*

Those first Winter months were spent in the warmth of Bristol Reference Library, often in the basement looking at old newspapers, where I regularly saw the same *'gentleman of the road'*, his worldly possessions in two Tesco carrier bags, engrossed in the current edition of the Financial Times! I never did pluck up the courage to ask him how his stocks and shares were doing.

My husband always came with me when ever I ventured from Bristol and thus one autumn day we found ourselves window shopping in Chancery Lane, London, heading for the Public Record Office. Now these were no ordinary shops, they supplied new or second hand wigs and gowns to the legal profession…a bit un-nerving when you know you will soon be holding the original documents to a family murder trial?

The years since the death of my grandmother and the realisation there was a murderess in the family have been full of surprises, discoveries and explanations, not to mention a need for a certain amount of understanding. It took four years, a barrister, two days in Bristol County Court, a great deal of anxiety and an overwhelming desire to commit a murder myself, before a sympathetic Judge decided I was the rightful owner of my grandmother's cottage. By then I knew my ancestress by marriage had not been so fortunate with her legal battle and, from the 'phone calls my father received, I was also aware how some older family members were not happy with my discoveries. With hindsight I understand their feelings, fortunately as the years passed so those initial fears disappeared and, unlike the 19th Century Worlocks, the present family know Rebecca was never a threat.

Gilbert and Sullivan wrote that a policeman's lot was not a happy one, well back in 1820 the same could be said about a woman, especially when she was married to an abusive drunkard whilst blessed with an uncontrollable temper herself. No matter how much research I do or how much information I unearth there is no way of knowing if or why Rebecca really murdered her husband. If she selfishly planned everything then she is guilty as charged but if she had no choice but to protect not only herself but her three young children from a violent man then maybe we should not judge her too harshly.

Sadly in those days she was either guilty or innocent, there was no allowance for a crime of passion or self defence. I therefore leave it up to you, dear members of the jury, to make your choice.